GHOSTS
IN THE
SUNKEN
GARDEN

GWENDOLYN SMITH ZIMMERMAN

Content X Design

P.O. Box 8754

Kansas City, MO. 64114

CXD
CONTENT X DESIGN, INC.

ISBN: 978-1-942005-46-9

FOREWORD

By Ellen Hansen & Ryann Brooks

The story of the Kansas State Teachers College – now Emporia State University – began in 1855, two years before the City of Emporia was founded and six years before Kansas became a state. Those early residents of the territory of Kansas saw a need for a public universities and envisioned places where young men and women could educate and enrich themselves, where students could celebrate literature and the sciences, and where, importantly, they could learn how to teach the next generations of young people. In an age when Kansans could not fully agree on slavery and statehood, they did agree on the importance of education. The search for the perfect locations for the public universities would turn into long and hard-fought battle, carried out in the context of the lead-up to the Civil War, westward expansion, conflicts with Native American Indians, and other tumultuous socio-cultural changes occurring in the mid-19th century.

Using newspapers and legislative records, Zimmerman tracked events in the years before the Normal School was established. Her work details the political maneuvering and wrangling that resulted in Emporia being chosen as the location of the new school, after Lawrence and Topeka had been top contenders for the honor of hosting it.

Zimmerman drew heavily on newspaper accounts for much of the story that follows in these pages. Emporia has a long tradition of newspaper publishing; indeed, *The Kansas News*, the original newspaper, was founded in 1857 as one of the city's first businesses (Emporia n.d.), while Kansas was still a territory. The newspaper was instrumental in promoting population and economic growth, and was actively involved in supporting the admission of Kansas to the United States as a free state.

When Kansas was admitted to the Union in 1861, it was not without controversy, though the majority of the population supported admission as a free state. This was expressed in an article in the Leavenworth *Conservative*:

Truly the people of Kansas have cause for rejoicing. With them it is the realization of a six year's anxious hope; the termination of a struggle for the Freedom of Kansas commencing with the passage of the Nebraska Bill in 1854, and ending by the triumph of Free Labor in our admission as a Sovereign State on the 28th day of January, 1861. Who, of the friends of Free Kansas; who, of the men who have helped to make her Free; who, of the people who have stood by her cause through gloom and darkness until it emerged into light and victory, could help rejoicing? Who could help huzzahing for the FREE STATE OF KANSAS? (Wilder 1861, cited in Kansas History 1961).

Although modern versions of the free-state/slave-state controversy might create an image of two unified sides opposing each other, in reality both sides had many different groups supporting and opposing admission of Kansas as a free state or a slave state, with a seemingly endless list of reasons (Cecil-Fronsman 1997). In addition to the conflict over slavery, Kansas was experiencing clashes between white settlers and Native American tribes in the territory and then in the state (Marchand 1993).

Cecil-Fronsman (1997) indicates the important role played by newspapers in the territory and the new State of Kansas and other parts of the Midwest in the mid-19th century. Gwen Zimmerman used the historical record of regional newspapers to create the context within which the Kansas State Normal School was established. Her research confirms that it was a tumultuous time, as is evident in the pages that follow. Still, three of the state's major universities were founded in the midst of turmoil, from the early discussions beginning in the mid-1850s to 1863 with the founding of The Kansas State Normal School and Kansas State Agricultural College (now Kansas State University), to 1866 when The University of Kansas held its first classes.[1]

Emporia was founded in 1857 and grew quickly; by the 1880s, the city had a population of just under 5,000 people. Two colleges were founded before 1890: the Kansas State Normal School in 1863 and the College of Emporia in 1882. Its two institutions of higher learning, along with it being the home of William Allen White, the "Sage of Emporia," led some to call the city the "Athens of Kansas" (Murphy 2007).

The Normal School burned in October 1878 as the result of an accidental coal fire. Student records, the museum, the university's archives and everything else went up in flames, but the university rebuilt.

These are the bones of the story that Zimmerman began researching in the 1970s. The manuscript was left unpublished, but now, as ESU celebrates 155 years of existence in 2018, her work has been rediscovered and is presented in this volume. She apparently planned to produce a definitive history of the first 60 years of ESU. Although the manuscript ends abruptly in 1877, Zimmerman compiled a detailed documentation of ESU's beginnings. The early history of Emporia and ESU is one of perseverance. It is a story of politics. Perhaps most significantly, it is a testament to the importance of higher education, from the early days of westward expansion in the 19th century, to current times.

WORKS CITED IN THE FOREWORD

Cecil-Fronsman, Bill. 1997. "Advocate the Freedom of White Men, As Well As That of Negroes": The *Kansas Free State* and antislavery westerners in territorial Kansas. *Kansas History: A Journal of the Central Plains* 20(2): 102-115.

Emporia Area Chamber & Visitors Bureau. n.d. History of Emporia. Retrieved on June 22, 2018, at https://emporiakschamber.org/history-of-emporia/.

Kansas History. 1961. When Kansas became a state. *Kansas History: A Journal of the Central Plains* 27(1): 1-21, transcribed by Jim Scheetz; digitized with permission of the Kansas Historical Society.. Retrieved on June 22, 2018, at https://www.kshs.org/p/when-kansas-became-a-state/13159.

Marchand, Michael J. 1993. The historic Indians of Kansas. *Tales Out of School*, October. Retrieved on July 16, 2018, at https://www.emporia.edu/cgps/tales/o93tales.html.

Murphy, Regina. 2007. Starting the new century off right: Emporia Recipes from 1900-1929. *The Emporia Gazette*, Dec. 5.

DAUGHTER'S PREFACE

My earliest memories of my mother are not of the highly intelligent researcher and gifted writer that she obviously was; rather, they are of her at home, cooking, working in the yard, sewing my clothes, organizing our home and making everything in my world possible. I was five and it was 1950. We had just moved to Colorado Springs because my father, who hade been working on his PhD in History at the University of Michigan, was suddenly called by the US Army to serve one year in Japan as part of the post-WWII occupation. My mother and I stayed in Colorado. She took a bookkeeping job and I started first grade. On weekends we would go up into the mountains to hike and picnic, exploring nearly every narrow gravel coal road that crisscrossed the western slopes of the Rockies at that time. My father returned and then in 1954 we moved back to his hometown of Emporia when he took a history position at Kansas State Teachers College (now ESU), his and my mother's alma mater.

I cannot remember when my mother began to research and write this early history of ESU. My sister was born in 1960 and so it was probably well into the 1970s before she would have had the time to devote to this project. I do remember her talking about her work, telling me that she had chosen to focus on the earliest period because the official records of those years housed at the university had been lost in a fire (the fire of 1878). She said she was afraid that if she didn't do it, no one else would be willing to take on the painstaking work of going back through the state historical archives in Topeka to dig out the lost details.

In many ways, this book stands as testimony to the multi-talented, highly educated women of the mid-nineteenth century. Products of first wave feminism and the gender leveling effects of two world wars, they had entered higher education where they participated alongside men, but then graduated into a world of work that was not yet ready to fully accept them. My mother left the tiny, central Kansas town of Pawnee Rock, in the dry, dustbowl, depression year of 1936 for Emporia and Kansas State Teacher's College. Just a few months after she arrived she met my father, who would be her life long love, companion and intellectual partner until his untimely death at the age of 66. Sometime during the years just before and after his death, my mother worked on this project. Not long before his death, my father was named University Historian and perhaps that helped spark her own interest in investigating those early years. Caught up in my own career and family, I had only a vague idea of what she was doing. I do remember her carrying around a briefcase with note cards and a manuscript, which she had typed with a relatively new typewriter that had a "memory."

Shortly after my mother's death in 2012, I found the manuscript for this book among her belongings, and realized how complete and detailed an account she had written. Until then, I had no idea of what she had accomplished. Her original title indicated she had been planning to write a history of the first 60 years; however, the manuscript itself covered just the first twenty-two of those years. Mother never sought the limelight, and so my sister and I were left wondering what she had intended to do with her manuscript. Of one thing I am certain--my mother was a true scholar. Her many hours of research and writing were primarily a labor of love, a process she found compellingly interesting and thought would benefit the university and posterity. I am sure she thoroughly enjoyed being immersed in her work. Focused intently on the job at hand, I doubt she gave a whole lot of thought to what would happen once it was finished. If she did, she never shared that with me nor for that matter revealed what she had accomplished. Always a deliberate decision-maker, she may well have put the manuscript aside while still considering her options. In any event, I am certain she would have been pleased that I picked it up about the time of her beloved ESU's 150th anniversary, and that I finally read it carefully--and with great admiration. She would be both surprised and grateful to see it finally published. In my view, nothing could be more fitting.

The publication of this book would not have been possible without the support and generous assistance provided by Dr. Ellen Hansen and Ryann Brooks as well as staff members of the Social Sciences Department at Emporia State University. I am particularly indebted to Professor Hansen for so willingly becoming a partner on this project and pursuing it with steadfast commitment and enthusiasm. Special thanks is also due Kristin Hatch and Delaina Miller of Content X Design for their advice and expertise in shepherding the manuscript along the final stages of production.

Mary K. Zimmerman
Overland Park, Kansas

Gwendolyn Zimmerman

PREFACE

> *The Emporia News* contains more interesting educational matter in the course of a year than any weekly paper in the State. This is because it is printed at the Educational center of the State.
>
> (*The Emporia News*, December 6, 1867)

The purpose of quoting the above statement is neither to agree with nor to refute it, but rather to point out that if the Emporia editors had not been committed to keeping the public well informed about the Kansas State Normal in its early years, and if those connected with the institution had not diligently publicized the school at every opportunity, this narrative would have been impossible to write. Only the various official state reports and a few scattered mementos of the first thirteen years exist because the school's records were destroyed by fire in the autumn of 1878. For that reason, we should be eternally grateful to Emporia editors Jonathan Hunt, Jacob Stotler, and their associates for having left us significant information about a struggling young Normal School in the as yet undeveloped state of Kansas, and the assistance rendered it by an equally struggling, undeveloped community.

Gwendolyn Zimmerman
Emporia, Kansas
(late 1970s/early 1980s)

TABLE OF CONTENTS

1855-1877:

GHOSTS IN THE SUNKEN GARDEN

At long last Emporia had its university. On April 18, 1977, Governor Robert Bennett signed into law the bill changing the three state colleges to universities, and Emporia Kansas State College, formerly Kansas State Teachers College and Kansas State Normal School, was renamed Emporia State University. The change became official on April 21 with the publishing of the Act and simultaneously the school's one-time branches at Hays and Pittsburg also became universities.

Emporia State University, the imposing institution that stands at the head of Commercial Street, was a decade and a half into its second century; but the full story of its conception and birth begins even earlier, before Emporia ever became a town site. Known for the first sixty years as the Kansas State Normal, the school was created by law in 1863. Neither its creation nor the subsequent door opening in 1865 can be fully appreciated, however, without some understanding of the earlier political tug-of-war over Kansas University. For that reason, this narrative history of E.S.U. – a story that has long needed telling – commences a full ten years before the first day of school.

CHAPTER 1

HOW IT ALL BEGAN:
1855-1864

As early as 1855, the idea of a public university was prevalent in Kansas Territory. Who imported the idea is not known, but, contrary to the myths which perpetuate the notion that only the abolition-minded immigrants desired homes, churches, or schools, the leaders of both pro-slave and free-state factions advocated these institutions.[2] Especially did both factions visualize an eventual university as is evidenced by an inspection of the voluminous territorial laws, legal and extra-legal, under which the territory labored during the discord years preceding the Civil War. Ironically, this ignoble period, which earned for the territory the gruesome name of "Bleeding Kansas," was also the period during which the educational dreams and aspirations of both sides were being clarified and translated into words.

The first territorial legislature was elected largely by adjoining Missourians recruited to vote in the Kansas elections by pro-slave newspaper editors and David R. Atchison, United States senator from Missouri, in order to insure for themselves congenial neighbors.[3] This legislature during July and August of 1855 rose to the challenge of Governor Andrew H. Reeder, newly arrived from Pennsylvania, who in his first address on July 3 called for that body to contemplate a territorial university. Those legislators complied by approving a university charter for the promotion of "literature and of the Arts and Sciences." This institution was to be located up the Kansas River several miles from

1

Lawrence at the town of Douglas, whose citizens were to donate a ten-acre site. It was to be operated by a legislature-appointed board of twenty curators and supported by a "seminary fund" derived from the sale of whatever lands the national government should donate to the territory. Although this Act to institute a territorial university was never implemented, the plan was detailed and specific as to who was to handle the finances, how often the faculty was to be paid, where and when the curators were to meet, and for how long they were to serve. Moreover, three commissioners were actually named to choose the university site.[4]

That first body of territorial lawmakers was declared a "bogus Legislature" by the free-state citizens who refused to be governed by them or their "bogus laws." In fact, the free-staters organized a convention in Topeka in the autumn of 1855, drew up a constitution by which they hoped to become a state, and set up an extra-legal government with Charles Robinson as governor. Their document requiring the General Assembly to provide common schools was less insistent about higher education, permitting rather than requiring the Assembly "to take measures for the establishment of a university." They were also permitted to provide for the "Support of Normal Schools, with suitable libraries, and scientific apparatus."[5] This mention of Normal Schools seems to be the first and only instance in which the idea of a separate Normal School in Kansas was officially articulated prior to 1863.

Long after Congress failed to approve the Topeka Constitution, the free-state faction referred to it as their instrument of government, and under it selected their own representatives and governor. They continued to meet in Topeka even after troops in 1856 forced them to disband. Meanwhile, the "bogus legislature" was recognized by both Congress and the President as the legitimate government of Kansas Territory. Nevertheless, the pro-slave Lecompton Constitution of 1857, which President James Buchanan endorsed, fared no better in Congress than had the earlier free-state document. It did, however, indicate that the idea of a public university was still alive. The legislators at Lecompton, without going into detail regarding higher education, upheld their earlier proposed university by requesting that seventy-two sections of state land be used for the seminary fund.[6]

A third abortive attempt at statehood came in May of 1858 when the free-staters drew up the Leavenworth Constitution, which sounded more ambitious towards education than their earlier Topeka document. This time they declared that as the State could afford to do so, institutions of a higher grade should be established by law in order to have a complete system of public instruction which would include primary, normal, preparatory, collegiate, and university departments.[7] The ordinance called for seventy-two sections of land for the university, and sixty additional sections for four district colleges to be located in four equal divisions of the State.[8]

Finally by 1859, pro-slave and free-state politics became dead issues. The "bogus" statutes were burned in a bonfire; Republican and Democratic parties were organized; and an election was called for a constitutional convention. The resulting Wyandotte Constitution, drawn up in July and adopted on October 4, 1859 became in January, 1861, the Kansas State Constitution. At last, the State University was more than a dream. The Wyandotte document required of the state such as an institution.

> Provision shall be made by law for the establishment at some eligible and central point, of a state University, for the promotion of literature, and the arts and sciences, including a Normal and an Agricultural department ...[9]

But calling for a university in the constitution was a far different matter than creating one by law as learned from the struggles of the 1861, 1862, and 1863 legislatures. Many Kansans today, vaguely familiar with the fight between Lawrence and Emporia for the university, are almost totally unaware of the fact that the very first state legislature on May 23, 1861, voted to locate that institution in Manhattan on the site of the foundering Blue Mont Central College, a Methodist institution with one building, a small library, and a large acreage. Governor Charles Robinson, fearful that his city of Lawrence might fail to capture top prize of the capital and thereby be left empty handed, vetoed the bill. The same legislature had just passed a bill reinforcing the constitutional requirement that the capital be located according to a majority vote of the people in the November general election.[10] To justify his veto, Governor Robinson explained that if Manhattan's offer had promoted the legislators' decision, then all portions of the state should be entitled to extend like offers. He also considered the decision to be premature in as much as there was as yet no available endowment. The Manhattan measure died, just two votes short of the necessary two-thirds to override the veto.[11]

Representatives from Lyon County (called Breckenridge until early in 1862) worked against the Manhattan Bill for reasons different from those of the governor, although when voiced the arguments sounded much the same. R.W. Could, representative from Waterloo, and Senators H.S. Sleeper of Neosho Rapids and E.P. Bancroft of Emporia, were identified as actively opposed to locating the university at that time in order to give the people an opportunity to be heard.[12]

In the meantime, Jacob Stotler, editor of *The Emporia News*, was also speaking out for postponement of the university question. On May 4, 1861, an editorial pointed out that Emporia was the ideal spot for the university, the central location to fulfill the Constitution's requirements. A week later, he declared that since the institution would not be needed for some time, he doubted that it would be located during the current session, but

> We would modestly suggest to the Legislature that when they locate these State Institutions that there is a country far to the south of Topeka, Lawrence, and Manhattan, and that the Kaw Valley is far from sixty to seventy miles north of the center of the State, and that there are almost 44,000 people north of that river while there are about 62,000 inhabitants south.

The next issue of the paper was critical of the bargaining and vote trading connected with locating the capital, university, and penitentiary. Not only legislators, but lobbyists and special interests groups were frantically bargaining and dealing in an attempt to get their pet measures passed. Lyon County (Breckenridge) itself had nine or more lobbyists on the scene.[13] Nevertheless, the Emporia editor predicted that corruption would outwit justice, and everything would be located in the Kaw Valley.

Thus it was that during and after the state's first legislative session, Emporia and Lawrence found themselves allied against Manhattan. Lawrence leaders preferred the capital above anything else; but failing that, Governor Robinson had knowingly saved the university for them.[14] Emporians were justified in their belief that the university should be located in the Neosho Valley to comply with the Constitution, but their reasons for supporting Lawrence as the capital site are less easily understood.

In the weeks preceding the November 5, 1861 election, many reasons why voters of Southern Kansas counties should support Lawrence instead of Topeka in the bid for the capital were published in Emporia. Foremost among them was the rather strange reason that for the present the farther away the capital was from the center of the state, the better. Lawrence was some thirty miles nearer the border than Topeka, so remote that surely the capital site would have to be changed after a few years. When that time came, ran the argument, the southern area of the state would be strong enough politically and well enough populated that the capital could be relocated to their advantage, preferably in the Neosho Valley. In the interim, there was no money for permanent state buildings anyway, and Lawrence with its hack routes and mail service was more accessible than Topeka; also there were more accommodations in Lawrence.[15]

Another argument for supporting Lawrence concerned the proposed railroad routes. The Leavenworth and Pawnee Railroad was expected eventually to extend service to Lawrence and on into the Neosho Valley, whereas the Atchison and Topeka Railroad was projected to go west, bypassing the Emporia area. Thus, a vote for Lawrence became a vote for local railroad service.[16]

The 1861 legislature apparently had spent considerable time discussing the desirability of annexing a portion of Southern Nebraska to the State of Kansas. Lawrence had opposed the proposal, but Topeka had endorsed it. According to the Emporia editor, a vote for Topeka would be strengthening the hands of those who would annex a portion of Nebraska. That would be the only hope Topeka would ever have of retaining the capital if the town should win it in November. Such a change in the northern boundary would, of course, be against the best interest of the Neosho Valley or areas to the south. A vote for Lawrence, however, could eliminate that threat. [17]

One reason given by the Emporia editor for voting on behalf of Lawrence proved to be almost naïve. It was based upon an erroneous assumption that because Lawrence representatives had voted against locating the university in Manhattan, they had voted for the interests of southern Kansas. Topeka, on the other hand, had voted to accept Manhattan's Blue Mont College. In his October 19 issue, Stotler asserted that

> Lawrence is now and always has been in favor of giving us some of the State Institutions. We think the State University should be located in the Neosho Valley. Lawrence will work with us in this. Topeka goes or a least did go last winter for locating everything on the Kaw River. We ought to recollect her at the ballot box on the 5th of November.[18]

By the time of the second legislature in 1862, Manhattan, Emporia, and

Lawrence all were grasping for the university, especially Lawrence who had lost the capital to Topeka. Again Manhattan offered Blue Mont College; Emporia offered forty acres of land; and Lawrence offered twenty acres of land, $10,000 worth of real estate, and $15,000 cash.

After much debate by the committee on public institutions, only the Manhattan bill was recommended for consideration. It easily passed the House by a vote of almost three to one, but became bogged down in the Senate where a power struggle was developing between the United States Senator James H. Lane and Governor Robinson. Senator Lane, seeking to guarantee enough votes to impeach the governor, was attempting to expel four senators sympathetic to Robinson on the charge of conflict of interest because they were holding federal military jobs. Using the university bill as a lever, Lane succeeded in getting a Manhattan senator to vote against the Robinson men by promising that they would be replaced by men who would vote for Manhattan's university bill.[19]

Senator Bancroft was one of the four men to be replaced. As early as October 19, 1861, a notice had appeared in the *Emporia News* stating that

> J.M. Rankin of this place [Emporia] was nominated to fill a supposed vacancy in the State Senate caused by the appointment of E.P. Bancroft to the position of Quartermaster of the Home Guards. Whether there is a vacancy or not, we do not know.

Bancroft and two others in question continued to serve in the Senate until March 1, 1862, at which time their seats were declared vacant. The fourth man had resigned a week or so earlier. In the case of Bancroft, Senator Rankin occupied his seat.[20] Although the Manhattan bill had previously been defeated by three votes; a motion to reconsider the bill passed by a large margin. Despite that trial vote, however, and the newly-seated senators, Manhattan lost again by a single vote. While Rankin had voted to reconsider, he, like his predecessor, voted against the bill itself. Senator Sleeper voted "no" on both counts.[21]

In the meantime, the editor of *The Emporia News* still disliked the idea of locating the university in Manhattan, preferring postponement because the State did not yet need a university, but maintaining that if the legislators would vote in accordance with the spirit of the Constitution, Emporia would "stand a better show than any other town, because it is nearest to the Center of the State."[22]

On February 8, the editor insisted that the only thing Manhattan had in its favor was an existing building; that since the Kaw Valley had the Capital and Leavenworth the penitentiary, the Neosho Valley according to justice should have the university. The following week, a convincing letter written to the *Topeka Daily Record* and signed "Justice" appeared in the Emporia paper. The letter extended the argument for Emporia as a university site. Statistics were cited comparing Lyon and Riley Counties in population, amount of taxes paid, climate, and the quality of agricultural lands. In the first two instances, Lyon County figures were enough larger to be quite impressive.

After the second defeat of Manhattan, the editor intimated that it was the local representatives who had kept Manhattan from getting the university. He also declared that "Emporia <u>now</u> stands a better chance for the desirable institution of learning than any other point claiming it."[23]

By late fall, Stotler was preparing his readers for the third legislative session. On December 6, 1862, there appeared a new provocative bid for the university. This time the editor reasoned that by locating the institution in Emporia, the legislature would also be opening up the entire southern portion of the State to growth and development.

The fight over the university might have continued indefinitely, had not the new governor unwittingly broken the three-way deadlock. In his message to the 1863 legislators on January 14, Thomas Carney urged them to establish a university, calling their attention to the Morrill Act of July 2, 1862, and indicating that by taking advantage of that Congressional Act, the legislature could provide an agricultural school and at the same time fulfill the Constitutional requirement of a university. He assured them that

> A wise combination of the interests of the State, and a just application of the means which the General Government should grant, will enable us to do for education all that an intelligent people could ask or desire. It is for you to perfect this combination, and by right legislation to receive the benefit of the Act of Congress of July, 1862, which appropriated to this State for educational purposes, ninety thousand acres of land.[24]

The Governor obviously was thinking of a single state university, but the legislature was still thinking in three directions. After agreeing to the terms of the Morrill Act, both houses agreed unanimously to accept Manhattan's third time offer of Blue Mont College, this time for an Agricultural School.[25]

After one part of the contemplated University of Kansas was bestowed upon Manhattan, the battle between Lawrence and Emporia became furious. As late as January 17, *The Emporia News* had surmised that not all of Douglas County's representatives would support Lawrence's bid. Indeed their offer was less than in 1862, twenty acres of land and $15,000 in cash that they did not yet have. Emporia had increased its offer of forty acres of land to eighty. The House committee on public institutions recommended that the Lawrence bill be rejected in favor of Emporia's bill. At this point, despite the committee recommendation, the Lawrence delegation, led by former governor Robinson, lobbied for passage of the Lawrence measure.

Emporia's weekly paper was continuing to support the town's bid for the university; but on February 7, the editor cautioned that "although the prospects of Emporia were never brighter than they have been this session, it is by no means certain that she will secure the prize." A week later, the paper announced that the university had been located in Lawrence. The editor was bitter in his denunciation of Lawrence for having "bought the University." He also complained that Emporia, who earlier had supported Lawrence for the capital, expected help on the university question. According to the editor, Emporia had fought almost alone against Manhattan, only to see Lawrence "reap the success."

Apparently, the telling argument used against Emporia in the House concerned the town's water supply. Professor William Foster of Douglas County, who recently had lived in Lyon County where he was a nominee for the legislature in the fall of 1861, declared before the House that for want of water Emporia was an unfit spot for the university.[26] Representative C. V. Eskridge staunchly defended Emporia's wells and cisterns, but when the vote was taken to strike Emporia and substitute Lawrence, there was a tie vote (33 to 33). A Lawrence sympathizer, Edward Russell, who was in the Chair broke the tie. On the following day by a vote of 38 to 32, the entire House passed the amended bill.[27]

Emporia fared no better in the Senate where a final effort by Lyon County's Perry B. Maxon to reinstate the original Emporia measure met with a resounding defeat (18 to 7). Next day the Senate voted 19 to 4 for the Lawrence bill. Governor Carney signed it on February 20, but it was not yet a bonafide law. As passed, the Act required no less than forty acres of land and an endowment of $15,000 to be deposited with the state treasurer within six months after the site was deeded to the state. Noncompliance on the part of Lawrence would cost them the university which would go to Emporia by default provided that community could come up with eighty acres of land.[28]

Lawrence needed the $15,000 by November 1, 1863. In October, they finally managed two-thirds of the amount, but only at the last minute when Governor Carney personally offered to advance $5,000 in cash for citizens' notes in the same amount was Lawrence able to comply with the law. It was November 2 before the governor could issue a proclamation declaring the state university to be permanently established at Lawrence.[29]

Scarcely more than two months later in his 1864 message to the legislature, Governor Carney appealed to the lawmakers to reimburse the hard-pressed Lawrence citizens who had contributed to the $5,000 gift. By stressing their recent losses suffered in Quantrill's raid, he set the stage for unanimous passage of a relief bill introduced by a Lawrence legislator. The relief money, totaling $5,167.00 was taken from the $15,000 endowment fund. It repaid Governor Carney and released the notes signed by Lawrence citizens, but left the not yet functioning university with less than two-thirds of its original endowment.[30]

Recent research supports the claims of the 1863 Emporia delegation who cried "foul" at the time of the Lawrence victory. It appears that there was indeed vote buying and much dealing between Lawrence supporters and the various railroad interests in Northern Kansas.[31] In light of today's knowledge, it is unfortunate [for Emporia] that the legislature failed to act upon Eskridge's plea for an investigation when he addressed the House on February 10, 1863. His resolution "relative to the location of the university" follows:

> Whereas, It is reported on the streets of Topeka that corrupt means have been resorted to, to procure the passage of Bill #81 [the Lawrence bill]; and whereas, the House owes it to itself, to protect itself against corruption and bribery, and also to protect its honest members from such infamous aspersions: Therefore Resolved, That there be a committee of five appointed by the Speaker, with power to send for persons and papers, to investigate said Charges, and report the result of said investigation to this House at an early day.[32]

Although an attempt to table the above resolution failed to pass in the House by a vote of 28 to 41, it nonetheless was rendered wholly ineffective by amendments. One amendment required that any investigation be done without any expense whatsoever to the state; the other, an amendment to the amendment, pronounced that "unless specific charges be made in regard to the offense, and the parties charged," the House would not entertain the resolution.[33]

In the aftermath of defeat, Eskridge and his colleagues remained resilient. Even before the university bill had been signed into law, Emporia's delegation was striving for a different institution. On February 19, 1863 Eskridge introduced the historic bill to establish, locate, and endow a State Normal School at Emporia.[34]

Contrary to the generally accepted notion that Emporia was handed the Normal School as a consolation prize is the fact that Eskridge failed in an attempt to get special treatment for this latest bill. With the designated date for adjournment fast approaching, he tried to hasten the second and third readings of the bill in order to insure a chance for passage but was forced to abide by standard procedure and wait for "the order of the day." Finally, at an evening session on February 26, the House passed the Normal School bill by a vote of 41 to 19. An amusing sidelight worth noting is the recorded vote of Professor Foster of Douglas County. Evidently no longer concerned about Emporia's lack of water, he was one of those casting an affirmative vote in behalf of the State Normal School.[35]

On the following day, the foregoing bill was read for the first time in the Senate. By March 2, 1863, it had passed by a vote of 23 to 0 and was in the hands of Governor Carney who signed it on March 3, the same day that the legislature adjourned. Upon publication in *The Emporia News* of March 7, the act became law.[36]

The Emporia editor registered neither surprise nor dismay over the Normal School bill. Following a brief announcement on February 28 that Eskridge had introduced such a bill, Stotler added caustically that

> We should think the bill would pass. We cannot see what object anyone would have in voting against it except that there are one or two points on the Kaw River—Tecumseh and Lecompton—that have not yet been provided for at the expense of the State.

If Stotler failed to be surprised or perplexed over the prospect of gaining a Normal School, he likewise lacked initial enthusiasm. In the same paper that carried the official publication of the Act, he briefly reported the results of the final vote and listed the names of those appointed to select a site: Isaac T. Goodnow, H. W. Fick, and LeRoy

Crandall.[37] In another related editorial, he explained that all three Lyon County representatives had voted for a Kaw River bridge bill (at Topeka, Lawrence and DeSoto) in order to get the Normal School bill passed. Much to Stotler's satisfaction, the bridge bill failed to pass. He admitted that he himself would have voted for "no Normal School" rather than to have voted for bridges.

Just who initiated the idea of a separate Normal School is not really known; nor can we be sure of the reason for it. Long afterwards, however, in newspaper stories, public speeches, and eventually in the written history of the early Normal School years, the popular belief was that while no one in Kansas in 1863 knew much about Normal Schools, Emporia's politicians accepted the gift because any institution was better than none.

Legend has it that Representative Eskridge, an otherwise knowledgeable man, knew nothing whatsoever about Normal Schools. His introduction of the Normal School bill supposedly was the result of his having been prompted by others. The generally accepted version of the tale names Isaac T. Goodnow as prompter—the one who attempted to ease the pain of defeat by suggesting to Eskridge that he try to get a Normal School for Emporia. In response, Eskridge supposedly uttered an oath and asked, "What in _____ is a Normal School?" Accompanying this story is that of a contrite legislature who, in their eagerness to console the defeated, passed the Normal School bill without opposition. The final thrust concerns the citizenry of Emporia and Lyon County who were inconsolable at first and completely indifferent towards the prospects of having such a school.[38]

Historical accounts of the day support very little of the above legend, but as early as 1869 at least one newspaper reporter began to weave the threads. In an otherwise complimentary editorial about Kansas State Normal School and Eskridge, who by then was lieutenant governor, the reporter explained that after losing the university despite a well-organized attempt to get it, Eskridge was desperate—afraid to face his constituents at home [Emporia] because the town had to have some public drawing card in order to survive. In an attempt to brighten the countenance of the disheartened representative, "someone" suggested a Normal School to which Eskridge responded, " Normal School! What's that?" The reporter further explained that there was scarcely a dissenting vote against the bill, the consensus being that the project would never be heard of again.[39]

There seems to have been no other mention of the legend in early day speeches or historical accounts of the Normal; but thirty-five years after the school was established, the legend surfaced. On January 17, 1899 in a speech before the Kansas Historical Society, Albert R. Taylor, president of K.S.N., spoke on "The History of Normal School Work in Kansas." After explaining that the movement in America was very young in the 1860s and practically nonexistent west of the Mississippi, Taylor asked,

> Is it any wonder then that when in 1863 State Superintendent Goodnow suggested that a state Normal School would comfort the people of Emporia, who had failed by one vote to get the state university, that it is said a prominent legislator wanted to know, in a blankety, blank way, "What is a Normal School, anyhow?"[40]

Goodnow, a transplanted Rhode Island seminary professor, could very well have been the one who sparked Eskridge's enthusiasm for a Normal School. A founder of Manhattan, he was deeply involved in the whole university struggle, first as president of Blue Mont College in 1861 and again as legislator in 1862. If he was responsible for the idea, however, he certainly did not indicate as much when twenty-five years later he responded to President Taylor's request for information concerning the origins of the institution. In a hitherto unpublished letter, Goodnow wrote in part:

> Manhattan, Kansas, Feb. 22, 1889
> A.R. Taylor, President etc.
> My Dear Friend,

> In reply to your favor of the 15th: The idea of a Normal School at Emporia was conceived & brought forth at the Sessions of the Legislature in 1863. The friends of Manhattan & Emporia had united to put the Agricultural College at Manhattan, & the University at Emporia in opposition to Lawrence who had been working for it for three years. At first Emporia was in the ascendant but finally Lawrence secured it by means of bribery it was thought! C. V. Eskridge, the champion of Emporia, introduced a Resolution into the House, inquiring into the means by which it was done. The friends of Lawrence, feeling well over their success & generous towards their rival & to stop the investigation proposed in Eskridge's resolution, put in a Bill to locate the State Normal School at Emporia & to endow it with 38,000 acres of "Salt Lands." Without this action the Normal School would have remained a part of the University. The Bill

was accepted by Mr. Eskridge and was passed almost if not quite by a unanimous vote; & no more was heard of an investigation. It was a great victory for Mr. Eskridge & Emporia after a terrible defeat; almost if not quite equal to the victory for Lawrence![41]

In spite of the above letter, President Taylor seemed intent upon crediting Goodnow with initiating the Normal School idea. Several years after he no longer was connected with the institution, Taylor on at least two occasions again publicly related the legend. Both speeches were given on the Emporia campus: one at President J. H. Hill's inauguration in 1906, and the other at anniversary festivities in 1915.[42]

Interesting and worth noting, although having no apparent effect upon the legend, is the fact that L. B. Kellogg, forty-five years after he himself as first principal had opened the school, gave what appears to be his only recorded mention of the legend, but with a different twist. Kellogg claimed that L. D. Bailey, justice of the Kansas Supreme Court, not only had suggested the Normal School but had actually written the bill; patterning it after the Massachusetts Normal School. Kellogg also attempted to tone down somewhat the supposition that Eskridge was uninformed. "It is said that Mr. Eskridge inquired 'What is a Normal School?'" Kellogg related, pointing out to his audience that

> Whatever may be said about Mr. Eskridge's previous knowledge of Normal Schools, it is to his credit that in the early days of the school the institution had no better friend than he, and that his services as a member of the Board of Regents were of the greatest possible service to the school.[43]

One irony is that nowhere on the campus or within the city can one find a tangible reminder of the man who by his tenacious courage brought the institution into being. For some reason that defies explanation, the memory of Eskridge's contribution towards Emporia's public school education and especially towards the Normal School has all but faded into oblivion. Yet as recently as 1927, William Allen White in his editorials was extolling the man's accomplishments and reminding Emporians of their debt to Eskridge.[44]

Emporia editors had not always been so kind, however. In the autumn of 1863, Stotler, angry over recent legislative action which reduced printing rates for official notices, decided to run against Eskridge for a seat in the upcoming legislature. He wrote stinging editorials about what Eskridge had done or had failed to do, especially in regard to the late university struggle. Stotler, nevertheless, lost the election. Earlier in the summer, Stotler's paper had sizzled with heated exchanges between Eskridge and Representative F. R. Page of Neosho Rapids, the latter reportedly having been less than wholeheartedly in favor of Emporia's university bid. Indeed, throughout 1863 Stotler was bitter over an unfair loss of revenue; Eskridge was eloquently insistent that his political maneuvers had only enhanced Emporia's chances for the university, while Page was bent on convincing constituents that his own efforts had been in the best interest of all Lyon County.[45]

Most Emporians, meanwhile, were mainly concerned with their own personal safety. Rumors of Indians and guerrilla bands sped across the prairies all summer long. As early as May, a citizens' guard was organized to protect the community from surprise attack. Citizens were particularly nervous about Quantrill who reportedly was in the area. To give everyone a sense of security, a "six-pounder" (a large gun) was installed in front of the *Emporia News* office.[46] Little wonder then that Emporians momentarily forgot about the Normal School. Stotler, late in the summer, admitted that "we have neglected to state that the Normal School has been located on Mr. Fick's farm adjoining town."[47]

All three commissioners presumably had met initially in the spring, but not until four months later was any official action taken. The twenty-acre Fick site, located between Ninth and Twelfth Avenues east of what later became the "Katy" tracks, probably had not been chosen for its desirability so much as to comply with the law. In any event, it was never used. Fick and his wife, Sarah, deeded their land to the state on August 17, the same day of the commission meeting. Apparently, only two of the land commissioners were present for the transaction.[48]

In retrospect, the concern is not that there was a delay in getting the Normal School under way, but rather that the institution came to life as soon as it did. The sparsely settled state of Kansas was caught up in widespread economic hardship during the early 1860s; yet its role in the Civil War was played with patriotic zeal. Kansans played an especially significant role in 1864 when General Sterling Price's rebel forces made their final western thrust over the Eastern border of the state. During that period, most able bodied men of the Emporia area were somewhere between Fort Leavenworth and Fort Scott, determined to repel the invaders.[49]

Fortunately for the future of the Normal School, the border warfare did not command full attention of the government until well after the 1864 legislature adjourned. By then the organization of the Normal had been accomplished and the first appropriation bill passed. Again, it was Eskridge who introduced and guided both bills through the House. Judging by the votes, neither bill met with much opposition. In fact, the Organization Act had but one negative vote, and that in the Senate. The appropriation bill passed in the House by almost three to one. There were no negative votes in the Senate. Called "An Act To Aid the Normal," it provided only one thousand dollars for salaries, but at least the Normal School finally was funded.[50]

The Reverend Grosvenor C. Morse of Emporia, in all probability, had been actively interested first in the university and then the Normal School from the very beginning; but not until during the organizational phase of the institution in 1864 did he begin to leave tracks that led to his immeasurable contribution.[51] As early as January 2, 1864, his pen was persuasively pointing out to Emporians the desirability of an early opening date for the Normal. In a lengthy article in the *Emporia News*, Morse insisted that he had nothing to say one way or another about the circumstances leading to the school's location in Emporia; but he was a staunch believer in Normal education as a means of upgrading the common schools which were, according to him, the college for the millions. He thought it only proper that Kansans should be proud of fine school houses, but he lamented the deplorable condition of the state regarding qualified teachers. The Normal School did not rival any other state institution but rather was the servant of all, according to Morse. He believed that despite the inevitable increase in taxes the school should be put into operation at once "for the purpose of providing a supply of teachers for immediate use." In yet another paragraph, he hoped that the legislature would "make the Normal a living thing at once."[52]

One indication of the extent of Morse's influence upon the Organization Act may be seen by comparing Section IX of the law, printed in full herein, with the aforementioned article which predates the 1864 legislature. In the article, Morse suggested that some students from all counties or districts within the state be admitted free to the Normal. Another indication of his involvement can be found in *The Emporia News*, July 23, wherein Morse pointed out that before the Normal could get under way two oversights must be taken care of: the Organization Act must be published in the Statute book as required by Section XVII of the

Act, and the Board of Directors must be appointed by the governor who, at the time, was absent from the state. In the meantime, according to Morse, preliminary plans were being made in order to help the directors when appointed.

A month later Governor Carney appointed six men to the Board of Directors: James Rogers, a legislator from Burlingame; T. S. Huffaker, Council Grove; J. W. Roberts, a judge from Oskaloosa; David Brockway, legislator from Topeka; Representative Eskridge and the Reverend Grosvenor C. Morse, Emporia. The three ex-officio members were Governor Carney, Superintendent Goodnow, and State Treasurer William Spriggs, thus completing the required nine-member board.[53]

Had not the Kansas-Missouri border military crisis taken precedence, the directors would have met in the autumn; but as it happened, December 8, 1864 was the earliest date they could get together. Superintendent Goodnow, chairman pro tem, called the meeting for ten o'clock that morning in Emporia. A permanent organization was effected with Governor Carney as president; Morse, secretary; and Spriggs, treasurer. Business at that first meeting included two resolutions: that, for the sake of uniformity, textbooks officially recommended by the state be used by the Normal, and that the board accept the offer of the upper floor of the new schoolhouse belonging to District #1 of Lyon County.[54]

The new district schoolhouse was the first tangible result of the school bond law that was destined to revolutionize the common schools of Kansas, thereby creating an insatiable demand for teachers that in turn was to force upon the non-viable Normal School a future growth beyond all expectations. It was indeed fitting that Eskridge, the man who championed both the bond law and the Normal School law, should be the one to speak out at Emporia's annual school meeting to resolve:

> That we tender to the State, free of charge during such portion of the ensuing year as may be necessary, for the uses and purposes of a Normal School, the upper room of our district school house, and hereby instruct the district school board to favor the object of the resolution.[55]

From the nine directors, Eskridge, Morse, and Rogers were elected to the executive committee whose first duty was to hire a principal for the projected Normal School. Morse was the member drafted to make the trip east for that purpose. How soon after December 8 he was able to get away is not recorded, but by the end of the month he was back in Emporia. An announcement of his successful quest appeared the day after his return:

> Rev. C. G. Morse returned by last night's stage from Chicago. He informs us that he succeeded in his mission to obtain a teacher for the Normal School at this place. He has secured the services of Professor L. B. Kellogg of the Illinois State Normal University.[56]

The arduous December journey made by Morse and the equally arduous journey a month later by Lyman Beecher Kellogg are both worthy of space in this narrative history.

CHAPTER 2

FINDING A "PRINCIPAL"

Kellogg, who lived beyond his allotted three score years and ten, told of his first journey to Kansas many times, but the brief five years left to Morse after his historic trip east were too full of plans and action to allow for reminiscing. Fortunately, however, Morse had a friend, the Reverend Richard Cordley, who later told his story.[57]

In 1865 the nearest railway station to Emporia was across the river from Leavenworth which was a three day journey by horseback. At the end of two days in the saddle, Morse rapped at the door of his colleague and friend in Lawrence. According to Cordley's account, a freezing drizzle had been falling throughout that December day, and when he opened the door, he found Morse standing there encased in ice from head to foot. Mrs. Cordley took charge of him while her husband stabled the horse, and before long, over hot tea, Morse was telling of his mission. He was enroute to Chicago to find a school man who would be willing to come to Kansas to head the new Normal School for one thousand dollars.

Of Morse, Cordley later said, "He took great interest in the opening and development of the State Normal School, and probably gave that institution more gratuitous labor than any other man."

Of the proposed salary, Cordley said that the thousand dollars was such an absurdly small appropriation that it is doubtful anything would have been done except for the faith and enthusiasm of Morse. "He was full of his plans for opening the school, and had no more doubt of his success than if he had ten thousand dollars instead of one."

Morse left on his horse early the following morning for Leavenworth where he crossed the river and boarded the train for Chicago. According to Cordley, Morse failed to get the man he had in mind in Chicago and went on to Bloomington.[58]

Fifty years after the event, L. B. Kellogg recalled that his invitation to come to Kansas to teach school occurred in this manner:

> When Mr. Morse got as far east as Chicago he called upon Perkins Bass, whom he had known as a fellow student at Dartmouth, and explained his errand.
>
> Mr. Bass, who was acting president of the Illinois Normal for a year after President Hovey went into the army, thought Mr. Morse could find someone at the Bloomington school, and recommended him to see Mr. Edwards, the president, and inquire for a young man by the name of Kellogg, who had been a student there when he, Perkins Bass, was acting as president of that school. Mr. Bass thought that Kellogg would be a good man for the place, if he was still at Bloomington or could be found.
>
> Mr. Morse accordingly, came to Bloomington from Chicago, saw Mr. Edwards, and inquired about me. Mr. Edwards brought him around to my room, and introduced me to Mr. Morse, and said Mr. Morse was authorized to employ a principal for a Normal School to be started in Kansas, and that both Mr. Bass and he had recommended me for the place, and that if I wanted to go he would get somebody else to take my place in the Model school and let me off.
>
> Referring to the recommendation of Perkins Bass, it was a great surprise to me, because while I knew him as acting president of the school, two years had elapsed since then. I did not know that he had ever noticed me in school; and did not suppose that he knew my name even, let alone remembering me in any manner. This is simply an illustration of how little we realize, upon what casual and unexpected things our whole course in life may be changed.
>
> My coming to Kansas seems to have been the result of Mr. Morse's stopping off in Chicago to see his old classmate, Perkins Bass, on his trip east. I do not know what it was that caused Mr. Bass to remember me. The recommendation of Mr. Edwards was easily explainable. I had been a student under him for two

years, and had done some teaching in the school as an assistant, and he, more than anyone else, knew about what might likely be expected of me as a teacher.[59]

Morse returned immediately to Emporia, according to Kellogg, in order to hasten arrangements for opening the school. Although the aim was for a January opening date, Morse soon wrote Kellogg that the opening date would have to be postponed until February because of a delay in getting seats for the school room. Morse also sent Kellogg specific travel instructions and a letter of introduction to his friend Cordley of Lawrence.

> I was to take the C. B. & Q. railroad from Chicago to Quincy, Ill.; then to cross the Mississippi river by ferry boat, unless blocked by ice, and then to take a small spur of the Hannibal & St. Joseph railroad to Palmyra Junction; thence on the main line of Hannibal & St. Joseph to St. Joseph, Mo.; thence by railroad down the east bank of Missouri River to Weston, the end of the track, nearly opposite Fort Leavenworth by ferry boat to the fort landing; thence by stage to Leavenworth. Stay overnight at the Mansion house, Leavenworth, instead of Planters house at the levee, on account of its greater respectability; the next day to go by stage from Leavenworth to Lawrence, and the same night at 9 o'clock, if I struck it right, to take the stage from Lawrence to Emporia. If I did not get to Lawrence the night the stage left for Emporia I would have to stay over at Lawrence for a day or two because the stage from Lawrence to Emporia was tri-weekly only.[60]

According to his own recollections and the newspaper account of his arrival, Kellogg was five long days enroute from Chicago to Emporia utilizing almost every mode of transportation available, including his own leg power. It was a mid-January morning when he boarded the train in Chicago and night before he arrived in Quincy, thus completing the first leg of his journey. Kellogg remembered vividly the dangerous but exciting second stage of his journey:

> The next morning it was reported that we should have to walk in crossing the Mississippi river on the ice, as the weather had turned warm, and it was not deemed safe to drive across the ice with a team, as had been done for several days before. The ferry boat had been out of commission for some little time on account of the river being frozen over.

There were something like 10 or a dozen passengers to cross the river that morning to take the Hannibal & St. Joe train on the Missouri side. We got along all right until about two-thirds of the way across, when we came to a break in the ice where the current of the main channel of the river was beginning to make an opening. The opening, however, was only two or three feet wide there, and by taking a running start we were able to jump it. It was believed that inside of half an hour it would be impossible to cross. The river appeared to be approximately a mile wide at Quincy. A small, dinky train was waiting for us, and took the passengers about 20 or 30 miles southwest down the river to what was called Palmyra Junction, where we waited for half an hour or so, until the train from Hannibal on the main line came along. It took until night that day to get to St. Joseph.

At St. Joe, I found a small hotel just across the street from the depot, and having found out the train I was to take down the east side of the Missouri River would leave at 4 o'clock in the morning, I went to bed with the understanding that I would be called at 3:30 in the morning. I remember waking up several times in the night and wondering if it was time to get up; but found that it was not. Finally, I woke with a start, and found it was 5 minutes of 4. I dressed hastily, hurried down stairs to the bar room, and found the boy who was to have called me fast asleep in a chair. I hurriedly shook and wakened him, paid for my lodging and ran to the depot, finding the train already started and pulling out with increasing speed as it went out. I chased the train down the track, and after great exertion and fast running, caught up with the train and climbed onto the rear platform wholly out of breath and exhausted from the running.

We arrived at Weston from St. Joe for a late dinner, and found a ferry boat waiting to take the passengers down and across the Missouri River to the landing at Fort Leavenworth. The Missouri River carried floating ice, but was open for the passage of the boat. At the landing a four horse stage was in waiting to take the passengers to Leavenworth.[61]

The Mansion house was thronged with guests and travelers the evening I arrived. I could get no sleeping place in the hotel proper, but was informed the hotel would accommodate me with a room in a building across the street, controlled by another guest. When I was shown to my room, I was told to leave my room door unlocked, unless I preferred to get up and unlock it to let the next man in, if he came. The hotel annex consisted of the upstairs portion of two or three store buildings, temporarily partitioned off into as many sleeping rooms as the space would afford. There was a constant tramping up and down the long hall leading to these rooms and people talking and coming and going to and from the rooms—at least that was the way it seemed to me. I did not know what kind of a crowd I had got into, and was somewhat apprehensive. After a while, a couple of men seemed to stop at my door and a stranger was shown in by the same hotel attendant who had brought me over. He lit the kerosene lamp, and looked to see if I was asleep. I was not, but seemed to be. The stranger, who was to be my roommate, said nothing, but after pulling off his coat, unstrapped from his waist a belt carrying a holster with a large revolver in it. He took out the revolver from its case, or holster, and examined it, apparently looking to see if it was loaded and in order, and then put it under the pillow on his side of the bed. He then undressed and climbed into the bed. I kept carefully to my side of the bed, and in the morning, I saw that he was a decent-looking fellow and while we were dressing I found out that he was from Council Grove, in business there, and had come to Leavenworth for supplies. . . .

I was informed that the stage for Lawrence would leave about 9 o'clock in the morning, and would come around to the hotel before starting. When it drove up, I hurried out, and attempted to climb in. The stage driver asked my name. I told him. He shook his head, and said I could not go; that my name was not on the waybill, and the stage was full. I ought to have gone to the stage office the night before or very early in the morning and engaged my passage, paying for it at the time. But I did not know this; and so had lost my opportunity to ride in that stage. The next regular stage would not go until the next day. I went back into the hotel disappointed. I concluded, however, to hunt up the stage office and engage passage for the next day. Arriving at the office, I was informed that there were some other passengers wanting to get over to Lawrence, and that if there were enough of them to make up a load, they could send out an extra stage that day. In the course of a half hour or so they had enough inquiries to make up a light stage load. So, about 10 or 11 in the forenoon I got safely off on the extra. We reached Lawrence at night, and I found that the Emporia stage would leave that night. My first errand was to book my passage at the stage office and was informed the stage would call for me at the hotel about 9 o'clock. . . .[62]

23

The final leg of Kellogg's journey (from Lawrence to Emporia) as described by Kellogg himself has been the inspiration for occasional feature stories through the years, especially during E.S.U.'s centennial observance from 1963 to 1965; but before Kellogg ever wrote his recollections an error that needs to be corrected had crept into the literature concerning the opening of the Normal. The often used history compiled in 1889 contains the misleading statement that "Mr. Kellogg reached Emporia by stage coach in time to address the citizens on the subject of Normal Schools on the evening before school was to begin."[63] The implication, of course, is that the new principal arrived the day of the lecture which had been scheduled for the evening before the school opened, whereas in reality Kellogg had been in Emporia almost four weeks before the February 14 lecture. At least one significant study, decades later, interpreted the above statement to mean that "Mr. Kellogg reached Emporia by stage coach the day before the Normal was to open its doors for the first time."[64]

Some of the confusion about Kellogg's arrival can be attributed to the low key announcement that appeared in *The Emporia News* the following day under the small heading "Distinguished Arrivals:"

Arrived by last night's Stage [Friday, January 20] Hon. J. R. Swallow [State auditor], Prof. L. B. Kellogg of the Illinois Normal University; Mr. Buchanan, treasurer of Chase County; J. C. Fraker, treasurer of Lyon County; D. S. Gilmore of the *Ilworth Times*; R. S. Crampton of Baltimore, and J. H. Hunt of *The Emporia News*. –all report favorable.[65]

If one counts the driver and assumes that Hunt listed all of the passengers aboard, there were eight people on that stage. Had Kellogg's recollections never been published, that figure would have stood; but half a century later Kellogg wrote that there were ten who shared in that historic ride.

There were two passengers with the driver on the outside or driver's seat, and there were six passengers, or three on a seat made for two, on the two inside seats, besides myself; making 10 of us in all to ride. . . . That stage ride from Lawrence to Emporia lasted all the rest of that night and until after dark the next day through a practically uninhabited country. Part of the time, I tried to sit on the sharp edge of the side of the coach bed between the two seats; part of the time some or more of us would get up and walk up grades to relieve our cramped limbs, and also lighten the load for the two horses. At other times I would sit on the knees of first one and then another of the six inside passengers. Nobody complained, and the time passed in conversation. The stops to change horses and for meals were welcome rests. To my astonishment the winter roads were smooth and dry, and to some extent dusty. There was no snow and no mud. The sun shone and it was warm like October in Illinois. . . . We arrived at Emporia about 7 o'clock in the evening; it being a late stage on account of the heavy load of passengers.[66]

Kellogg also recalled that it was Hunt who first had invited him to sit on his knees for a portion of the ride. Others whom he remembered to be on the stage were Gilmore and Fraker. But if he remembered the person who perhaps was the most "distinguished" passenger of all, he did not admit to it in his recollections. It was left to the renowned editor of *The Emporia Times* by means of parenthetical information to remind the world that his mother had come to Emporia on that same stage.

One of the passengers on that stage was Miss Mary Ann Hatten of Galesburg, Ill., who was coming to Kansas to teach school. She afterwards married Dr. Allen White. The editor of this paper is their offspring. —Ed. *Gazette.*[67]

If anyone ever identified the tenth occupant of that stage, this writer is totally unaware of it.

The intervening weeks between Morse's triumphant return from Illinois and the initial opening of the Normal's doors were busy ones for Morse and his persuasive pen. As board secretary, he issued the official announcement that L. B. Kellogg had been hired to head the Normal School which was projected to open about February 1. "Meanwhile," he pleaded, "let every friend of our common schools endeavor to interest as many as possible to engage in fitting themselves to do honor to the Teachers vocation and subserve the cause of popular education."[68]

A week later, in the paper that told of Kellogg's arrival, Morse stated that the Normal School's success would depend to a great extent upon the efforts of Emporians. He shared with them several glowing recommendations written in behalf of the new principal, declaring that "We have, we think, secured the first condition of success, i.e., a Normal teacher of the first order." But Morse, for all of his enthusiasm, was at least in one area pragmatic. Anticipating the problem of housing, he asked how students were to be accommodated with board at low rates when so few Emporians had spare room.

> We should put ourselves to considerable inconvenience and share our best with the students, putting everything at the very lowest possible rates, so as to encourage the enterprise. Let no student be kept away for want of accommodations, or high prices. Let the ladies take hold of the matter, each one see how many she can accommodate.[69]

Morse explained that some students would require both room and board, some bringing their own bedding; others would want a room only and would board themselves. Because of the generosity of Emporians, he concluded, "the Directors will not hesitate to say to all, Come!"[70]

Nearly four years were to pass before boarding houses actually came into being, but it is worth noting that they were a part of the overall plan even before school commenced, as evidenced by Morse's mention of them in the same article. He optimistically stated that "We are happy to know already that arrangements are being made to erect boarding houses the present season."

In the same paper, Morse discussed another vital part of the Normal School under the caption "The Model School." Actually, the article amounted to an editorial about the philosophy, theory and practice of teaching. Referring first to Section Six of the 1864 Organizational Act creating such a school, Morse called it a "necessary apprentice shop to the Normal School." He discussed the manner in which the Illinois State Normal had procured their model school—by first using the district school for experimental purposes until their need outgrew the facility, necessitating that they build. "Shall Emporia have such a school?" he asked.[71]

Morse's editorials on education at this time undoubtedly paved the way for town support of the projected Normal School and contributed significantly to the successful launching of the institution. Another contributor was J. H. Hunt, editor of *The Emporia News*, who from time to time indicated his wholehearted support of Kellogg and the Normal. A week after Kellogg's arrival, Hunt wrote about the great need for qualified teachers, complaining that many inferior ones were teaching and that all of them should have at least one term in the Normal.[72]

By the first of February, details regarding the opening of the Normal had been worked out, as indicated by the advertisement which appeared in both the February 4 and February 11 issues of *The Emporia News*.

Accompanying the notice was a letter from Superintendent Goodnow to the clerks of the various counties of Kansas regarding the opening of school and Kellogg's qualifications.

Another Morse article also appeared. Writing under "School Economy," Morse maintained that thousands of dollars were being wasted annually upon incompetent teachers, "a very cogent reason why the Normal School should receive special interest. We want a corps of trained teachers in every county in the State," he declared. According to reports from county superintendents, 85% of the state's teachers were incompetent. But, as Morse pointed out, even worse than the waste of money was the fact that children were not getting the instruction they should have—"an irreparable loss to themselves and the State." In a lighter vein, the same paper carried an invitation to the public to hear the lecture (Tuesday evening, February 14) on Normal Schools by Kellogg in the Normal room with a "Sociable" following.[73]

Others than the readers of the Emporia paper were made aware of the new State Normal School through the pages of the February issue of *The Kansas Educational Journal*. Three pages of that magazine were devoted to the institution: the same advertisement that had appeared locally; a reprint from *The Illinois Teacher* listing Kellogg's exceptional qualifications, his experience, and his suitability for the job at hand; and a welcome to Kellogg from the teachers of Kansas, pledging to him their full cooperation, and encouraging would-be teachers "to avail themselves of this favorable opportunity of attending the State Normal School and fitting themselves for better positions."[74]

By today's standards it seems incredible that a young man not yet twenty-four years of age had been chosen to head the Kansas State Normal School; but if at the time there were any qualms about Kellogg's lack of maturity or his ability to handle the job, no record of them survives. All through the West in the 1860s monumental tasks were being performed by the young, and Kansas was no exception. Preston Plumb was not yet twenty when he helped to found Emporia. Eskridge was thirty when he championed the Normal School bill; Morse was thirty-six; Bailey, forty-four; and Goodnow, forty-nine.

The nearest thing to doubt about Kellogg's ability, that has been found, is in a chronicle by one of his first students who twenty-five years later wrote:

. . . A few of us only had met the new principal, and somehow we felt that he was not equal to the situation. How deceiving appearances are sometimes! . . .

. . . The most of us were of that age when we really thought that the world would hardly move along without us, and really thought we could get on the blind side of the new teacher. But somehow we never found it.[75]

The night young Kellogg arrived in Emporia he was met by the Reverend Morse and a few curious townspeople for what Kellogg later called "a little reception in the hotel parlor." Instead of staying at the hotel, the new principal rode home with Morse in a spring wagon pulled by one elderly horse. The Morse family lived on a farm about two and one half miles southeast of Emporia, and Kellogg for the first few months resided with them, walking to and from the Normal School. Later he boarded with Jacob Stotler at the northeast corner of Seventh Avenue and Merchant Streets.[76]

The young principal wasted no time in becoming a part of the community. The day after his arrival he accompanied Morse to a safety meeting where the town citizens discussed the need for protection from a feared Indian band. A few days later, according to Kellogg's memoirs, he and Morse journeyed to Topeka by wagon to visit the legislature. It was there that Kellogg for the first time met Senator Eskridge. Presumably, he also met Jacob Stotler, speaker of the house, and Representatives R. H. Abraham of Emporia, and F. R. Page of Neosho Rapids.

Whether or not Kellogg's and Morse's visit had any positive results cannot be assessed accurately from this distance, but the projected Normal School did share with the Agricultural College in a little-publicized appropriation bill which Governor S. J. Crawford signed the day before the initial opening of Kansas State Normal School. Entitled "An Act For the Payment of Teachers and Professors of the State Normal School, the State Agricultural College," the law provided $2,000 to the Board of Directors of the Normal for salaries at the institution during 1865. It was scheduled to go into effect after being published in the *Kansas Educational Journal.* It was duly published, but no mention of the act ever appeared in *The Emporia News.* Nor is it referred to in any history of the school. For that reason, a copy of the act appears within the pages of the appendix of this history.[77]

On another occasion prior to the opening of the Normal School, Kellogg was driven by Morse to Council Grove to present a lecture on education. On that trip the transplanted Illinois schoolman saw Indians for the first time. The Kaw Indian Reserve, at the time, lay between Americus and Council Grove where the Agency was located. Kellogg not only saw them on the Reserve, but he observed them at the Agency.[78]

CHAPTER 3

IMPLEMENTING THE ORGANIZATION ACT AND OPENING THE DOORS: 1865-1866

The opening of the Normal School apparently had been postponed once for want of furnishings; but, nevertheless, when the advertised date, February 15, 1865 arrived, there still were no seats or desks for the schoolroom. They had been delayed in transit, presumably in Leavenworth.[79]

It is curious that what must have been considered a minor inconvenience and at most a temporary arrangement should have found a prominent place in the permanent history of the school. Indeed, the description of the first day has been recited down through the generations until it has become a litany. Unlike much of the legend which had little factual base, the description of that February 15 came from Principal Kellogg, himself. Although his 1870 five-year report to the Board of Directors is usually the source cited, an earlier description comprised a portion of the historical sketch which Kellogg outlined for his audience at the dedication of the first Normal School building. Inasmuch as this dedicatory address of January 2, 1867 appears to be Kellogg's earliest record of that historic first day, it seems worthwhile to relate it here.

On the fifteenth day of February, 1865, eighteen students—fifteen more than were greeted by Father Pearce, in Lexington, when the first Normal School of Massachusetts was opened, and one less than President Hovey had at the beginning of the Illinois University—were gathered in the room I have before spoken of as granted to the school by the kindness of Emporia. Out of doors, were all sorts of rumors concerning an expected rebel invasion from Texas, and another of Indians from the Territory, under Stanwaitie. In doors, the eighteen students had settees borrowed from a neighboring church, and the teacher's seat was a yellow painted chair borrowed from the County Treasurer's office. There were two stoves in the room, no teacher's desk or other furniture, no text books, maps, or other appliances. No visitors. The parable of the sower was read, the Lord's Prayer repeated; and so the Normal School of Kansas was opened. We were all hopeful, and, ere long, hard at work. Very soon the school room was well seated, and reasonably furnished. The number of students increased day by day, until there were forty-two; and all were earnest, faithful and enthusiastic. The discipline was all that could be wished, and little said about it. The school was much visited, and much talked about at home and in the newspapers. I do not know how far knowledge of that term's work extended, but it is certain that the Kaw Indians were reached; for, one morning, shortly after devotional exercises, a painted warrior of that uncivilized tribe favored the school with a visit.[80]

Nowhere in *The Emporia News* was there any mention of the dearth of furniture or equipment for the new Normal School, but in the first issue following the official opening, Editor Hunt, who had been away for a couple of weeks, wrote optimistically about the institution.

Despite the storm and mud, the Normal School opened as had been advertised, on Wednesday the 15th int., with a goodly number of candidates for teacher's honors. We are assured that in Mr. Kellogg we have a teacher that is <u>all a teacher</u>—just the man for the place. Now is the time for every individual to become a teacher, or desire to improve himself in that vocation. We have now the beginning of a real Normal School, and no humbug.[81]

Still known as "the original eighteen," those students who showed up that first day in spite of adverse weather and the unreadiness of the facilities included fifteen young women and three young men, all from Lyon County except two. Because their presence made history on that stormy February 15, their names deserve a place in this narrative:

Zeruah P. Allen, Lawrence; Mary Bay, Dry Creek; Laura Burns,

Emporia; Ellen M. Cowles, Fremont; Clarissa Fawcett, Heloise Hunt, Emma Hunt, Bettie Maddock, Sarah Mentor, Mattie Nicholls, Josephine Slocum, Emporia; Adaline Soule, Eagle Creek; Elmira Spencer, Margaret C. Spencer, Mattie P. Spencer, Frank Gillett, Albert T. McIntire, Emporia; and John F. McClean, Illinois.[82]

Historical accounts emphasize the humble beginnings of the Kansas State Normal School, pointing up the lack of revenue, accommodations, and library, marveling that in spite of such deficiencies the institution survived and managed to grow. Contemporary accounts, however, took a different tack. The early proponents of the Normal School never ceased in their public relations effort, continuing long after the school was launched to voice enthusiasm and a sense of pride in the embryonic institution. Eskridge and Morse, both directors of the school, and Editor Hunt threw their unqualified support behind Principal Kellogg, an extraordinarily able educator, who was too young to know defeat. These men had a dream that even the tenuous national problems of 1865 could not obliterate. The draft almost removed Morse from the scene in March, but upon investigation by officials of the town, it was determined that Lyon County volunteers were more numerous than the draft quota; thus no one had to be conscripted.[83]

Perhaps the aura of optimism that enveloped and nurtured the Normal School can best be summed up in the words of Hunt, who, less than three weeks after opening day, wrote that the school had opened under very favorable circumstances. The teacher was able and experienced; the building was good; equipment, comfortable and convenient; and new students were applying daily. Hunt wrote:

> . . . . This school bids fair to become one of the fixed and living institutions of the State and was located here through the indefatigable exertions of the Hon. C. V. Eskridge (after Lawrence, by the aid of money, had swindled us out of the University) . . . .
> It is emphatically the people's school—each representative district in the State has a right to send one student tuition free, to be chosen by the representative, by the provision of law. . . .

Hunt ended his enthusiastic editorial with a hint of pride in what had been accomplished locally, at the same time daring to ask of Lawrence a question that probably many Emporians had been asking themselves if not each other.

> We would inquire of our Lawrence friends, without any invidious feeling, what has become of the State University and

the $15,000 donated?[84]

By the time the first term had been in session six weeks, publishers began to donate textbooks, and Kellogg was receiving letters of encouragement from prominent educators who commended the young State of Kansas for inaugurating the Normal School. Editor Hunt proudly stated that "Our School is moving on." He also declared that

> Prof. Kellogg is running our Normal School handsomely, and to the entire satisfaction of all, which is a rare circumstance in the history of Schools.[85]

Since 1863, Lyon County had been conducting a semi-annual Teachers Institute. The fifth such event was held at the Normal School early in May, 1865. The four-day session which had been given much advance publicity was open to all teachers of the county and anyone else interested in attending. No fewer than twenty-five persons were involved in the presentations at this particular institute, many of whom were students at the Normal. Kellogg played an important role in the proceedings as did Morse who had been involved also in the previous institutions.[86]

Morse was one of the committee of four whose job it was to draw up the many resolutions by which those who had made the Institute possible were thanked. One of those resolutions was

> Resolved—That we hail the successful opening of our State Normal School with feelings of unmingled satisfaction, and we believe that under a continuance of its present administration it will prove an invaluable auxiliary to our educational interests, and should receive the hearty support of the friends of common schools throughout the State.[87]

The May Institute resulted in the far reaching decision to switch from semi-annual to annual institutes which were to be held in the fall of the year. For more than three quarters of a century, public school teachers in Kansas were subsequently involved in fall institutes just prior to the opening of the new school year.

Another outgrowth of this particular institute was the emphasis thereafter placed upon physical exercise as an essential ingredient in the common school curriculum. Kellogg, who believed that an active body made for an active mind, already had his Normal School students involved with physical exercises insofar as was practical without special facilities.

He led the Institute's discussion of the benefits of introducing gymnastics into the common schools, and while general agreement was reached, not all participants believed as fervently in strengthening the body as did Kellogg. Morse favored physical exercise primarily as a means of waking up the mind.[88]

By the end of the first term in late June, there were forty-two students enrolled at the Normal. Although the initial announcement of the school's opening had encouraged students to be present from the first day, there apparently was no cut-off date for enrolling, thereby allowing students to enter the Normal whenever they were able, provided, of course, that they could meet the other qualifications.

The Normal had begun quietly without fanfare, but its first term closed with quite a flourish. Whether by accident or design, the closing festivities, June 27–28, 1865 coincided with a railroad promotional meeting which brought to Emporia prominent persons from throughout the state, many of whom attended the end-of-school activities.

Ten days before the event, *The Emporia News* carried an imposing notice about the closing exercises. The governor was scheduled to speak as were Superintendent Goodnow and Professor Kellogg. The examinations of the students and other exercises were to be open to the public. Judge D. G. Brewer of Leavenworth was to be the main speaker, and the finale was to be a "levee"—a students' reception on the final evening. In an editorial, Hunt extended an open invitation to all to come see for themselves the Normal School in action.[89]

For two weeks after the close of the first term, the local paper was full of news pertaining to the festivities. Although a rainstorm had cut down on attendance at the evening reception, it had failed to dampen the gaiety of the occasion. Many visitors, strangers to Emporia, swelled the audience attending the exercises; but some dignitaries were unable to be present, among whom was Governor Crawford. Ex-Governor Carney and U.S. Representative Sidney Clarke sent Senator Eskridge letters of regret which were published in the paper. Judge L. D. Bailey, chairman of the Board of Visitors prescribed by law for the Normal School, was present for the festivities. Superintendent Goodnow, whose topic concerned the English language, and Judge Brewer spoke as advertised. Brewer's speech, "The New Profession" became the first in a long series of anniversary addresses, and as such was published in full on page one of *The Emporia News*.[90]

At least one out-of-town visitor was a news reporter from the

Atchison Free Press. Remaining anonymous, he, like the local boosters, wrote glowingly of the close-of-term activities. He also was the first to voice the hope that the legislature would provide for a new building in which to house the growing Normal School.[91]

Editor Hunt, although he had attended the festivities and announced that he found them very interesting, left the writing of a full review to Morse. In fact, Hunt's editorship came to an abrupt end in mid-July when O. J. and E. L. Hunt, publishers, sold back *The Emporia News* to Jacob Stotler and his new partner, David S. Gilmore. In announcing the change of ownership, the Hunts maintained that their motto had been "Independent in all things—neutral in nothing." Certainly, they had shown no neutrality in regard to the Normal School during the brief ten months they operated the local paper. Their enthusiastic support undoubtedly played a significant role in the early rapid growth of the school.[92]

When the Board of Directors of the Kansas State Normal School met for the first time on December 8, 1864, their permanent organization ruled that they were to meet thereafter at the call of the executive committee. The first such call was for a meeting in Topeka, February 27, 1865, which was attended by five of the nine directors: Governor Crawford, Goodnow, Eskridge, Morse, and David Brockway. Their second called meeting was held in Emporia, June 26-28, in conjunction with the close of the first term. Already one of their number had changed. Brockway, who had resigned sometime following the Topeka meeting, had been replaced by the governor's appointment of former senator J. M. Rankin, professor of Ottumwa Christian College.[93]

An examination of the Minutes of the June meeting reveals that the Board actually convened four times while in Emporia, the first meeting adjourning for lack of a quorum. Again, no more than five were present: Goodnow, Huffaker, Rogers, Eskridge, and Morse. Decisions made by these men support newspaper claims that the Normal was in demand. The Board voted to ask the principal to see on what terms he could obtain an assistant teacher with ability to teach music and to report his findings to the executive committee. Because already more space was needed, the Board also authorized the executive committee to provide a recitation room by "whatever means that may be at their disposal."

Whereas in February the age limitation for students had been set at fifteen for females and sixteen for males, by June that requirement was raised to sixteen and seventeen respectively, the first of innumerable changes through the years to upgrade the institution. In order not to eliminate all younger students, however, the Principal was given "discretionary power" to admit pupils under those ages where sufficient maturity of mind was indicated and "where the pupil proposes to complete the course before teaching."

Prior to adjourning, members of the board indicated their pleasure with Morse's choice of a principal by passing a resolution that said in part:

> We very cheerfully express to Prof. Kellogg our entire satisfaction as to the manner in which he has discharged his duties as Principal of said school, and congratulate the State upon having secured his services for this important position.[94]

The executive committee apparently soon began seeking a benefactor, and by late July the local paper announced that John Fawcett was about to erect "a building near the school house for an additional recitation room for the Normal School." Fawcett's daughter Clarissa was one of the original students, but by the end of the year three other daughters, Maggie, Mary R., and Lavina, were enrolled.[95]

Vacation time notwithstanding, students as well as their principal and the board secretary worked diligently during the summer of 1865 to further the cause of the Normal School. Fourteen persons journeyed to Atchison to participate in the State Teachers' Association meeting July 26, 27, and 28, an impressive delegation when one considers that two weeks were required for the round trip and convention. Although Lyon Countians outnumbered any other group except for Atchison, Emporia lost its bid for the 1866 convention site to Lawrence by two votes. If, however, prolonged rains and swollen streams had not prevented another six or more Lyon Countians from getting there, in all probability, the emerging State Normal School would have hosted the organization the following summer.[96]

President Kellogg, acting upon the request of the Board of Directors, was en route east to search for an assistant capable in music; but he traveled by way of Atchison to take a significant role in the teachers' conference. He not only addressed the assemblage regarding the history of Normal Schools and their present condition in the United States, but he drilled them in calisthenics. Others from Emporia who actively participated were Mary Jane Watson, who served as a critic; Ellen Plumb, a member of the credentials committee; and Reverend C.G. Morse, chaplain. Morse was also elected vice president of the organization and Miss Watson was named treasurer.[97]

Going east to Kellogg meant Illinois where he spent the month of August with family and friends while seeking an assistant principal. Kellogg's choice of Henry Brace Norton, superintendent of schools in Ogle County, Illinois, proved to be as fortunate for Kansas State Normal School as had been his own selection less than a year earlier.

Like Kellogg, Norton was a product of Illinois Normal University where in 1861 he graduated with honors, remaining there a year as principal of the model school. Previously, he had attended school in Rockford, Illinois, and Beloit College, Wisconsin. He was a man of many capabilities and a variety of interests ranging from natural science to literary skill both in creative writing and editing. His poetic bent endeared him to his colleagues, students, and the local citizenry in general.

Although Norton was five years older than Kellogg, he and his new principal were not strangers to one another. Their years at Illinois Normal had overlapped. According to Kellogg's memoirs, he had at first admired Norton at a distance and then had been greatly impressed by his friendliness when they later chanced to meet.

The two men, whose ideologies were similar, complemented each other in their professional endeavors but were completely opposite in their physical make up. Kellogg was small of stature but endowed with an almost endless supply of energy; Norton was tall, lanky, and rather Lincolnesque, but plagued with faltering health whenever he overextended his physical or mental exertion.

Unlike Kellogg's arrival in Emporia, which has become a significant portion of the literature of the school, Norton's arrival has remained obscure. Indeed, any recording of the circumstances surrounding the event seem to be nonexistent. Yet, the local newspaper of the day gave almost identical attention and coverage to each man, the editor in each case assuring his readers that the man in question was a worthy addition to the community.[98]

It was early September by the time Kellogg returned from his Eastern trip, but more than a week elapsed before the public knew he had found an assistant for the Normal. Jacob Stotler, now the editor of *The Emporia News*, by his own admission had failed to report the fact earlier. He made amends by voicing his approval of Kellogg: "The unexpected success of the first term of the school proves that the right man is in the right place." He continued by explaining that Kellogg, who had been authorized by the Board to hire an assistant principal, had secured the services of H. B. Norton, a graduate of Illinois Normal University, who would arrive in a few days to begin his new duties. Norton, however, did not arrive quite early enough for the opening of the fall term on September 13. It was a few days later before he and his family arrived from Bloomington.[99]

When the second term began, the Kansas State Normal School enrollment was more than three times what it had been on that historic first day of school in February. By the end of the term, it had quadrupled.[100] Mr. Fawcett's donated school room was needed desperately long before it was finished sometime near the middle of the second term. In mid-October 1865, the local editor announced in a progress report that "the new building to be used for recitation purposes is rapidly approaching completion."[101] Probably, it was put to use shortly thereafter. In any event, Kellogg described the addition in his 1865 report..

> Accommodations—The apartments now occupied by the school are as follows: 1st. The assembly room is 32 X 36 feet in the clear; height of ceiling, 14 feet. It is well lighted, ventilated, and an easily warmed room in the second story of the stone edifice recently erected by the citizens of Emporia for their village schools. This room contains the seats and desks of the pupils, and is their study room. It also contains the reference and reading tables on which are found books for consultation and the leading newspapers of the State. It furnishes accommodations for seventy students. At the entrance to the assembly room are two cloak or dressing rooms for the use of the students. They are furnished with hooks for clothing, wash stands, and other appliances necessary to neatness and a tasty [sic. tasteful] attire. These three rooms have been surrendered, by vote of the school district, for the present use of the Normal School. 2d. A frame building 18 X 34 feet, one story in height, used for recitation purposes. This is placed near the stone building and is connected with it by an easy passage way.[102]

Although created primarily for teacher education, the Kansas State Normal School from its very infancy attracted more than potential teachers. Forgers of the Organizational Act showed both foresight and wisdom by not restricting enrollment to student teachers, yet encouraging those students in particular to enroll. The act merely restricted admissions to persons of "good moral character" who could pass an examination, the nature of which was determined by the Board of Directors. To encourage statewide utilization of the school, the act provided scholarships to a certain number of promising future teachers by specifying that each representative district be entitled to recommend one student each twenty-two week term to attend tuition free, provided the foregoing qualifications were met, and provided the student sign a declaration of intent to teach in the common schools of Kansas. Whether other students planning to teach could attend without paying tuition was left to the discretion of the Board. That body, moreover, was alone responsible for excluding or including other than potential teachers. The Board had a broad base from which to operate the school.[103]

Inasmuch as the Board of Directors was expected to operate the Normal School without expense to the state, it is to their credit that prior to the opening of the first term the members advertised that students other than those eligible by law for gratuitous instruction would have their tuition waived provided they filed their intent to become teachers. Tuition for others would be fifty cents per week.[104]

The admissions policy was more precise by the second term. By then, the principal was authorized to admit a limited number of students who did not intend to teach, provided they paid tuition in advance. He also was authorized to accept, tuition free, all qualified students who planned to teach if they would sign the following pledge:

> I hereby declare that it is my intention to become a teacher in the schools of this State, and that my object in attending the Normal School is the better to prepare myself for this important work.[105]

Principal Kellogg, in his 1865 year-end report, mentioned for the first time the provision that tuition-free students were required to teach for a period equal to the time spent in the Normal School. A student, therefore, who completed the full three-year course would be required to teach in Kansas for three years. According to Kellogg, the honor of the student was at stake in fulfilling this requirement.

During 1865, forty-five students, scarcely more than half of the seventy-eight enrolled, subscribed to the pledge. The others paid twenty-five dollars in tuition per year. Kellogg reported that there had been an increase in tuition since the first term and that another increase was being considered. The reason given was to lessen the number of non-professional students who, whenever it became necessary, would be required to give up their places to those who planned to teach.[106]

Whatever else was lacking in Kansas education at the end of 1865, two primary needs were brought out in a lengthy, well-written review of the examinations and festivities that marked the closing of the second term of the Kansas State Normal School. The first great need, of course, was for more and better qualified teachers for the common schools of Kansas; the second was the need for sufficient space in which to accommodate the growing number of students wishing to attend the new Normal School. Editor Stotler on this occasion eloquently declared that

> In the original establishment of this Institution the State Legislature, wittingly or unwittingly, entitled themselves to the gratitude of all good citizens for the zeal thus manifested in behalf of our common schools. Let them now take the next step and appropriate the necessary means, and erect a building that will suffice for the purpose of the school for at least ten years and they will add larger measures to the gratitude of the rising generation and of the friends of education generally.[107]

In his year-end report, Principal Kellogg pleaded for a new building to accommodate the increased number of students—a building that after five to ten years could be used by the Model School. He also pointed to a related problem, one that Morse had addressed at the very beginning, that of how and where to house and feed the student population.[108]

Since early summer, friends of the Normal had been agitating for a new building which the school could call its very own. There was dissatisfaction, however, with the established site, and by December 1865 a movement to change the location gained momentum. According to the local editor, the Fick site had never really been an "eligible" location for the Kansas State Normal School because of the unsightly and low-lying terrain which was all but inaccessible in wet weather. The commissioners, without any serious attempt to find other sites, had chosen Fick's tract as a matter of expedience in order to comply with the law. Pointing out that a change of location would aid the future of the institution, the editor urged that any change be made before a dollar was spent for building or improvements. Before the year ended, at least one public meeting of Emporians was called to consider changing the location.[109]

During the first days of the 1866 legislature, Senator Eskridge pushed through a bill to change the site of the Normal School. By January 11, it had already reached the house where it was shepherded by

Representative Stotler who afterwards explained through his newspaper that the rules were suspended and the bill passed in a "jiffy." Thus, by mid-January the bill became law.[110] It called for the site to be changed to the head of Commercial Street to a narrow strip twenty rods wide extending north about one-half mile from what is now Twelfth Avenue. Still referred to as the Filley tract in official physical plant records at Emporia State University, the acreage was donated by Giles C. Filley of Saint Louis to the State of Kansas for the Kansas State Normal School.[111] Although Filley was allowed three months in which to transfer the deed, Lyon County records show that it was recorded on March 20, 1866. The law also specified that the Fick land be deeded back to the former owner.[112]

Jacob Stotler, who three years earlier had seemed totally disinterested in the Normal School, was now one of its staunchest supporters. Indeed, it was fortunate for the school that, after being speaker of the house in 1865, Stotler was defeated for that position in 1866. By his own admission, he had not campaigned for the job because he believed he could better serve his home district from the floor. Certainly, the Normal School benefitted.

At the same time that Stotler wrote home about the successful attempt to change the Normal School location, he also reported that he was certain there would be an appropriation "to keep our Normal going in good shape." But he was less sure about getting the amount necessary to erect a building. Appropriation bills already had been proposed in the amounts of $50,000 for a new Capitol and $7,000 for the non-viable state university. Yet, a week later, Stotler introduced an appropriation bill for the Normal in the amount of $13,000, ten of which was for the new building and three for salaries, and within two weeks the bill had passed both houses. By the following week, the governor had signed the bill and the Board of Directors were already busy with bids.[113]

The day after Governor S. J. Crawford signed the Normal appropriation bill, the Board of Directors gathered in Topeka for its semi-annual meeting. In addition to the three ex-officio members, Crawford, Spriggs, and Goodnow, both Eskridge and Morse were present. Principal Kellogg also attended in order to present plans for a school building. After considerable discussion, T. H. Lescher's plan with an estimated cost of $9,360.00 was adopted. The executive committee, Eskridge, Morse, and Rogers, was designated as the building committee, and Kellogg, an advisory member, was instructed to proceed to Lawrence to secure the full specifications for the proposed building.[114]

By April 1866, when bids on the project were taken, the architect's estimate proved to be considerably below what the various builders considered adequate. Indeed, less than three months after the $10,000 appropriation was approved, a contract to build the State Normal School building was awarded to John Hammond, an Emporia builder, for the sum of $15,300. This amount included carpentry, stone work, plastering, and painting with a promise that part of the building would be ready by the following January.[115]

As scarce as money was in the young State of Kansas, it seems surprising from this distance that any responsible committee would deliberately enter into a contract calling at the outset for an expenditure that exceeded the appropriated amount by more than fifty percent. One can only assume that the executive committee, comprised of Eskridge and Rogers, both legislators, and Morse, who already had demonstrated his reliance upon faith, were confident that additional funds would be provided. Their official report submitted to the Board of Directors in January, 1867, contained a plausible explanation of the decision to overspend and an itemized list of needs not yet met. The latter included furniture and apparatus, a cistern or well, outbuildings, a fence enclosure, and, of course, completion of the school building itself.

According to the report, Hammond's bid had been the lowest and the best of several bids submitted from a sizeable area of the state. Nothing but delay and additional expense would have resulted from rejecting the initial bids and advertising anew. To have reduced the size of the building to fit the appropriation would have defeated the purpose which, of course, was to provide sufficient space for a growing institution. Thus, the committee determined that by accepting Hammond's bid the best interests of both the State and the school would be served. Considerable negotiating, however, took place before the contract was awarded. Hammond agreed to enclose the building and finish it as far as possible with the funds already at hand, specifically agreeing to finish the assembly room and two recitation rooms by the first of the year and the rest of the building when the means were forthcoming.

The committee was pleased with Hammond's cooperation and that of Edward Borton whom they had chosen to superintend construction, and their report commended both men for quality workmanship. That the committee had an eye for aesthetics as well as for utility is evidenced by their authorization of an additional three hundred dollar expense for a decorative cornice and centerpiece of stucco on the unusually high ceiling of the assembly room. At the time of the report, Hammond had been paid a total of $9,950 which included the ceiling décor. The remaining fifty dollars of the original appropriation went for the architect's fee, specifications, and advertising. In spite of his initially slow start because of heavy early summer rains, Hammond managed to keep his promise. By the first of the year, the Normal School moved into the assembly room and two recitation rooms, once again borrowing furniture—this time from the Emporia public school.[116]

The most complete descriptions of this first building to appear were in the Principal's report for 1866 and the report of the Board of Visitors, both of which were reviewed in December 15 issue of *The Emporia News*. The latter reported that the structure was about half a mile from the center of the town, a 40' X 60' limestone building consisting of two stories above the basement, and crowned by a lofty cupola. The entire upper story was the main assembly room, a high, well-lighted hall capable of seating comfortably at desks about 120 persons. (Kellogg, in his report, said it would accommodate 150.) The ground floor was divided into four rooms, three of which were to be recitation rooms for the Normal School students and one for the projected model school. Two of these rooms were as yet unfinished as were the dressing rooms located in the basement.[117] But perhaps the description that best paid tribute to the untiring efforts of those early citizens and the one that can best ignite the imagination of today's reader comes from a letter to *The Lawrence Tribune* on December 8, 1866 from Burlingame:

> The Normal School building is a great credit, not only to Emporia, but to the State of Kansas. Built of stone, it stands on a fine elevation and can be seen for ten miles or more from town.[118]

During the busy months of planning and construction, Normal School students and their faculty of two had continued to spend long hours at their studies and in self-improvement, the fruits of the latter soon becoming a primary source of enrichment for the entire community. In October of 1865, a literary society was formed at the Normal for the purpose of practicing debate, declamation, reading, writing, and singing. From the first, it was intended to be a permanent part of the institution and although regular meetings were not open to the public, as early as December 8 the group gave its first public performance. In addition to group singing and dramatic readings such as excerpts from "The Merchant of Venice," the crowded audience heard a timely debate on Negro suffrage. According to the local editors who registered surprise at the members' proficiency, "Excelsior" was their motto.[119]

By March 21, 1866, when the students gave a second public performance in conjunction with the end of the winter term activities, the organization had become the Normal Literary Union. Now its program and goals were more ambitious, and an admission fee was charged for the purpose of beginning an organization library. Called "Penetralia," the event was held in the Methodist Church where more than three hundred persons congregated to hear a varied program that included Shakespearian readings by Professor Kellogg and students. Kellogg read the parts of Macbeth and Falstaff, the latter characterization reportedly bringing down the house with applause.[120]

The talents of the new assistant principal added measurably to the success of the "Penetralia." A follow-up review in *The Emporia News* lauded Norton for the improvement in the singing during the six months he had been on the scene. But Norton's primary contribution, and one that prompted nearly two-thirds of Emporia's population to attend, was the reading of his poem "Into the Wilderness," written especially for the occasion. Norton, an able poet with some publications, had been working for some time on the poem, and for several weeks Stotler had been promising that Norton would present it at the program.

Nearly two months after the event, the poem appeared in Stotler's paper with the explanation that finally "Professor Norton yielded to the requests of many of our citizens to have it published." Although it is lengthy and obscure in meaning for today's reader, the poem must have spoken clearly to Norton's audience caught up as they were in the pros and cons of equal rights for the newly-freed slaves. Employing Biblical imagery, the poet pleaded for total liberation rather than a return to the barren wilderness of bondage. Although Stotler expressed a wish that the poem be published throughout the land, there appears to be no evidence that more than one paper copied it.[121]

Norton's various talents were continually drawn upon for the benefit of both school and community. At the second annual anniversary exercises, June 18-20, 1866, Norton wore several hats. Not only did he assist Kellogg in the public examinations of the students, and direct the singing of the Literary Union, but he presented the anniversary address. Although there were yet no graduates, much careful planning went into the three-day event. Almost a month in advance, the local editor had applauded the choice of Norton as main speaker, at the same time voicing the hope that as many strangers as possible be present to witness the examinations and other festivities for proof that "the Normal School is the best institution of learning in the State."[122] When the end of the term arrived, however, heavy rains and floods kept people from other areas of the State from attending. Even so, the occasion was successful enough to merit a two-column story in *The Emporia News*.[123]

Summer vacation had scarcely arrived before the Normal faculty, students, and friends focused their attention upon the approaching state teachers' meeting in Lawrence, July 3-5, 1866, a combined convention and Fourth of July celebration. Teachers from throughout the area then considered to be southwest Kansas were urged to attend, partially in order that the area might be able to secure the next year's convention. The local newspaper claimed that if a proper effort were made, the next meeting could be in Emporia.[124]

Although the hope for Emporia was premature (the 1867 convention went to Topeka), the meeting nevertheless proved to be a boon to the Normal School. Approximately one hundred teachers, the largest attendance to date, adopted a resolution in behalf of the institution:

> Resolved that the great educational need of our State is a large number of teachers fitted for their work by thorough mental and moral development, and by special professional study; and that we rejoice in the abundant evidence we have that our State Normal School at Emporia by the energy and ability of its principal and teachers is laying the foundation of a noble work; and that it has our most hearty sympathy and support.[125]

Ministers, legislators, lawyers, and educators from the populated areas of the state participated in the three-day convention. Significantly, one of the most eloquent proponents of the new Normal School was from another institution. J. W. Horner, president of Baker University, warmly endorsed the work of the Normal in what was the first of his many testimonials in behalf of the school. Both Kellogg and Norton read papers before the receptive assembly, and Norton's was ordered to be published in the organization's official magazine, *The Educational Journal*.[126] Of the three state institutions of learning created by the 1863 legislature, only the Kansas State Normal School was fulfilling its role at this time. The university whose first building was finally under construction had not yet begun to function, and the agricultural college had developed neither an agricultural nor a mechanical arts department. Its course was still strictly classical. According to their president Joseph Denison, who addressed the Kansas teachers in Lawrence, the term agricultural as it applied to land grant colleges really was a misnomer. Such schools were called agricultural colleges out of deference to the large agricultural interests throughout the country.[127]

Kellogg headed for Indianapolis in August to attend the national teachers' convention where he spoke before the American Normal Association on the "State of Normal Education in Kansas." His paper was one of four presented from various Normal Schools to the association, the president of which was Illinois Normal University's president and Kellogg's mentor, Richard Edwards. During the meeting at which thirteen states were represented, Kellogg was elected secretary. His was a singular honor for a young frontier educator who had not yet turned twenty-five.[128]

Before the fall term opened on September 12, 1866, it became more apparent than ever that if the Normal was to serve all young Kansans wishing to attend, thereby insuring its permanency, something had to be done about housing them. In Kellogg's absence, Norton pleaded to Emporians to provide additional accommodations for students, pointing out that more applications than ever were arriving and that the successful establishment of the Normal would be a "permanent business advantage to Emporia." On the first of September, the local paper reported that several persons had been in Emporia looking for boarding places for their sons and daughters who planned to attend the Normal. At the same time, Kellogg announced that one of the business houses was offering free use of dishes if desired, and groceries, provisions, and fuel at "first cost prices," to all students renting rooms and boarding themselves. In September, too, came the decision of N. S. Storrs, proprietor of the town's only hotel, to convert the Emporia House into a readymade clothing store, a move that complicated what already was becoming a critical housing problem. Storrs was closing his hostelry not because there was a lack of business but because there was too much.[129]

CHAPTER 4

STRUGGLING TO HOUSE STUDENTS: THE STATE NORMAL SCHOOL BOARDING HOUSE ASSOCIATION

From the outset, G. C. Morse espoused the boarding house concept as the best means of providing inexpensive accommodations for incoming students. Whether the scheme would have progressed more rapidly had the immediate need been greater is an unanswerable question, but the historical fact is that Emporians, who were quick to support the Normal School in other endeavors and were willing to share their homes with students for a reasonable fee, were either unwilling or unable to lend sufficient financial support to the Boarding House Association. One can only assume that there were too few local citizens of sufficient means to become stockholders even on an installment plan. At any rate, what seemed to be a sound idea flourished for a time but eventually floundered. Not until the fall of 1868 was there any semblance of a boarding house, and it not only proved to be temporary but quite inadequate. During the struggle of the stock company, what initially had been a plan to house a hundred students, was eventually cut to twenty-five.

Morse had first mentioned the boarding house in January of 1865, but it was summer before the scheme was ready for implementation. The proposal, made public in June, was to form a joint stock company for the purpose of erecting a ladies' boarding house to accommodate students from all parts of the state. If the school were able to serve only the nearby area, the legislature would "very coolly reply to our request for an appropriation next winter."[130]

Just what was accomplished at the first organizational meeting of the stock company was never made public, but a few days later at the closing exercises of the Normal's first term, Morse presented the boarding house plan to the audience. Maintaining that such a building was necessary to the existence of the school, Morse also revealed that since the organizational meeting, the matter had taken "a definite form and will, we trust, be pushed with vigor." Shortly after, in a preliminary announcement of the fall term, the availability of board was spelled out in detail. Boarding could be obtained with private families on reasonable terms, or students could rent rooms and board themselves at cheaper rates. Then as if to reassure potential students about future facilities, the notice read "Arrangements are now making [sic] for the erection of a large building to be used as a boarding house."[131]

On July 22, 1865, *The Emporia News* announced in an editorial that a meeting was being held that very day to organize the company. The editor revealed that approximately $4,000 in shares of stock had already been subscribed, and that when $5,000 was reached, the work would commence. Morse was identified as the solicitor of subscriptions. In behalf of the venture, the editor made three valid points: (1) The Normal School would be of little benefit unless a means of inexpensive board for the students could be provided; (2) Nothing would benefit Emporians more in dollars and cents than the fostering of the Normal in every possible way; (3) The state would not appropriate money to sustain the school unless students from all parts of the state could be accommodated.

A temporary organization resulted from that July 22 meeting. Trustees were appointed to seek the best terms possible for securing a building site, and three separate committees were appointed to draw up articles of incorporation, rules for the association, and to solicit stock. Already, forty-eight subscribers had pledged seventy-two shares of stock. Enthusiasm appeared to be running high. Barely a week elapsed before the trustees called a mass meeting on August 8 to effect a permanent organization.[132]

At the August 8 meeting, by-laws were adopted. The official name chosen for the company was the State Normal School Boarding House Association, officers of which were a president, secretary, treasurer, and a four-member Board of Directors whose president was the president of the company. All seven of these persons were to be elected to serve one year or until successors were duly chosen. Membership was restricted to subscribers of one or more shares of stock, and only those members would be eligible for a position in the company. Each share was worth fifty dollars and one vote for the stockholder. Elections were by ballot, but other business could be conducted by voice vote unless ballots were called for by a majority of those present. Members present could vote for absentees by proxy up to ten votes if the ones present had authorization to act. Ten members were to comprise a quorum, and annual meetings were to be held in June. The treasurer, who was to be bonded, needed also to furnish two references as sufficient securities. The other rules pertained to authorized withdrawals of money and the expenditure thereof.[133]

At their next meeting, on August 22, John Hammond, one of the four directors, presented a building plan which subsequently was adopted. The estimated cost was $12,000. At this time nearly $6,000 in stock had been pledged, and by Christmas the full amount was expected. Work on the project was to commence at as early a date as practicable. Stotler, the newly-elected secretary of the stock company, through his newspaper made an impassioned plea for everyone who could afford it to invest in the venture.[134]

After the initial meeting, nothing more appeared in the newspaper regarding the location of the boarding house. When the site was agreed upon is uncertain, but it probably was about the same time that Hammond presented his building plan. In any case, stockholders were called to an October 17 meeting for the purpose of incorporating the association as a preliminary to placing the building under contract. According to a Normal School news story at this time, $8,000 in stock had been solicited and the contract was soon to be let.[135]

No mention whatever was made of the boarding house when the announcement was made of the opening of the winter term, December 27, 1865, but a week later an advertisement appeared in *The Emporia News* with regard to the taking of "sealed proposals" for the project. Bids for stone and carpentry work were to be received in the office of E. Borton, county clerk, until midnight Tuesday, January 16, 1866. Construction bids were opened on schedule, and there was an optimism in the early weeks of 1866 that surely must have helped the Normal in its quest for building funds from the legislature. Local artisans were awarded the initial boarding house bids: the firm of Hughes and Jones for stonework at $4,600; and John Hammond, woodwork at $7,400. The latter figure included painting but no plastering.[136]

Towards the end of January, company officials began asking that subscriptions be paid. In order to ease the process, an installment plan was adopted. Twenty-five percent of the stock was due on the first of each month until paid in full, the first to be paid on February 1. The total pledged apparently was as yet unchanged from the October figure of $8,000. Paying up was less than satisfactory, and within a couple of weeks, there appeared over the signature of seventeen concerned stockholders, who believed that both the house plan and the bids were entirely beyond the means of the association, a notice of a meeting to be held on February 23 for the purpose of reconsidering the plan and adopting one that the association could afford. In an editorial the next week, Morse, who was not one of the signers, pleaded for funds to build the boarding house. Although he sounded confident that more money would be forthcoming, he also admitted that if those who thought the cost of the building could be diminished could actually do so and still provide the necessary accommodations, he would be in favor of it. His primary concern was for adequate housing, a must for the continued success of the Normal.[137]

The advance announcement about the opening of the 1866 spring term on March 8 included the assurance that arrangements had been made for extra seats in the school and for additional students to board with pleasant families. There still was no reference to the boarding house, probably because the project was in jeopardy. The following week a significant story appeared in which the editor, presumably Stotler, asserted that while there was no doubt at all about the Normal School building being constructed that summer, not much was being heard about the boarding house "of which so much was said and done a short time ago." Although there was now absolute evidence that such a structure would soon be needed, interest seemed to be lagging. According to the editor, the Kansas State Normal School in Emporia was a fixture, and Emporians needed to follow the lead of Normal School cities in other states where it had become necessary to erect boarding houses.[138]

Finally, there came a notice that the contract for the revised boarding house was to be let on May 29, the cost of which was expected to be $10,000. This information was announced after at least two abortive attempts had been made to hold a mass meeting to consider matters pertaining to the welfare of the Normal. Friends of the school from elsewhere in the state were to have addressed the local citizens, but an unusual return of winter-like weather "froze out" the meeting. Only "four men, a boy, and another fellow were there." The meeting was rescheduled for the following night, but it fared no better. The editor hoped that the stockholder's meeting the coming week would be well attended. "Don't let the thing freeze out entirely," he pleaded.[139]

With the beginning of June, the outlook of the boarding house proponents brightened momentarily. Contracts had been awarded on Tuesday, May 29, to John Hammond for carpentry; Howe and Griffith, masonry; and J. V. Randolph, plastering. By Thursday, ground was broken for the foundation. The intent was to push hard on the construction if subscribers made their payments on time. Only the failure of the stockholders to keep up with their payments stood in the way of the building being completed at the same time as the Normal School structure.[140]

The same floods and heavy rains that cut down on the attendance at the June anniversary exercises temporarily held up the work on both the Normal building and the boarding house, but by July the weather was no longer a deterring factor. In the large advertisement about the autumn term that appeared in *The Emporia News* as early as July 21, the boarding house was mentioned with a cautious degree of confidence. "A large Boarding House is now building [sic] for the use of Normal students. It will be finished as soon as practicable—by the 1st of January, it is believed."

In a progress report in August, Norton reported that the first story of the Normal School building was up, and the structure would be ready by the first of the year. His report on the boarding house, however, was less positive. The first story was almost completed and work was to be pushed as fast as the money was paid by the stockholders. Presumably payments were sporadic, necessitating the work to be correspondingly sporadic. In late November, a two-line brief in the newspaper indicated that work had been resumed on the project.[141]

Progress in the meantime was being made in another area of Emporia housing, that of a hotel. Since September the town had been without public housing, and strangers often were forced to move on unless they were fortunate enough to be invited to stay with Jonathan H. Hunt, former editor of *The Emporia Times*. Hunt, who lived near Sixth Avenue on Exchange Street, had an increase in visitors as the weeks passed. Towards the end of the year, he made plans to build an addition to his stone house and convert it into a hotel.[142]

During their annual visit to the Normal School late in 1866, members of the Board of Visitors inspected not only the nearly completed school building but also the boarding house site. In their report, they revealed that the walls of the large stone building, intended to accommodate fifty boarders, were nearly finished. Somewhat later, Kellogg also spoke optimistically of the boarding house although the Normal already had moved into its new building without any indication as to when the housing facility would be ready. Kellogg paid tribute to Morse, the authorized agent of the stock company, as the originator to the enterprise and thus far the primary force promoting it.[143]

Whatever the expectations were, the ill-fated boarding house was destined to remain unfinished throughout 1867. Early in the year John Hammond was preparing to install door and window casings, but as late as October the building was still not enclosed. Lack of money undoubtedly was the reason, for in late July the Boarding House Association issued a warning to delinquent stockholders. The company had made its last call for unpaid assessments and was threatening to go to court to collect.[144]

At last the inevitable occurred. The town could stretch its hospitality no further, and when the 1867 fall term opened, at least four eligible students were compelled to return home for want of rooms with self-boarding facilities. Hope for the boarding house was either dwindling or a need for additional facilities was being anticipated, for in November, lot owners in the northern part of Emporia were being asked to consider improving their vacant lots by building houses upon them for student rentals. Such a move, it was thought, would be beneficial both to the State and to the lot owner.[145]

Whether construction of the boarding house continued into 1868 is not known, but apparently it was May before the association met. At the request of an undisclosed number of stockholders representing twenty shares of stock, the secretary, Edward Barton, called a special meeting for May 12. Regarding the tenor of that meeting, the local editor made the following observation:

> The State Normal Boarding House Association had rather a stormy meeting on Tuesday. There appeared to be more than the usual amount of combustible materials present. A committee was appointed to investigate the affairs of the association and report at a future meeting.[146]

The regular annual meeting of the association was held on June 9 to consider among other things "what further disposition shall be made of building." Regardless of considerable opposition, the association traded its property for Jonathan Hunt's residence-hotel on Exchange Street, giving the association an unencumbered building worth as much as the unfinished project. The Normal School now had a boarding facility to accommodate twenty-five students for the fall term, and the city gained a new hotel. Hunt was to convert the boarding house into a hotel, for his other one had not been large enough for his trade.[147]

At the time of the property trade, G. C. Morse, architect of the joint stock company and from its inception one of its dedicated supporters, was no longer in Emporia. In late April or early May, he had accepted a call to the Grasshopper Falls Congregational Church. (That community became Valley Falls in 1875.) Morse was one of the three directors of the association replaced at the annual election. The new directors were C.V. Eskridge, L.B. Kellogg and John Wood. Reelected to office were G.D. Humphrey, president; Edward Barton, secretary; R.B. Hurst, treasurer; and William T. Soden, director. All were prominent early day Emporians except Wood, who was comparatively unknown.[148]

By late August 1868, the plan for operating the boarding house was ready, and *The Emporia News* published the following:

> The Normal School Boarding House Association hereby announces the opening of the boarding house to Normal students for the fall terms upon the following liberal terms: Rooms and suits [sic] of rooms will be rented so low that each student will pay at the rate of 25 cents a week. Students will furnish their rooms and board themselves which can be done at small cost, or, furnishing their room, will club together, engaging some women to cook for them such provisions as they themselves provide; or, having rooms in the boarding house can engage their meals of the family in it, or of families near. The boarding house will be under the supervision of a kind, responsible family living in it, of whom the students can obtain meals and whose duty it will be to attend the safety of the building and the comfort of the students.[149]

According to both the principal's report for 1868 and the Board of Visitors' report, the boarding house while of great benefit to the Normal School was already inadequate to meet the demand. Kellogg described the boarding house as a coeducational venture. His report indicated that "the students usually club together, two, four, or six ladies, or gentlemen in the same way, forming a 'family' and board themselves, which is done at a small cost." The visitors described the building as a stone structure of two stories and a wood addition of the same height which appeared to be kept in good order by the family residing in it.[150]

The year 1869 began a strong surge in Emporia's growth. Not only was the town becoming a supply post for emigrants searching for land claims in southern Kansas, especially in the lower Walnut and Arkansas River valleys, but it was being viewed as the end of the trail for an increasing number of settlers who were impressed by the State Normal School, the stone and brick buildings that were supplanting the temporary frame structures of the town, and especially the likely promise that service from at least one railroad would be forthcoming before the year's end. In fact, Emporia's population had more than quadrupled since the winter of 1866-67 when the population was about six hundred. Most of the increase came in the two years just prior to the 1870 census, which listed Emporia as a town of 2750 persons.[151]

Unfortunately, construction could not keep pace with the rapid influx of people, and Emporia experienced a housing shortage that threatened every avenue of progress. By September, 1869, Stotler was pleading for two or more public boarding houses in order that strangers might have a place to board and newcomers a place to stay while building. The Nation House, Hunt's hotel which had been the boarding house association's property, was crowded all of the time although it had been in operation less than nine months.[152]

The Normal School had continued to flourish beyond all expectations, and in its fifth year of existence Kellogg and the directors were struggling not only with the perennial problem of where to house students and how to board them at prices they could afford, but also with the problem of how to accommodate the increasing number in the Normal School building proper. In his 1869 annual report, Kellogg stressed the magnitude of the problem. He pointed out that the primary cost of the students' Normal School education was the room and board. The latter had increased to five dollars a week, posing a burden for many students eagerly seeking to rent the few available rooms with self-boarding arrangements in the Normal boarding house in order to cut their board costs in half or more. To Kellogg the crux of the problem was "how to secure board at such rates as will not virtually close the doors of the institution to many worthy pupils." What with Emporia's extraordinary growth, there seemed little chance that the situation would become better unless the Board of Directors could devise some way for the school to supply its own needs in rooms to rent and cheap board. Kellogg outlined his own proposal for solving the problem: Ask the state to erect a row of small cottages, 16' X 24', one and a half stories with two rooms on the ground floor and two above, constructed simply and economically at a cost not exceeding $1000 for each dwelling built on Normal School grounds convenient to the present buildings. Each cottage could accommodate from eight to twelve students whose rent would be nominal to cover insurance and upkeep. A few (or one or two) could be built at first, then more as funds became available.[153]

Members of the executive committee of the Board of Directors were in favor of Kellogg's proposed cottages, but because of the State's desperate need to economize were unwilling to seek funds for building them. The Board of Visitors, composed of former Governor S.J. Crawford, E.B. Peyton, and W.R. Brown, likewise approved Kellogg's proposal. Two or three cheap boarding cottages for female students, they maintained, would yield large returns by adding to the usefulness of the Normal; but they, too, stopped short of recommending the expenditure because of state finances. The visitors who were pleased with the Normal School declared it to be what its founders had intended – a first class institution. They reaffirmed, however, what Kellogg had reported about the lack of adequate housing and the reasons for the continuing problem. Their visit to the boarding house, moreover, had been less than satisfactory. They were critical of the overcrowded conditions there, although according to Kellogg, quite a number of applicants had been turned away for want of room.[154]

It was the visitors who revealed in their 1869 report that a majority of the stock of the Normal School Boarding House Association had been bought up by one stockholder. They neither disclosed the stockholder's name nor gave any explanation of why or how he had been able to purchase the shares. If there was any impropriety, the newspaper chose to ignore the fact. The first newspaper reference to the matter came in the spring of 1870 in a brief account of two stable fires across the alley from each other. One of the stables belonged to the Normal School boarding house owned by John Wood.[155]

No indication of the status of the boarding house was included in the announcement of the opening of the winter term on January 3, 1870; only the usual assurances that Kellogg would assist students in arranging for room and board appeared. The newspaper, a couple of weeks later, issued a notice that Emporians needed to take in more students, or some would be forced to return home as they had been last fall. If the Normal boarding house was used at all in 1870, it was for only a short time. Early in June, a review of the stock company's efforts written by Stotler, or his new partner, mentioned that what had been too big a house was traded for a smaller one which now was closed by the man who bought up all of the stock. Thus what had been a five-year joint struggle by prominent Emporians and friends to provide the Normal School with much needed housing finally ended in total defeat.[156]

CHAPTER 5

"A YEAR OF SUBSTANTIAL PROGRESS": 1867-1868

Official records of the early Normal School were long ago destroyed by fire, thus making it difficult to determine the actual enrollment at any given time during the first years. Official state reports, however, sometimes include enrollment figures, and newspaper accounts occasionally reflected the enrollment situation. The principal's reports, which were submitted near the end of each calendar year, usually gave the total number of students for that year instead of for each term. Kellogg, however, made exceptions in his first reports. Perhaps with a sense of history, he recorded in 1865 the total number of students who had enrolled during the first term of the Normal. In 1866, he stated that about seventy students were in class at the time (presumably December). Stotler, who frequently visited the Normal School to see for himself how it was progressing, reported in the fall of 1866 after one such visit that about seventy students were attending the session.[157]

Anticipating a further increase in enrollment and an enlargement of the curriculum once the Normal moved into its open quarters, the Board of Directors added a third member to the faculty sometime during the fall of 1866 when Abbie G. Homer became the Normal School's first female teacher. A graduate of the Westfield, Massachusetts, Normal School, she had been teaching since September in Lyon County's North District school, later known as Rinker school. The Board of Visitors referred to her as "having training almost identical to the present teachers." Although Miss Homer did not begin at the Normal until January, 1867, Principal

Kellogg listed her as a member of the faculty in his 1866 report. He listed himself as teacher of history, government, and the theory and practice of teaching; Norton, associate principal, as teacher of the natural sciences and English; Miss Homer, teacher of mathematics and geography. What Kellogg did not reveal, however, was that by the time the Normal School would have moved into its new building and the winter term begun, Miss Homer would be Mrs. L. B. Kellogg.[158]

The Normal Literary Union activities, especially those at the close of a school term, had become a delightful source of entertainment for Emporians and those who crowded into the Methodist Church on Wednesday evening, December 19, 1866, were not disappointed. There was the usual debate, this one on the question of whether President Andrew Johnson should be impeached; choral singing, directed by H.B. Norton; varied student readings and musical selections, plus the added attraction of the newly formed silver cornet band. Then came the event that was "the finishing stroke of the term of the Normal" – the marriage of Professor Kellogg. Three days later, Stotler had this to say of the occasion:

> The event of the evening and the one that brought such a large audience together was the marriage of the Principal of the School to Miss Homer. They entered the church at the close of the other exercises. Rev. G. C. Morse performed the ceremony in a solemn and impressive manner. The audience were then dismissed and the congratulations of the students and friends followed. All will join with us in wishing this happy union of the Faculty of our State Normal School many blessings, and a long life of continued usefulness and unalloyed happiness.[159]

January 2, 1867, dawned clear and cold in Emporia, promising a continuance of the first sub-zero weather of the winter; but fortunately for those who had traveled to attend the dedication ceremonies of the Normal School building, a south wind began to moderate the temperature and by the following day the light snow cover had completely disappeared. How many had been discouraged by the bitter cold from making the trip is not known, but a record number of first day students were on hand for the formal dedication, an event that also signaled the opening of the winter term.[160]

For the most part, the formal ceremony featured local citizens who were special friends of the institution. Eskridge had been selected to be the presiding officer, but he was unavoidably absent and Judge J. H. Watson became his substitute. Morse gave the opening prayer; J. H. Leard, the benediction. The guest speaker was J.W. Horner, president of Baker University, whose topic concerned the general education system. Kellogg reviewed the history of the institution and explained the purpose of a Normal School. In a departure from the printed program, Morse also addressed the assembly. According to Stotler's account, Morse "treated the audience to some interesting reminiscences of the effort to start the school, procure a teacher, etc."

Worthy of the occasion was the ceremonial music which included the students' glee "We Love Our Native Hills," and the featured Dedication Hymn. Words of the latter were written especially for the occasion by H. B. Norton and set to music by M. J. Stimson. The hymn, sung by selected students and citizens, appears as a poem in the Appendix (page xiii). Adding zest and fanfare to the opening and closing moments of the formalities, the Silver Cornet Band made their second school appearance. According to Stotler, theirs was "soul stirring music" and "not the least interesting part of the program, by any means."[161]

So long as the embryonic Normal School was confined to temporary quarters, only encouraging and enthusiastic voices were heard from the public; but once the institution moved onto its own twenty-acre preserve, a subtle change began to take place. Critics from out in the state began to speak up until never again would the institution be completely free of controversy. The very first public attack came before the glow of the dedication had faded. It began, however, as more of a heckle than a criticism.

Governor S. J. Crawford in his 1867 annual message to the legislature had stated that although in operation for two years under many disadvantages, Kansas State Normal with its new building, a third teacher, and ninety students, would doubtless now become what its founders had intended it to be. Crawford also declared that "if ends aimed at in the establishment of this school are in a fair way of being realized, it should then receive the fostering care of the State...."

The governor's remarks were not only ambiguous, but they differed substantially in tone from his positive statements concerning Kansas University which had only begun to function the previous September, and the agricultural college which for the most part was still following the classical curriculum of its predecessor. It is not surprising, therefore, that some state editors should raise inquiring eyebrows and pose the question of what is wrong at the Normal School.

Undoubtedly, officials and friends of the Normal were puzzled by the governor's remarks. Whether Stotler would have protested publicly had he not felt compelled to defend the school is uncertain, but circumstances promptly stung him into action. The *Leavenworth Bulletin* answered the governor's appraisal almost immediately with the blunt statement that "There is evidently a screw loose in the Normal School." Stotler's reply was a masterful rebuttal. He voiced surprise and regret over Governor Crawford's ill-chosen words suggesting, however, that the Leavenworth editor may have misinterpreted the remarks, hastily reading into them what was not in the governor's mind at all. The governor, who was an ex officio member of the Normal's Board of Directors, after all had fully endorsed board action at the January meeting. Since he had been unable yet to visit the school, his information about the institution had to come from newspapers, official reports, or from others who had visited the school. Stotler knew of no newspaper in the state that had ever printed any but favorable comments about the Normal. The official reports had been positive, and visitors seemed always to have approved enthusiastically of what they had observed. But since suspicion had now been aroused, Stotler called for a joint commission of inquiry to be appointed from both houses of the legislature to determine the truth about all of the state institutions. "Let there be Light!", he proclaimed.[162]

Kellogg, too, had been concerned about the governor's speech and the newspaper reaction to it. In a letter to Governor Crawford, Kellogg included newspaper clippings to underline his concern. Crawford replied promptly to Kellogg, denying that he had intended any detriment to the Normal School. He had worked diligently for two years in the school's behalf, both as a director and as governor. Crawford assured Kellogg that he had no complaints about the management. In fact, he was entirely satisfied and he intended to continue working to advance the school. The letter, which was published in *The Emporia News*, placated both Kellogg and Stotler, and calm was restored.[163]

In the meantime, the Normal School directors were striving for state funds with which to complete the new building. At their regular January meeting, they endorsed a list of expenditures which had been recommended by the executive committee to accomplish that end. The total amount of the appropriation request was $14,000. The itemized list included the following: completion of the building, $5,650; furniture and apparatus, $1,500; teachers' salaries, $4,000; model school, $1,000; fencing of building, $1,000; well or cistern and outbuildings, $850.[164]

The appropriation bill passed the legislature with little difficulty and Governor Crawfordng signed it on February 19,[165] May arrived before there was any public mention of the Normal School improvements then in progress. Furniture from the H. M. Sherwood Company of Chicago arrived, thus enabling the return of pieces borrowed from Emporia's district school. Constructed of cherry wood of the "very best pattern and highest finish," the new furniture included double desks, chairs, recitation seats, and "all other essentials for normal and model schools." With the approach of the school's first commencement came a flurry of activity in an attempt, presumably, to complete all improvements. Two cisterns were dug and pine palings installed to front the campus, but landscaping, which entailed breaking the prairie ground and planting trees, had to await another season.[166]

The weather, always a force to be reckoned with on the plains, had been particularly harsh during the winter of 1866 and the spring of 1867. Storms prevented the Normal Literary Union from presenting its ambitious end-of-term program on March 26 as scheduled. Initially postponed for a month, the event did not take place until the end of the following term. In the meantime, the winter session closed with written examinations instead of the usual oral ones. Except for the reunion of students and friends on Tuesday night, March 26, there were no festivities marking the close of the term.[167]

In a notice about the opening of the Normal's spring term, April 10, 1867, Kellogg revealed what must have been the birth of the school's Placement Bureau. He pointed out that with the new building no one would be excluded for lack of space, and that the only expense would be the cost of living inasmuch as tuition and textbooks were provided by the state. He admitted that although no students had yet completed the course of study, several were suspending their work in order to teach. He then declared that "School officers who wish to employ Normal students should confer with Principal, who will, so far as possible, recommend to their schools suitable teachers."[168]

The city of Emporia even in the early years often helped to enrich the lives of the Normal students. One such occasion was on April 17, 1867, when Lucy Stone Blackwell, accompanied by her husband, lectured on the importance of Women's Suffrage. Not long thereafter, a local impartial suffrage league was organized with at least two Normal School teachers being involved. H. B. Norton became the league's first corresponding secretary, and Mary Jane Watson, vice president.[169]

During the first term in their new home at the head of Commercial Street, Normal students had suffered for want of sidewalks to and from the town site, but Emporians sought to improve the situation. In April, editor Stotler asked "When shall it be built?" October came, however, before materials for the boardwalk were hauled to the site.[170]

Meanwhile, memories of the treacherous winter soon were superseded by a once-in-a-lifetime experience for most of the students and faculty as well as for the town's citizens. On Wednesday, April 24, 1867, there came a low rumble as of distant thunder; groceries jiggled on the shelves; and Emporia was in the throes of an earthquake. Two days later, Stotler described the students' situation thus:

> At the Normal School the students made a grand rush for the door, and in the hurry and scramble to get downstairs, some of them were more or less injured, but none seriously.[171]

The first commencement exercise of the Kansas State Normal School took place two years to the very day after the historic first term closed in celebration. Although three years of study was the regular requirement for graduation, two young women, Mary Jane Watson and Ellen Plumb, were able to graduate six months earlier because of their past experience "of accredited character," and because both had done extra work while enrolled at the Normal.[172]

The two-day observance opened Thursday morning, June 27, with the end-of-term oral examinations. According to firsthand accounts, all was as usual inside the Normal School. Students were in their places with the females noticeably in the majority. The room was large, well ventilated and appropriately furnished with everything in order. School opened precisely at 9 o'clock with a few spectators on hand. First came the devotional exercises, then Kellogg announced the order of the day's examinations: five hours of examinations, each lasting one hour; two subjects scheduled for each hour, one on each floor.

> The professor [Kellogg] then taps his office bell with a pencil, which is the signal of attention. At the second tap those who are to leave the room for recitation rise; at the 3rd tap face about and march out of the room. There is something almost military about the promptness, unity, and precision of their movements, as in all of the daily routine.[173]

Recitation rooms and the Model School room were encircled by blackboards, chalk and erasers, an "indispensible auxiliary" to the demonstrations which were important audio/visual aids in Normal education. Problems, maps, music, drawings in mathematics, botany, and sketching found expression here, and all were subject to criticism from both students and teacher. On this particular day, the closing of the school's seventh term, the town editor who had attended all previous examinations noted "substantial progress." [174]

Sensing the historical significance of the occasion, Stotler provided 2,000 extra copies of *The Emporia News* at five cents per copy in order that Kansans could send them to family and friends elsewhere. The issue also contained a great deal of information on the positive attributes of the surrounding country. In fact, the feature story about commencement contained an idyllic description of the countryside.

> Everything outside seemed to be in keeping with the occasion. From the windows of the school building – a noble edifice just completed on an elevation adjoining town, and overlooking miles in extent of the valleys of the Cottonwood and Neosho – preparations for the Farmers Commencement could be seen on every hand. Miles square of wheat in a never ending golden circle as far as the eye could reach, were nodding in impatient readiness for the reaper. Other miles square of oats, corn, and potatoes, regal in such a green as painter never limned, filled up the magnificent promise of the Harvest; realizing for Kansas what Sidney Smith said of Australia: 'Tickle the earth with a hoe and she laughs with a harvest.' [175]

The second day of festivities began with the Board of Directors' annual meeting in the forenoon and a lecture before the Literary Society. The commencement program, for which a large crowd of spectators had gathered, began at two o'clock in the afternoon. Eskridge, representing the Board, opened the historic occasion by announcing that Judge L. D. Bailey would preside. Bailey in turn announced the program that previously had been published. There was a prayer, an anthem, speeches by both graduates, music by the Silver Cornet Band, an address, an awarding of diplomas by the Reverend G. C. Morse, and the benediction. The gala occasion ended with a students' reception that evening.[176]

Scarcely had the commencement crowd dispersed before Kellogg, his faculty, and a number of students journeyed to Topeka to participate in the July 2-3 meeting of the State Teachers' Association. This was the third annual convention in which the Normal School had participated, and it soon became apparent that the fledging institution was gaining in prestige throughout the state. Not only did Kellogg and the others appear on the program, but they were rewarded with important offices. Miss Watson was elected secretary of the association, and Kellogg became chairman of the executive committee. He and Norton were chosen editors of the organization's official magazine for the coming year, and Emporia was designated as the site of next year's convention.[177]

Almost immediately the local editor registered his pride in the outcome of the Topeka meeting. On July 26, Stotler claimed that Emporia was fast becoming the educational center of the state, especially so because the head faculty of the Normal were to publish the *Kansas Educational Journal* there. Stotler, whose newspaper contracted to print the journal, continued his enthusiasm despite the fact that his printers were hard pressed to produce the first issue in addition to their regular work. When the journal was ready for distribution, Stotler declared that the first issue from the new editors was "much better filled than it has been heretofore."[178]

Another educational event, which added to the stature of both the school and community, took place at the Normal in the fall of 1867. A statewide teachers' institute was held from September 9-13 for teachers who were unable to attend the Normal on a regular basis. The institute which coincided with the opening of the fall term was also attended by the students whose regular school work was postponed a week.

The first official announcement of the institute, which presumably had developed from an order by the Board of Directors, appeared in the Emporia newspaper on August 2. The Announcement stated that instruction and books were to be free, the enrollees' only cost to be for travel to and from their homes. Emporians would entertain institute members free of charge. In a separate article, a plea was made to citizens to volunteer their hospitality. As a list of thirty or more families who had volunteered to be hosts was also published, it is apparent that much ground work already had been accomplished on this latest enterprise.[179]

Coming at the same time that Emporians were being urged to take in at least one Normal student for the fall term to alleviate the critical housing situation, it is surprising that the above arrangement met with such success. Institute members were instructed to report to Kellogg's home when they arrived in Emporia in order that the principal could personally direct them to their hosts' homes. Attendance exceeded sixty members including numerous prominent educators in the state.[180]

The 1867-68 school year opened under the directors of a newly-appointed board, the old one having served it three years. Reappointed to a second term were Morse, Eskridge, James Rogers, and T. S. Huffaker. New members were L. D. Bailey and S. S. Prouty, replacing J. M. Ramkin and J. W. Roberts. Ex officio members were Crawford, McVicar, and Springs.[181]

A change had also occurred in the student body of the Normal. Whereas in 1865 scarcely more than half the students had subscribed to the teachers' pledge, thereby waving tuition costs, by September 1867 virtually all of the students had enrolled as teachers. Presumably, school policy played a significant role in the marked change of direction. The curriculum was deemed more valuable for teachers than for others. Moreover, theory and the art of teaching classes were required of all students regardless of where one planned to teach, resulting in a gradual decline of other than would-be teachers. According to one observer, "And this is as it should be. The entire energies of the school should be devoted to the instruction of teachers."[182]

By 1867, too, a concentrated effort was being made to encourage attendance from all portions of the state. School officials played up the fact that each representative district was entitled by law to send one delegate to the Normal. Interested persons were instructed to apply to their particular representative. In the event a district had more than one eligible applicant, by contacting the Normal School principal, it was possible that "by special favor" two or more delegates from the same district could enroll. To further encourage enrollment, a suggested form of appointment accompanied the advertisement.[183]

In the two years and a half that the Normal had been in operation, only two persons had graduated with valid diplomas to teach. Thirty-seven others, however, had suspended their studies to teach. At least one community, after hiring a Normal student for assistant principal of their new school, authorized Kellogg to supply them with a "Competent school principal to be paid a salary of $1,200 per annum." That request undoubtedly pointed to a growing need for in-state trained school administrators.[184]

The most important change in the Normal during 1867 was the long awaited opening of the Model School. Created by the Organizational Act of 1864 (Appendix, p iii, sec. 6), the Normal had thus far been missing one of its vital parts. The new building had been so constructed as to accommodate the Model School, but not until September were the facilities ready. Designed as a model for teachers, the school was to be limited to thirty pupils divided into two grades: one group consisting of those who were nearly old enough for the Normal but not sufficiently advanced academically; the other group consisting of children ten to thirteen years of age who already had a "fair" education. Pupils were welcome from all parts of the state, and intent to teach was not a condition for admittance. Under a February 16, 1867 Act "to provide for the maintenance and education of the orphans and destitute children of soldiers," the Normal already had announced that such students would be permitted to enroll. Presumably, they likewise were eligible to attend the Model School.[185]

According to the Principal's Third Annual Report, December 1867, seven states and twenty Kansas counties were represented by the 157 students who attended the Normal during the year. This number included twenty-seven Model School pupils. Kellogg explained that the latter school served a double purpose: that of a school of observation and a school of practice. Although a woman from the Oswego, New York Normal School had been hired as permanent teacher of the Model School, Mrs. Gorhm had been in charge during the fall term. Her report was incorporated into that of the Principal. The two grades or groups were about equal in number. The goals of the school were to teach elementary branches of an English education in the best way known, and to conduct an experimental or training school for students to test theories learned in the Normal by actually doing the teaching. Thus began a long line of practice teachers at Emporia State.[186]

Kellogg's 1867 report, while positive concerning the growth and progress of the normal, raised for the first time a question about the high ratio of students per year, a problem that has plagued the institution to this day. According to Kellogg, the Normal's ratio of students per teacher was so high that requests from county superintendents for faculty help with institutes and other educational ventures had to be ignored because no one dared to leave during school. He maintained that it would be time well spent if the principal or his associate were allowed time to work outside the Normal walls to conduct institutes, lectures, write for the press, or otherwise promote the cause of education.

The school in order to function properly had other needs which Kellogg lumped into six categories. Second after references books, especially encyclopedias and dictionaries, came the request for a school catalog. The most revealing category, however, was the sixth on the list marked miscellaneous. Two cisterns had been provided for the Normal but no pumps, nor was there a well. The new building was not only without lighting, but three additional stoves were needed before the next term began on January 8, 1868. Three lightning rods had been recommended, one of which was installed but still unpaid for.[187]

In spite of the dearth of lighting and heat, the Normal School building was in demand for other than school functions. The Ladies' Mite Society of the Congregational Church held its festival and fair there on Christmas Eve and the Methodist Church had its festival there on New Years' Eve. Such use, however, was short lived. At their January meeting in Topeka, the Board of Directors voted to restrict the use of the building to functions connected with the school.[188]

Before the winter term began, new rumblings were heard concerning various public institutions, among which was the Kansas State Normal School. The new cry was for economy, and consolidation of the schools at one central location was being voiced as the best solution to the problem. A hint of what might be expected had occurred in the late summer when a Kansas newspaper ran a story depreciating the scattered locations of the state institutions. That editor advocated the removal of all of them to the state capital except the university, agricultural college, and the penitentiary. By the process of elimination, that left the State Normal School; the school for the Deaf and Dumb in Olathe; the Blind Asylum in Wyandotte; and the Insane Asylum, Osawatomie. All of the latter should be removed to Topeka, he maintained, for two reasons: (1) in order that they could be visited by the legislators during the annual session, thereby making known the needs as well as exposing any lack within the institutions; and (2) to prevent the current tendency of the scattered areas combining their strength in the legislature to gain unreasonable appropriations for maintenance or whatever.

Stotler rebutted with a lengthy article in his *Emporia News* condemning the concept of consolidation. He published excerpts from the above story, observing that the three excluded institutions would qualify for the reasons given more so than the remaining ones. He reviewed the statutes which had established a precedent for scattered locations, pointing out that Nebraska alone had its institutions in one area. Stotler declared that competition among Kansas institutions had been good. They had become better as the various local communities strived to improve them.[189]

In an editorial titled "Economy," Stotler went on record as open to any combination of the state institutions. He was in favor, however, of each one standing on its own merits and receiving "that alone to which it is thereby entitled." He maintained that appropriating money had become a political issue. Democrats especially were opposed to the high taxes, and some Republicans feared that if appropriations were made, the state would go Democratic. Stotler admitted that he would be disappointed if taxes were not reduced, but he would be so also if the state institutions were not provided for.[190]

The Normal School's appropriation seemed modest, the total amount coming to $7,367.00. According to the executive committee's report, salaries for the faculty members, Kellogg, Norton, Gorham, and Pitman, comprised $5,600 of the total. Perhaps more disturbing to certain critics than the appropriation sought was the Board's decision to seek release from the obligation to reimburse the state for appropriations thus far received, mainly the appropriations for the new building. The Board, which was preparing to offer the endowment lands for sale, believed that if the school could be absolved of past debts it could soon become self-supporting.[191]

In any case, a second editor north of the Kansas River was soon heard from. Earlier, having lashed out against the state institutions declaring that they were not beneficial to anyone, the editor of the *White Cloud Chief* had urged the legislature to vote down all such appropriations. On January 30, he denounced all state institutions as swindlers, pointing in particular to the Kansas State Normal School whose appropriation, he claimed, was to be used to run the *Educational Journal.* The caustic editor also wondered why, if the school were a success, were not the students paying to support it. As was usual, Stotler wrote a reply explaining every point.[192]

Kellogg went to Topeka late in January to attend a special meeting of the State Teacher's Association, one which he himself had called as chairman of the executive committee to consider educational bills proposed for the current term of the legislature. He also attended the January 30 meeting of the Normal School's Board of Directors. On that evening, he and Norton both addressed a large audience of educators and legislators in the Hall of Representatives. Others who spoke at that gathering were Joseph Denison, president of the Agricultural College, and Professor Robinson of Kansas University.[193]

On February 12, 1868, Senator N. C. Clark of Columbus, Doniphan

County, introduced Senate Bill #101 concerning consolidation. Upon the second reading, the Act providing for the concentration of certain State institutions was referred to a special committee of five: William H. Dodge of Holton; L. F. Green, Baldwin City; Issac B. Sharp, Wyandotte; James Rogers, Burlingame; and P. B. Maxson, Lyon County.

On February 15, 1868, three years to the day after the Normal's doors first opened, and three days after having received the assignment, committee chairman Dodge presented the majority report. The committee recommended passage of the bill. Concurring with Dodge were Green and Rogers, a member of the Board of Directors of the Normal School and its executive committee. The proposition considered in the bill was to concentrate the University, Normal School, and Agricultural College at one point, and the Deaf and Dumb, the Blind and Insane asylums at one point. Senator Sharp, who with Maxson recommended that Bill #101 be rejected, presented to the senate the minority report.[194]

Abiding by the recommendations of the majority of the committee, Bill #101 was referred to the Judiciary committee to remodel some sections of the bill and to add others in order to carry out "the subject of the bill at the earliest practical moment." The Judiciary committee, however, recommended passage of a substitute bill.

On February 27, Bill #101 came before the senate for a third reading, but Senator Sharp moved to postpone further consideration of the bill until March 25. The ensuing vote was a 12-12 tie. Sharp then moved to postpone consideration indefinitely, a motion that passed 13-10.[195]

A decision about the institutions had been postponed, but nerves in some quarters continued to be edgy. Emporia was no exception. Soon after the legislature adjourned, Stotler accused the legislators of purposely reducing Professor Norton's salary to a ridiculous sum. In an editorial he declared: "In the war on the State Institutions during the last session of our State debating society, the salary of our associate principal of Kansas State Normal cut down to $600." He admitted that the action was rumored to be a mistake; but why, he asked, such a blunder?[196]

The following week under "A Correction," Stotler answered his own query. While wholeheartedly apologizing for his earlier hastily written story, he denied intending to cast aspersions upon the representatives. He published a letter of explanation from Representative Plumb and an accompanying one from John T. Morton, chief clerk of the House, explaining what had been a regrettable clerical error. Morton included his assurance that the next legislature would correct the mistake, perhaps even to paying interest.[197]

Meanwhile school at the various institutions continued as usual. Students and faculty of the Normal were determined to have some kind of musical instrument for their assembly room. With that project in mind, they sold tickets to the literary entertainment being planned for the close of the winter term. Later in the spring, they staged a floral festival and sociable to earn money. Both ventures were profitable enough that by late June the school had an organ.[198]

The Normal's second annual commencement exercises were scheduled for June 29-30, 1868. The graduating class of four was double that of the previous year and again all female. Of the four students, only Josephine Slocum had been among the original eighteen. Mary Elizabeth Ela, however, had been a student since sometime in 1865. The other two women, Alice L. Norton and Josephine L. Patty, apparently had entered the Normal later. One of the highlights of their graduation was the class song they wrote and sang for the occasion.[199]

Coinciding with commencement was the annual meeting of the State Teachers Association. Such scheduling had been a tactful move on the part of the Board of Directors for the purpose of getting teachers and administrators from over the state to Emporia while the Normal was in session. Although the real work of the Association was not to begin until Wednesday, July 1, many of the delegates arrived in time to witness the examinations and attend the Sociable and Literary Society on Monday evening. A special feature of that event was the reading from Macbeth by Richard Edwards, LLD, president of Normal Illinois University, and Mrs. Gorham.[200]

All of the week, Emporia lived up to the title the local editor had given it: the educational center of the state. The town, full of prominent educators who not only were observing the Normal School in action, meeting with its Board of Directors, and participating in the Teachers convention, but also sharing by its chronic scarcity of housing, was able to play the part of gracious host only by requesting that its citizens open their homes to the visitors and take them in as guests.[201]

Probably, the most prestigious guest was professor Edwards of Normal, Illinois, who gave the commencement address. Speaking before a packed assembly with aisles and all available standing room occupied, President Edwards held his audience "spell bound for an hour" even though they were tired and warm. The assembly room was festive for the occasion.

Over the platform in a circle in well-shaped letters of evergreen, was the State motto, "Ad Astra per Aspera." The hall and windows were trimmed in green. On one of the front seats sat the 4 young ladies dressed in white.[202]

Judge Bailey of the Board of Directors presided at commencement. On the stage with him were other Board members and distinguished citizens on the program. The only change from the program as advertised was in the invocation. Board President Joseph Denison of Manhattan gave the opening prayer instead of Peter McVicar, superintendent of public instruction.[203]

The educational week had been an unqualified success for both the Normal School and the community. Kellogg and Norton were designated to edit the *Kansas Educational Journal* for another year. Also important to the Normal was the selection of Norton by the teachers to be their nominee for state superintendent of public instruction. While Emporians were reading complimentary reviews of the week's activities which Stotler had lifted from area newspapers, the Normal faculty took a brief well-earned rest.[204]

In mid-August the Normal advertised the September 9th opening of the fall term. In addition to the regular three-year teacher or Normal course, there was a new preparatory department for which tuition of six dollars per term was charged. Although the organization of this new department had been announced by the executive committee prior to the opening of the spring term, it is not clear whether any students had actually enrolled then. The reason for the department was to enable young men and woman of limited education to prepare themselves for joining the regular teacher's department whenever they could qualify. Students irrespective of their future career plans, however, were admitted. All applications were made through the principal. Preparatory students were subject to the same discipline as other Normal students, and they enjoyed the same privileges. They, like the Normal students, had assigned seats in the assembly room.[205]

What with the preparatory program enabling students to enroll who otherwise would have been ineligible, and the opening of the boarding house providing cheap board for the first time, the State Normal School in the fall of 1868 was within reach of more young Kansans than ever before. Enrollment figures soon began to reflect that fact.

Also advertised for the fall term was the Model School, tuition for which was five dollars per term. This important segment of the Normal had opened the year before only to have been suspended during the spring of 1868. The temporary suspension had been necessary, apparently, because of the resignation of the teacher just prior to the opening of the term, and because a number of the student teachers had dropped out of school to teach summer schools. Subsequently, the Board of Directors at their June 29th meeting hired Ellen Plumb, who was teaching in Leavenworth, to take charge of the Model School for the fall term. In late August, a special announcement in the local paper by Miss Plumb stated that children from eight to thirteen years of age would be welcome in the Model School. Twenty-six could be accommodated.[206]

There seems to have been no effort to implement the plan for a primary department during the fall term. An attempt to organize such a department for the spring term had failed. According to the spring announcement of the executive committee, a primary class of fifteen boys and girls from ages five to eight was being organized to commence on April 8. Tuition was to be four dollars per term. The class, under the control of Mary R. Pitman, Model School Teacher, would be taught morals and manners in addition to book learning, signing, writing, and inventive drawing. Applications for admissions were to be made to Principal Kellogg.[207]

With more beginning students than previously, enrollment for the fall term was promising in spite of the Model School being somewhat short of its capacity. No complete breakdown of the 1868 fall enrollment has been found, but the preparatory department and Model School combined numbered twenty-seven students. Ninety-eight enrolled in the Normal School proper, all but three of whom signed the pledge to teach, making a grand total of 125 students in the fall of 1868.[208]

The term had no more than begun when Kellogg and his family left for the East on a three-month leave of absence to visit Mrs. Kellogg's family. Kellogg himself was to visit other Normal Schools, especially those of New England, for the purpose of studying their procedures. In his absence, Mary Jane Watson was hired to assist Norton. Although the Kellogg's had returned by December 15, the principal did not participate in the public examinations at the close of the term, leaving that to the teachers Norton, Gorham, Watson, and Plumb.[209]

A minor triumph occurred early in 1869 when the Normal School's first catalog became a reality. Dated for the year ending December 31, 1868, the catalog was published in January, 1869, by the *Emporia News* Book and Job office. Information of interest in the thin booklet included the names and towns of the Board of Visitors; the graduates due date and where they were teaching, and the list of faculty members (see footnote 208).

All students during 1868 were listed in the catalog according to classification and gender. Considering the graduates to date had been female, it is surprising that the enrollment of the sexes was nearly equal: seventy-eight female students and seventy-five males. Listed were four graduates; twelve seniors; sixteen middle; eighty-five juniors; twenty preparatory; and seventeen model school.[210]

A unique feature of the first catalog was the inclusion of the scholastic record of each student as an aid to various school administrators in selecting Normal students for teachers. Published therein were the individual marks of each student in attendance, department, and scholarship. The rest of the catalog consisted of information concerning the three terms per year: winter, twelve weeks; spring, twelve weeks; and fall, fourteen weeks; and a list of requirements and opportunities for the students. For example, students were expected to worship on the Sabbath at some local church; they were expected to take at least one hour of exercise in fresh air each day, and to retire at 10 p.m. "Unreasonable" rising and study were forbidden; and unless permission had been obtained previously from the principal, no tardiness nor absences were permitted.

Opportunities included the literary society which held meetings every two weeks; social gatherings of students, teachers, and citizens once or twice each term; and gymnastic exercises for both students and faculty. Music lessons in piano and other instruments were available from teachers near the Normal. Emporia society was pictured to be of an "elevated character," there being no dram shops [taverns] in town. Graduates were allowed to remain for a limit of one additional year to review and assist in Normal teaching. The diploma earned after three years' study was by law a perpetual teachers' certificate to teach anywhere in the state without examination by the county superintendent.

Applicants to the teachers' department were required to furnish character recommendations from a responsible person in addition to signing the written pledge to teach. Tuition remained free for teachers. Other Normal students were charged eight dollars per term. Everyone paid an incidental fee of two dollars. Rooms in the new boarding house where students could board themselves were quoted at prices from twenty-five to fifty cents per week. Such arrangements, presumably, were reflected in the wide range of estimated expenses for the full school year. Cost estimates for forty weeks ranged from $103 to $194. Board alone ranged from $80 to $160 for the same time period.[211]

By the time the 1868 catalog went to press, another change had occurred in the Board of Directors. James Rodgers of Burlingame, a member of both the Board and its executive committee since 1864, and a proponent of the state institutions consolidation bill of 1868, had for some unspecified reason resigned. Appointed to replace him in both positions was Jacob Stotler. A year earlier, the Board had added to its number by making the Normal School principal an honorary member. Interesting but unexplainable is the fact that in the 1868 catalog both Kellogg and Norton are listed as honorary members of the Board.[212]

C. V. ESKRIDGE.

PROF. H. B. NORTON.

GEORGE W. HOSS, LL. D.

LYMAN B. KELLOGG.

REV. G. C. MORSE.

C. R. POMEROY, D. D.

FIRST BOARDING-HALL, 1868.

WALTER M. ANDERSEN
COLLECTION

Stone Building, 1867-1878

Old Administration Building, 1873-1878

"The morning of October 26, 1878"

**First graduates: Class of 1867,
Ellen Plumb (right) & Mary Jane Watson (left)**

CHAPTER 6

FINANCING AND ENDOWING THE NORMAL

By 1869, the Board of Directors had become persistent in its efforts to develop the somewhat confusing but unique third portion of the Act to establish, locate, and endow the Kansas State Normal School. Thus far, the School's endowment had been merely talked about in terms of the future. No income had yet been realized from the so-called "salt lands" set aside in the 1863 Act for the institution's livelihood. Although indebted to the astute framers of the Act for their farsightedness in endowing the institution—the first Normal School in the United States to receive such a gift in government lands—early officials of the Normal had but a vague notion of where the lands were located, their value, or even the acreage involved.

The endowment had been possible because of the two legal documents which had enabled Kansas to become a state. The ordinance, which prefaced the Wyandotte Constitution of July 29, 1859, had first spelled out the general acreage. Section five of that document provided that: All salt springs, not exceeding twelve in number, with six sections of land adjacent to each, together with all mines, with the lands necessary for their full use, shall be granted to the State for works of public improvement.

The subsequent Admission Act granted all of the salt springs not to exceed twelve in number, with "six sections of land adjoining or as contiguous as may be to each." Thus, there perhaps were to be as many as seventy-two sections of land "to be used or disposed of on such terms, conditions, and regulations, as the Legislature shall direct." The specific lands were to be selected by the governor within a year after Kansas became a state.[213]

By 1863, when the Normal School Act was passed, it had been established that there were indeed seventy-two sections of land in the state grant. Nevertheless, Section three of the Act creating the Normal was written in the same general terms as was the Admission Act. All of the so-called salt lands were to be set aside as a perpetual endowment for the support and maintenance of the Normal School "save and except the salt springs, and the section of land upon which each of the said salt springs are located, and one additional section...." (Appendix, p. i).

In the beginning there seemed to be little confusion about the acreage of the endowment lands, which were located along the Republican and Saline Rivers in Mitchell, Lincoln, Saline, Cloud, Jewel, and Republic counties. The local newspaper, the Board of Directors, and the governor of the state, all referred to the Normal School's endowment of fifty-nine sections of land or 37,760 acres.[214] As early as 1868, however, the phrase, "and one additional section" began posing a problem, presumably over which section to delete. In an attempt to solve the problem, the Board of Directors recommended that the legislature add the extra section to the Normal School lands. No action was taken, apparently, for the following year the directors repeated their request. They

> Voted to reaffirm the recommendation of the last year that the ambiguity with regard to the Normal lands occasioned by the expression "one additional section" as found in the law donating said lands to the State Normal School be removed by requesting the State to add the one additional section to the endowment of the school. (Minutes, January 20, 1869).

The legislature responded by passing senate bill #78, "An Act Supplemental to an Act to establish a State Normal School." Governor James M. Harvey approved it on March 3, 1869.[215]

Although the ambiguity of the language had not been corrected, the endowment lands now numbered sixty sections. Hereafter, any questions about the original acreage would be purely academic. Thirty years later, while president of the Normal, Albert R. Taylor gave his interpretation of the "one additional section." His was a different view from that of the men on the scene in the 1860s. Taylor determined that for every salt spring section an additional section was to be kept by the state.[216]

During Taylor's term of office, the 1886 legislature, having long before determined that the minerals upon the salt springs sections were worthless, relinquished the state's claim to the twelve salt springs by adding them to the Normal School's endowment. Finally, the Normal School had acquired the full seventy-two sections of the state grant.[217]

Contrary to the Act creating the Normal School, which designated the salt lands as a perpetual endowment, "the principal of which shall remain forever undiminished," the 1866 appropriation bill stipulated that the amount used for the new building was to be deemed a loan to be repaid from funds derived from the sale of school lands. The 1867 appropriation bill, passed in order that the structure might be completed, likewise stipulated that all of the appropriated amount except the portion used for teachers' salaries be deemed a loan to be repaid from land sales. The funds, moreover, were not to be used for any other purpose until the state had been reimbursed.[218]

The 1866 legislature had also passed a law regulating the sale of the Normal lands, an indication that the loans were not intended to be of long term. Section four contained explicit instructions to the Board of Directors about repayment of the building loan, defrayment of the school's current expenses, and the investment of any residue. Accordingly in June, the Board made its first move towards disposing of the lands by voting to employ a suitable person to appraise the land. H. D. Preston was chosen for the job. He was to divide the sections into the smallest legal sub-divisions of forty acres (sixteen parcels per section), and make a full description of each as to number, quality, whether timber prairie, upland or lowland; if prairie, how far from timber and water, how near to stone quarry, what slope, and the like. Although there is no known record of his findings, his report was presented to the Board the following year and termed satisfactory.[219]

Nevertheless, none of the lands sold at that time. Adding the nebulous "one additional section" to the endowment apparently had little if any effect upon the Board of Directors' ability to sell the lands. Availability of homesteads and the ever present speculation that new areas were soon to be opened for settlement probably kept incoming settlers from purchasing land except as a last resort. In any case, not until the 1870s were any of the salt lands sold. By then, the 1866 land sales act had been repealed and a land agent appointed by the Board to handle the disposition of the endowment lands.[220]

Regardless of what lay ahead for the Kansas State Normal School, 1869 was a year of accomplishments for the four-year-old institution. Being able to occupy its own building and grounds was a source of pride not only for faculty and students, but for the community and the state. The boarding house had become a reality; the model school was functioning; and the faculty was contributing to the field of education on both the state and national levels. Also, there was continued growth in enrollment, albeit a high turnover in students. Already by early 1869, as many as one hundred and fifty former students were engaged in teaching.[221] Perhaps a quotation from the *Topeka Daily Commonwealth* best sums up the high esteem held by the Normal School at this point.

> What West Point is to our army, the Normal School is to the school system in Kansas; not as supplying all the officers or teachers, but as giving tone, system, coherence, to the whole, introducing and disseminating new ideas and improved methods, and furnishing instructors of unequaled aptness and professional enthusiasm, whose work may furnish a model for general imitation.[222]

The institution fared well, too, at the hands of the legislature. Professor Norton's back pay was taken care of; additional land was granted to the school's endowment; and the full appropriation asked for by the Board of Directors was approved.[223]

The third annual commencement, June 23-24, 1869, was a milestone in the history of the institution.. In January, the senior class consisted of four women and eight men, but by June three of the latter had dropped out. Nevertheless, for the first time, male students were among the graduates and the nine students who remained to graduate represented an increase of more than one hundred percent over the previous year.[224] The anniversary festivities were somewhat affected by rainy weather which discouraged travel, but attendance, nevertheless, was rated as good. Examinations of the Model School were held on Tuesday, June 22, a day prior to those of the Normal proper. The main attraction of the Literary Society meeting Wednesday evening was a debate of the question "Would the United States be justifiable in declaring war with England?"[225]

Thursday, June 24, was an especially full day what with nine graduate addresses during the morning and the formal commencement at two o'clock. The afternoon program opened with special music by the cornet band. T. D. Thacher, editor of the Lawrence *Republican Journal,* gave the anniversary address in which he considered benefits of higher education to the state. Governor James M. Hervey was on hand to issue the diplomas and Kellogg spoke on what the Normal students owe to the state, a speech that was published in *The Emporia News,* September 10, at the onset of the fall term. Festivities ended Thursday evening with a graduate reception.[226]

The Normal had no more than closed its doors for the summer when its faculty and some of the students headed for Manhattan to attend the annual state teachers' meeting. The adventures of one group are preserved in a letter to *The Emporia News.* On Monday morning, June 28, at eleven o'clock, a large covered wagon drawn by four horses rolled northward down the hill towards the [Neosho] river. Leading the party were professors Kellogg and Norton riding ahead on horseback. In the wagon were coachman Douglas and seven women: Misses Nicholls, Slocum, Ela, Huddleston, Norton, Medill, and Towner. By dusk, the party reached Council Grove where some stayed at Mr. Mather's place and the rest at a hotel. At noon the following day, they all lunched under a grove of trees twenty-tree miles northwest of Council Grove. About two o'clock, the rain came, relieving the monotony of the trip for the wagon passengers, but certainly not adding to the comfort of the two horsemen. They were soon dripping, and the mud became stickier with every passing minute. Late that night, the party reached the Kansas River opposite Manhattan to find the water too high to cross at night by ferry or skiff. Thus, they retraced their steps half a mile or so to a large farm house to seek food and shelter. On Wednesday morning, they crossed the river in a little skiff, wandered through the mud to the hotel, and repaired themselves for the approaching meeting.[227]

Announcements of the opening of the 1869 fall term at the Normal began to appear by mid-August. In view of the statistics given by the Board of Visitors in their 1868 report – that all but three of the ninety-eight students in the Normal department last term [fall of 1868] had taken the pledge to teach – the editorial "Good For All," urging parents to send their children to the Normal School whether or not they intend to teach, is of special interest.[228] The irony of the situation was that although the sole mission of the Normal School was to train teachers, the administration having consciously attempted to attract would-be teachers (see text at footnote #105), the greater the number of students signing the intent to teach, thereby exempting themselves from paying tuition, the less income there was from students. Stotler, recently appointed to the

Board of Directors, apparently sought to improve the school's finances by appealing to all potential students who were interested in getting a good education. When the fall term opened on September 13, 1869, one hundred and twenty-five students were enrolled in the Normal. By November, Kellogg reported to Stotler that of the 127 students then enrolled, 96 were teachers. The others were in the preparatory and model departments. In his fifth annual report, Kellogg gave figures that showed a significant increase in the overall 1869 enrollment.[229] Aided considerably by an earlier report of the joint legislative committee assigned to inspect the State Normal School, Kellogg was able to declare by late 1869 that the building improvements requested of the legislature had been accomplished. Included were improvements such as removal of defective plaster and installing a ceiling of pine paneling; repairs of the leaky roof around the cupola; repair of a leaky cistern; and the planting of maple trees as a start towards landscaping.

The above-noted joint committee, composed of Senator M. V. Voss of Bourbon County, Representative I. T. Rankin of Johnson County, and Judge L. D. Bailey, was one of several such committees appointed the previous January to inspect conditions at the various state institutions. Rankin, a former member of the Board of Directors, and Senator Voss had spent two days early in February visiting the Normal School. Judge Bailey, a current Board member and frequent visitor to the campus, did not arrive until after the two legislators had departed.[230] Their report to the legislature pronounced the Normal School a credit to the state. They had been pleasantly surprised to find that in spite of a scanty endowment, a sparsely settled state, and the newness of the school, the Kansas State Normal compared favorably with "the best Eastern schools of the kind." They were especially complimentary of Kellogg and Norton.

> The Principal is by nature adapted to govern. Mild and urbane in his manner, but firm, determined and just in his purpose
> The profound and erudite associate principal, with his fine scholastic attainments, and his peculiar faculty of imparting instruction, is equally indispensible to the Institution and State.[231]

Turning from the school itself to the building and grounds, salaries, and incidental expenses, the committee concurred that it was but one step from the "sublime to the ridiculous." They reported a financial condition that was anything but flattering and described in detail the building areas that needed immediate repairs. As for the barren prairie grounds, landscaping was essential to the inspectors who thought it inexcusable that beautifying the grounds had been ignored for so long. Finding that all heretofore appropriations to the Normal had been extended legitimately, the committee urged that the full amount asked for by the Board of Directors be appropriated. That amount ($8,630), they believed, was essential for the continued existence of the school. They would have liked to recommend additional needs but dared not do so because of the state's financial situation.[232]

Perhaps the wants of the Normal, as spelled out in Kellogg's 1869 report, more clearly depicts the status of the Normal than any other surviving document. According to Kellogg, there had been no great need for languages being taught heretofore in the Normal, but with the educational growth of the state in its material progress, common schools were no longer enough. A classical education was now necessary since a demand had been created for high school teachers and for persons qualified to handle academies. Although the main work of the Normal was to supply better common school teachers, the school could not stop there. It must continue to fit its students for the highest positions or its reputation would fall and its usefulness diminish. Kellogg considered the need for a department of classics and modern languages and an additional teacher to take charge of it important enough to place it at the top of his list. The Board of Visitors supported his request for a language department. The Board of Directors, however, did not. The executive committee refrained from recommending extra professorship, not that it was unimportant, but because of the cost at a time when the state needed to economize.[233] Only Kellogg's report predicted a new era of expansion and usefulness for Kansas State Normal with the coming of the railroads. That era began with the close of the 1869 fall term.[234]

CHAPTER 7

THE RAILROAD AND OTHER SEEDS OF CHANGE: 1870-1871

When the winter term opened in January 3, 1870, Normal students from the upper Neosho valley and areas of northeast Kansas were able for the first time to "ride the cars" to Emporia. The railroad, which became the Missouri, Kansas, and Texas line soon after reaching Emporia, began stretching its rails into southeast Kansas before spring. With summer, the Atchison, Topeka, and Santa Fe arrived, scarcely pausing in Emporia before penetrating the southwestern portions of the state.[235]

Along with Emporia's improved transportation came an intensified housing problem, especially in the shortage of hotel rooms and the increased demand for boarding facilities. In mid-winter during what usually was a slack season, all three of the town's hotels were crowded. Even the governor, James M. Harvey, went so far as to report to the 1870 legislature in his annual message that the Normal School was in great need of suitable boarding arrangements for students who already were in attendance. [236]

Both the Normal School and the community looked to the 1870 legislature to chart their future. The issue of consolidating the state institutions was still alive, but no proposal to remove the Normal School surfaced during the legislative session. In fact, the feeling seemed to be that two or three additional Normal Schools were necessary in order for the state to keep pace with the ever increasing demand for qualified teachers. There was, however, a proposal to remove some of the other institutions to the capital. It was tabled by substantial majority.[237]

Emporians had begun to consider the benefits of becoming a city of the second class, and by February a petition was being signed in preparation for the city election scheduled for the first Monday in April. Also being circulated was another petition asking the legislature to grant Emporia, whenever it should become a city, the authority to issue bonds, if the people so elect, to the amount of $6,000 to build a boarding house for the Normal School.[238]

At the same time, Emporians were striving to get rid of Washington Park, land set aside by the town company for civic or county buildings, but land which had proved to be so poorly drained that in rainy weather it was a quagmire. In March, the legislature passed an act enabling the town authorities to vacate the park. Because it had not been used for its original purpose, the land reverted to the original town company. According to the agreement, half of the thirty-two lots were to go to the town company and half to the city of Emporia.[239]

At the April 8 city election, Emporians voted to become a second class city, the fourth ward of which was Washington Park. From the first ward, Eskridge, who had just completed his term as lieutenant governor, was elected councilman. The following day he was elected president of the city council, a position that proved to be beneficial to the State Normal School whose executive committee he also served. One of the council's first items of business concerned boarding houses for the Normal.

In May, the council adopted an ordinance to issue bonds for the purpose of building the boarding houses. The election was set for June 16, 1870. The plan proved to be a controversial one, especially with the boarding house keepers whose cause was espoused in a letter signed by "Justice" in *The Emporia News*. On May 28 in a public meeting at the court house, Kellogg addressed the crowd who subsequently voted to allow the council to hold the bond election.[240]

In a second rebuttal, "Justice" explained that he was not opposed to education nor to boarding houses. He was opposed to the city getting into the boarding house business. On June 16, Emporians voted down the bond issue. They were uncertain about whether the bond money would complete the structures, and whether the houses once built would remain city property. They were also uncertain about who would pay interest on the bonds.

Within a week, a new petition calling for another election was being circulated. It was presented to the city council in July. The new petition asked that the $6,000 bond issue be re-submitted to the vote of the citizens with the following stipulations: that the houses remain city property and that they be under the control of the Normal School only for so long as they were used as boarding houses; that the amount voted upon must complete the buildings; that the student rent be sufficient to pay interest on the bonds; and that at least two houses be built, one for each sex exclusively.[241]

The council was unanimous in its decision to hold a second election, July 26, 1870. This time the bond issue carried. A special committee from the council was appointed to work with the executive committee of the Normal School on the sale of bonds and erection of the boarding houses. The appointed councilmen were also authorized to choose the building sites.[242]

Within a month after the bond election, plans for two frame boarding houses were in the hands of potential contractors who had until September 3 to submit bids. The houses, located on either side of Commercial Street below Ninth Avenue, were under construction by mid-September. They apparently were occupied before the end of November, for a local news item on November 25 told of a young woman spraining an ankle in a fall down the outside steps of one of the boarding houses.[243]

A description of the boarding houses appeared in Kellogg's report for 1870. Kellogg referred to them as neat, substantial two-story frame buildings, 22 feet by 60 feet, well finished, plastered and painted, provided with cisterns, cellars, et cetera. Conveniently located about midway between the middle of town and the Normal School, the boarding houses were connected to the Normal School by plank sidewalks. Kellogg also reported that rooms rented for as little as twenty-five to fifty cents per week per occupant. Students united in clubs of three to five members for the purpose of boarding themselves. Their entire expense was from $2.00 to $2.50 per person per week, about half the usual price for board with private families.[244]

Aside from the strides being taken by the railroads and the community, life in 1870 continued much as usual for the Normal students. Crowded conditions had become a fact of life. That condition was alleviated somewhat by the purchase of additional chairs for some students without desks who sat in the aisles and propped their study books upon the window sills.[245]

Bi-weekly meetings of the Literary Union continued to be a primary source of recreation and entertainment for students. A local reporter, after visiting one such meeting, wrote an impressive account of the occasion. In his opinion, the presiding officers were competent; business was disposed of systematically; good deportment prevailed; and the order of exercises arranged well. The main portion of the program, which also included music and oratory, was a reading contest wherein one selection each from American and English literature was chosen to be read in each of the four categories: patriotic, pathetic, descriptive, and humorous. Three judges in the audience determined the winners.[246]

In late May, a Normal School picnic was staged for faculty, students, and invited guests. An undetermined number of townspeople, all friends of the school, received printed invitations to the picnic. Among them were Mr. and Mrs. Stotler. In his newspaper, Stotler left an interesting account of that event. All comers were to meet at the Normal School with a basket of lunch at ten o'clock in the morning to start for the banks of the Neosho. "Needlessly early," Stotler wrote, "the smiling Normalites, in their best dress, were seen gathering at the school building." The picnic was held in "a very lovely place, being in the belt of timber north of the Neosho, above the railroad bridge [M. K. and T. Bridge]." The editor saw the spot as a good place for a real park with a potential 100 acres for rowing, fishing, hiking, and the like. Entertainment before dinner included boating, riding, walking, games of croquet, and "tete-a-tete by the pair and in groups." Dinner was served in "fine style" with people seated in groups on the grass in the shade of the "grand old trees."

Following the meal, there was music and various toasts, one of which was not on the program according to Kellogg, but one which the students and friends of the Normal thought should be there. It was senior student J. M. Spangler's toast to Professor Kellogg: "The log that has for so long furnished fuel for the fires of enthusiasm in the State Normal School." The Reverend G. C. Morse responded. Eskridge replied to the following toast of gratitude to the City Fathers:

> With true parental regard, they are providing for us a tabernacle in which to dwell; by their magic power they shall cause water to flow from some yet unsmitten rock; and from the gas of some yet undiscovered coal mine, they shall evoke light to dispel the gloom of our darkened path.[247]

For an unknown reason, the 1870 Normal commencement was not a part of the June festivities. It had been postponed until the end of the fall term. Nevertheless, attendance at the closing exercises on June 22-23 was larger than in previous years, according to Stotler, who as usual reviewed the examinations and the program of the Literary Union. In his resume of the foregoing events, Stotler explained that the date of commencement had been changed in order to accommodate the teachers. The following week, however, he ran a correction as to the reason. The change, he said, was to benefit the teachers and others in the state who might wish to attend but could not because of obligations at conflicting commencements at other institutions.[248]

Early notices of the September 12, 1870 opening of the fall term assured potential students that ample accommodations for boarding would be provided. Nevertheless, applications were apparently sluggish, for on September 9, Kellogg announced that he had heard students were not applying because they thought all seats were full. He assured them that there still was room in all departments. Only the Model School, which was to open on September 14, had room for but one more student.[249]

After a couple of weeks, Stotler made one of his occasional visitations to the Normal School which he subsequently lauded in his newspaper as the "leader and head-center of Kansas School teachers"—the acknowledged leader of western states in education. A month later, he ran a very positive tribute to the school and town from the *Topeka Commonwealth*.[250]

The fourth annual commencement exercises, scheduled for December 20, 21, and 22, followed the same format as previous ones held in June. After two days of examinations, the evening literary program was a much needed change of pace. Stotler wrote his usual enthusiastic review with one exception. He was critical of the parts being read instead of memorized by those taking part in The Merchant of Venice. At the same time, he was complimentary of the acting, in particular, Kellogg's portrayal of Shylock.[251]

Although extremely cold weather delayed the beginning of commencement activities on the morning of December 22, participants and audience soon arrived and the program began. Lt. Governor Eskridge presided. From twenty-two senior students who had attended the Normal during some time in 1870, there were six graduates. One of those, Henry N. West of Waveland, Shawnee County, was graduated posthumously. He had died in August. The remaining five gave their graduation essays. Mary L. Duren of Garnett spoke of the Prussian system of education in a speech titled "Good Wine Needs No Bush." David M. Bales of Toledo, Chase County, spoke on "Uses and Abuses of Ridicule." Nellie A. Storrs, Emporia, defended her intense interest in music with a speech "Music In and Out of School." John M. Spangler, also of Emporia, chose "The Apostle Paul as a Teacher;" and Sarah H. Hawkins, Virgil, "Kansas Expects Every Teacher To Do His Duty." The morning speeches ended with a brief address to the graduates by Kellogg.[252]

In the afternoon, the graduates received their diplomas from Governor J.M. Harvey. The guest speaker, the Honorable I. S. Kalloch of Lawrence and an accomplished orator himself, spoke of the value of public speaking. Emporia's new Congregational minister, Thomas Jones, who had given the morning invocation, gave the afternoon benediction. With a graduate reception that evening, the December commencement of 1870 became history.[253]

Changes in the Normal School personnel began to occur in 1870 and the first half of 1871, resulting in a complete turnover of faculty and the Board of Directors. First had come the resignation of Ellen Plumb who, after the first term of 1870, gave up teaching to open a local book store. She was replaced in April by Mary E. Baker of Decatur, Illinois. Miss Baker, a teacher of eight years' standing, was a product of Illinois State Normal University where she had served three years as model school principal before serving in the Decatur High School for five years.

H. B. Norton, after becoming president of the Creswell Town Company, made several trips to and from Arkansas City before moving there for the summer. He took a leave of absence from the Normal during the fall term at which time R. B. Dilworth of Leavenworth replaced him. When Norton decided to resign his position, Dilworth, a graduate of Princeton College, was hired in his stead.[254]

Tragedy struck the Board of Directors on July 13, 1870, when the Reverend G. C. Morse died as a result of an accident while cleaning a well on his farm. His replacement, the Reverend C. R. Rice of Emporia, was not appointed until the following January. By then, Stotler, who only recently had resigned from the board, was replaced by the Reverend R. M. Overstreet, newly-elected member to the state legislature and a former Presbyterian minister of Emporia. Thus the critical year of 1871, when Kellogg was hoping to add a fourth year to the Normal School curriculum and a new building to the campus, began with two new members on the Board's executive committee. The third member, Eskridge, who was finishing his term as lieutenant governor, suddenly found himself a minority of one in matters pertinent to the welfare of the Normal. Eventually Governor Harvey appointed a completely new board, but not until a combination of political and religious jealousies, personality conflicts, and character assassinations erupted, creating a situation that ultimately forced the resignations of the Normal principal and preceptress.[255]

Shortly after the winter term got under way on January 2, 1871, there appeared in *The Emporia News* an optimistic and detailed account of the progress of the Normal School. Although twenty or more potential students decided not to come for fear there would not be room, the total enrollment was 130. For the past three terms, entry requirements had been tightened until the most current students, according to the newspaper, were among the most mature and diligent students in the state. The writer, presumably Stotler, declared that

> All in all, the Normal School is in a more prosperous condition than ever before. We trust that it may receive from the Legislature this winter the aid and encouragement which its merits so richly deserve.[256]

By the middle of the month, Overstreet and Senator Stotler were involved with the new legislature. Both men were in positions to benefit the Normal School: Stotler, on the education committee and Overstreet, public institutions. Overstreet, moreover, had received his appointment to the Board of Directors in time to attend their January 18 meeting in Topeka. It was this particular meeting that marked the end of Eskridge, Morse, Kellogg triumvirate. Consensus no longer would come as readily as heretofore.

Board members, while unanimous in their decision to ask the state for appropriations for a new building to cost $75,000, balked at adopting the executive committee's recommendations for salary increases. They voted not to allow any future back pay for teachers, a means previously used to rectify the differences between the teachers' negotiated salaries and the actual pay they received. The board likewise refused to add a second assistant teacher to the faculty.[257]

On January 25, a second meeting of the Board of Directors was called, presumably at the request of Kellogg or Eskridge. Like the earlier meeting, it was held in the state superintendent's office. Seven members including Kellogg were present. Kellogg was asked to submit the estimates of appropriations he deemed necessary for the ensuing year. He also took the liberty of presenting a statement from the faculty requesting that the board reconsider its earlier action regarding the request for a second assistant teacher, a position the faculty believed essential for the growth of the Normal. The statement bore the signatures of Kellogg, Mrs. Gorham, and Dilworth.

According to the Minutes, Overstreet was overtly opposed to hiring a second teacher as well as being opposed to increasing the other salaries. Eskridge was equally vocal in his favor of both. He succeeded in getting the Board to reconsider each item separately, the end result of which was an increase of $2200 in salaries over the amount voted for at the January 18 meeting.[258]

In the meantime, Senator Stotler introduced his $50,000 appropriation bill for a new Normal School building. The bill asked that $25,000 be appropriated from current 1870 funds and $25,000 from 1871 funds on condition that the city of Emporia raise $20,000 towards the project in 20-year bonds at ten percent. At about the same time, the legislature determined that there would be no pay raises nor back pay for faculties of the state institutions.[259]

Shortly, Stotler revised his appropriation bill downward to $25,000 in order to get it through the senate. It passed that body on February 15 but was destined to die in the house in March by a vote of 37 to 33. The legislature, according to Stotler, was bogged down with money requests from all of the state institutions. Being more inclined to lower taxes than to increase expenditures, the members voted down all building appropriations except for $40,000 to the insane asylum.

Three weeks went by before Stotler wrote on the front page of his paper an article regarding the two board meetings. He maintained that Kellogg had furnished the executive committee with estimates for salaries and other current expenses for the ensuing year. In these estimates, the principal's salary was raised $500 in back pay. Instead of one assistant at $900, as heretofore, two assistants at $1000 each were asked for, and the salary of the model school principal raised $300. Since there were but two members on the committee, they could not settle the matter, according to Stotler. Thus, it had been taken to the regular board meeting on January 18.

Although he was no longer a member, Stotler gave as one of the reasons for the board not raising salaries the fact that the teachers would no longer be suffering a "heavy shave on state scrip." Stotler purportedly was surprised to learn of the called meeting. According to him, Rice was not notified of the meeting, and Overstreet learned of it only after a quorum failed to show up. Stotler maintained that the question was which of the two meetings to take as the authority. He believed that under the circumstances those in charge of appropriations the legislature should do as they please—give just what they think is right and no more.[260]

Stotler's threat stung Kellogg into writing "The Normal School Again," an article in which he referred to Stotler's small controversy with the Board of Directors. He took Stotler to task for threatening to abuse his legislative power. Kellogg considered the January 18 meeting to have been poorly attended. Stotler as secretary had not notified those members outside of Topeka and only four voting members plus the chair [Governor Harvey] were present. The meeting, Kellogg asserted, was not as "regular" as one might think. He considered Overstreet to be Stotler's man. The lesser salary figures, he believed, were Stotler's. Overstreet insisted that they be voted upon, and each time there was a tie. McCarty protested the proceedings, according to Kellogg, as did he himself, especially in regard to eliminating the second assistant teacher. At the second meeting, according to Kellogg, Overstreet's was the only negative voice present.[261]

What had begun as a verbal exchange between Stotler and Kellogg over their assessment of the recent board action soon grew into what Kellogg called "Our Personal Wrangle." The week following the first exchange, Stotler was no longer able to write dispassionately. Kellogg's earlier referral to the small controversy so angered Stotler that he wrote caustically upon the subject declaring

> The gun from which it [the controversy] comes is small and scatters badly, and no harm has been done.

In another instance, Stotler referred to

> This little fellow's repeated attempts to ignore the action of the Board of Directors at its first meeting,...

And as he warmed to his topic, Stotler admitted

> I do no longer propose to be dictated to as to the annual raise of salary demanded by this little man.[262]

In the more rational portions of his diatribe, Stotler revealed that he had resigned from the board several days before the first meeting, and that he with several other citizens had solicited Overstreet's appointment. Kellogg had not been approached because choosing a board member was not considered the principal's business. There had been enough of the "ring" business in Normal School management, and if he [Stotler] could prevent it, there would be no more of it. Stotler also declared that as a board member he had almost always opposed the salary estimates presented by Kellogg but had gone along with them because he stood alone. This time, however, he [Stotler] was backed by the board. Since the members had contradicted themselves in the two meetings, Stotler vowed to do as he pleased about appropriations for the Normal School.[263]

One complaint made by Stotler surely did not aid the cause of the Normal School in the attempt to acquire more space. He maintained that the Normal had 150 to 160 students instead of the 243 which Kellogg "falsely" claimed. It is not fair to count the number that has [sic] attended during the whole year instead of those in attendance at one time.[264]

Kellogg, in "Our Personal Wrangle," exemplified some of the traits which apparently had helped him develop a viable institution in spite of many adversities. He refused to stoop to vindictiveness. He diagnosed Stotler's ridicule as part of a plan to develop a newspaper controversy. He dismissed Overstreet, who had written a caustic article accusing Kellogg of writing untruths in the *Topeka Commonwealth*, as being too volatile and gross in his attack to deserve an answer. But most significant of all, he removed Stotler's sting by announcing that "being a little man," he would write only one column in answer to Stotler's two. Kellogg's grievances remained consistent. At the January 18 meeting, he protested the elimination of a second assistant teacher and the fact that he himself and the preceptress were given no salary increases. He reprimanded Stotler for flaunting his and Overstreet's legislative powers by quoting to them Section five of the Organization Act which gave to the Board of Directors the right to fix salaries.[265]

Before long, Stotler referred to the matter as "Kellogg vs. the State Treasury." He dwelt upon the principal's request for a $500 raise, all but ignoring the request for an additional teacher and the other salary increases. In spite of the fact that the vote at first board meeting was 3 to 2 against salary increases and at the second meeting 4 to 1 in favor of the increases, Stotler declared

We have the right on our side, and as long as we are defending the interests of the people against the overreaching demands of one man, we are willing to go ahead. But we submit that the small game will not require the wasting of much of our powder.[266]

Overstreet, whom Kellogg had declined to dignify by answering, originally became embroiled in the dispute because he believed that the article in the *Commonwealth* regarding the board's first meeting carried "the footprints" of Kellogg. In all probability, Kellogg did have a hand in the story; but Editor Prouty, who apparently favored salary increases, was present at both meetings. He certainly was in a better position to write the story than was Kellogg. In any case, the account centered around the fact that the majority of the board were new members who had repudiated the executive committee's recommendations.[267]

Kellogg was finished with the argument, but Overstreet and Stotler soon found themselves on the defensive against Eskridge who lashed out at them over the failure of the appropriation bill. Stotler's reply was a mild article in which he surmised that Eskridge was not really upset with the legislative action. His was the first blast of a new campaign. He predicted that Eskridge would be a candidate for the legislature in November, explaining that his tactics were to tear down all potential candidates. Overstreet, however, tore into Eskridge; first by ridiculing him for being so late in coming to Kellogg's rescue, then by denouncing him for having foisted two Normal clubhouses upon the local taxpayers, and finally by concentrating on the issue of $850 paid to Eskridge for Normal fencing. The latter issue was debated in the newspapers between Overstreet and Eskridge well into October, 1871.[268]

On April 12, 1871, a new reason for protest occurred when an accusation appeared in *The Emporia Tribune* referring to the Normal Boarding Houses as "houses of assignation." Professor Dilworth wrote a strong protest in *The Emporia News*, criticizing the editor of the *Tribune* for slander against the Normal School. Nearly a month later, Stotler published a resolution passed on April 13 by the Normal students denouncing the April 12 accusation as false. In the same issue was a notice dated May 1 from the faculty stating that the students' meeting had been authorized and held with faculty consent. It was signed by the entire faculty who were in sympathy with the student resolution. On the same day, the executive committee of the Board of Directors approved the action taken by the students in defending themselves against the unwarranted and scandalous charge. That notice carried the signatures of Eskridge and Overstreet.[269]

Unlike previous years, Stotler devoted very little space to Normal School news in 1871. The first information to appear concerning a school activity was on May 26, a week after the event was held. The notice gave no specifics other than that the Literary Society was pretty largely attended and that as usual the exercises were good. Graduation again had been scheduled for December, but if there were any closing exercises at the end of the spring term as there had been in the previous year, no one bothered to publish the fact in *The Emporia News.*

Early in June, Stotler announced the members of the completely new Board of Directors appointed by the governor. They were E. P. Bancroft, Harvey Bancroft, and S. B. Riggs of Emporia; E. S. Stover, Council Grove; J. W. Horner, Chetopa; and Edwin Tucker, Eureka. As previously, ex officio members were Governor Harvey, Hayes and McCarty.[270]

The new board convened in Emporia on June 22 with everyone except Tucker and Hayes present for the one day meeting comprised of three sessions, morning, afternoon, and evening. The initial session concerned the swearing in of the members by Governor Harvey and election of officers. Governor Harvey was elected president; E. P. Bancroft, secretary; and the three Emporians, the two Bancrofts and Riggs, were elected to the executive committee. After hearing Kellogg's report on the appropriations for the current year, the amount expended, and the amount on hand, the board adjourned until one-thirty p.m.[271]

At the afternoon session, both Stotler and Eskridge were invited to make statements concerning the last board's action on the subject of appropriations and expenditures. The executive committee was instructed to examine charges made against Eskridge in regard to improper use of funds appropriated for fencing Normal School grounds (see footnote 267) and to report at the next board meeting. They also were asked to check into the sale of land belonging to the institution before the next meeting. A committee was approved to examine the subjects of faculty salaries, the school year, and the propriety of retaining the present faculty, and report at an evening session. McCarthy, Horner, and Stover made up the committee.[272]

The evening session opened at eight o'clock with Governor Harvey presiding. By invitation, Overstreet spoke in regard to the differences between the former executive committee and certain members of the faculty in regard to salary. The special committee appointed in the afternoon recommended through their chairman, J. W. Horner, that: The Secretary be instructed to notify Professor L. B. Kellogg that his resignation as Principal of the State Normal School at Emporia, will be accepted, to take effect June 30, 1871.[273]

The same committee recommended that the Model School be discontinued; that the remaining four salaries for the ensuing year be set at the following figures: principal, $2500; assistant principal, $1600; preceptress, $1200; and assistant teacher, $1000; and that the secretary be directed to notify Mrs. J. H. Gorham that her resignation to take effect June 30, 1871, would be acceptable. The board accepted the report and dismissed the committee before considering each recommendation separately. In the end, the full report was adopted unanimously.[274]

Thus were Kellogg and Mrs. Gorham dismissed. No headlines in *The Emporia News* drew attention to the fact. Stotler, in a brief report of the Board of Directors meeting merely announced that the two had resigned, their resignations to take effect immediately. At the same time, he also announced Kellogg's replacement.[275] Although Kellogg technically did resign, Mrs. Gorham did not. The notice of her resignation appeared in the local paper a day before she received the letter asking for her resignation. In an indignant letter to Stotler, she corrected his story of the previous week by informing him of that fact. She added, "I have been dismissed from the position. No reasons have been given me for the dismission."[276]

Not until the end of July did the Board of Directors find a new principal for the Normal School. He was George Washington Hoss, professor of English Literature and the theory and practice of teaching at Indiana State University. He formerly had taught mathematics at Northwestern Christian University in Indianapolis, having resigned after eight years to become superintendent of public instruction. He authored the law establishing the Indiana State Normal School and edited the *State School Journal.* In the local announcement about Hoss having accepted the head position at Kansas State Normal School, he was described as about forty years of age, a man of good personal appearance and one of "pleasant address;" a thorough scholar and a Christian gentleman. A few months earlier, he had written a letter congratulating Emporians for their temperance triumph.[277]

CHAPTER 8

NEW FACULTY, NEW BUILDING, NO HEAT: 1871-1873

When the 1871 fall term opened, school was kept much as usual despite publicity that the Normal School had been entirely reorganized. The primary change was that while they were once again without a model school, students were to use the city schools for observation. Although the course of study had been extended to four years in order to allow for the study of languages, the executive board stated quite clearly in the school circular that "the present limit of the Normal School course in ancient and modern languages[is] to prepare [students] for the Freshmen class in our best universities." All students were charged the two dollars incidental fee; but in the fall of 1871, those other than potential teachers found that tuition increased from six to eight dollars per term. The increase, however, was short lived, for in the 1872-73 catalog, tuition for non-teachers had reverted to six dollars per term.[278]

As a fitting welcome to the new principal who had come to Emporia mid-August, special exercises were arranged for Monday evening, September 11, the opening day of the school. Governor Harvey and Superintendent McCarty were to have been part of the program, but they were unable to be present. Nevertheless, the event which was well attended by the school's ninety-one first day students was an impressive welcome to the new faculty from the Board of Directors and the citizens of Emporia. In addition to Hoss, Amelia F. Brewer was new to the staff, having been hired as preceptress to replace Mrs. Gorham. Dilworth and Mrs. Philbrick were holdovers. S. B. Riggs called the gathering to order.

There was singing and a welcome address by Major E. P. Bancroft. Professor Hoss responded with the main address of the evening "The Normal School – Its Aims, Relations, and the Means of its Efficiency." A social following the formal program climaxed the evening.[279]

Hoss appeared to have no difficulty in getting adjusted to his new job nor in being accepted throughout the state. The Methodists in state convention at Junction City extended him a hearty welcome by resolution: ...in behalf of education, truth, and sobriety—knowing he is a ripe scholar and eminent educator and an earnest worker in the cause of Temperance. In late September, he addressed the Lyon County Teachers Institute at Reading. By then, more than one hundred students were enrolled at the Normal.[280]

The new principal became actively involved in the temperance movement, serving as an able speaker at local meetings and a director of the Temperance Alliance. He also addressed his Normal students from time to time. Midway in the fall term, he initiated an important weekly lecture series for students on Friday afternoons. These lectures, forty-five minutes in length, concerned the laws of health with special reference to the health and habits of students. While most of the early lectures were delivered by Hoss himself, at least one was given by an Emporia doctor, W. T. Vail. Hoss and Dilworth were both speakers in a new civic lecture course devised to raise money for Emporia's needy families. There were six speakers in all at twenty-five cents each, $1.50 for a course ticket being sold by clergymen of the city. In addition to his many local lectures, Hoss spoke frequently in outlying areas, primarily to promote the cause of the Normal School and public education in general. One of his first out-of-town speeches was called "Why Do We Educate?" delivered in Council Grove.[281]

Although the economy measures passed by the new board had initially limited the Normal faculty to four teachers, a fifth became essential before the end of the fall term. M. C. Lamprey, a graduate of Dartmouth College and a former high school principal and superintendent of city schools, came from Iowa in November to teach languages and mathematics. When "Santagio" visited the school, he reported in an 1871 letter to the editor that Lamprey's lesson on fractions was explained so well that all students could comprehend the lesson. He described the new recruit as a young promising teacher, full of energy and "up with the times."[282] In fact, the reporter was favorably impressed by the entire faculty. He described Dilworth as not very communicative to strangers but a live, active teacher; Miss Brewer, a superior teacher well fitted for the responsible duties of preceptress; and Mrs. Philbrick as one who seemed to have more energy than most teachers. He assessed Hoss as a mature man, physically, intellectually, morally, and religiously, who needed only to be seen to be admired. A better president could scarcely be found, he thought. "What a glorious army of disciplined educators [who] in a few years will march out of the literary West Point of Kansas, and wage a war against ignorance. . . ."[283]

In December of 1871, there was no graduation even though the catalog schedule called for one. It probably is safe to assume—in view of the school's continued attempt to adopt a double course of study of two and four years instead of the earlier three year course—that there were no candidates for graduation. Moreover, in late June the new board had ruled that the school year should revert to the original schedule of beginning with the fall term and ending with the spring term.[284] The usual end-of-term public examinations, however, were held on December 19-21 although all of them except reading and elocution were written. Presumably, the latter examinations took the place of the traditional literary entertainment. In any event, nearly all of the students by this time belonged to either the Literary Union or a second society just being organized. Those students certainly would have been a part of the classes being examined orally. Perhaps even more important was the fact that as a result of the recent changes, the Normal was without a vocal teacher. Significantly, the board at its called meeting of December 14 authorized the executive committee to employ the services of a teacher of vocal music.[285]

Also in December, the Normal administrators had an unexpected assist in their struggle to get a new building when a reporter by the name of Pangborn from the *Kansas City Times* came to town to write a story about Emporia. In his lengthy recital of the community's rapid growth in population, at the time about 3,000, the number and variety of business houses, transportation routes, churches, and schools, Pangborn referred to the Normal School building, which five years earlier had seemed so commodious, as a "small and contracted edifice, by no means adequate to the requirements."[286]

The President's Annual Report likewise dramatized the dire need for more space. Hoss reported that classrooms built for twenty-five were being used by forty students; that an assembly room for 100 was being used by a student body of 120. Only sickness and other absences had made that possible. Lack of room necessitated the continued absence of a model school which to Hoss was a serious loss. "Without a Model School," he maintained, "a Normal School is shorn of much of its strength."

At a special meeting of the Board of Directors in Emporia on December 14, called by Governor Harvey even though he was unable to attend, the following resolution was unanimously adopted:

> Whereas: the great educational demand of our State is an increase of better qualified teachers, and
>
> Whereas: The present Normal School facilities are insufficient to meet this rapidly growing demand, and
>
> Whereas: the present building accommodations of the State Normal School at Emporia are totally inadequate to meet the pressing necessities of the school; therefore Resolved, That the Executive Committee, with the full endorsement of this Board, be authorized and instructed to present the necessities and claims of the Normal School, to the State legislature and ask for an appropriation of fifty thousand dollars, to erect suitable buildings for said school.

The executive committee was instructed to prepare plans of a proposed building which in their judgment would best present the subject to the legislature.[287]

When the winter term opened on January 2, 1872, there were 120 students present and enough letters of intent from others to indicate that enrollment would swell to 140 or more in a couple of weeks. Since there were not enough seats for those in attendance, all seats were taken up and replaced closer together in order to install another tier. Such an arrangement crowded the room beyond comfort, but it was essential in order to accommodate the increased demand upon the institution. It was thought that there would have been 200 students by this time had it not been general knowledge that there was a lack of space.[288]

A new feature appeared in Stotler's newspaper at the beginning of the year. Under the head " Normal School Essay," such class exercises of Normal students as seemed worthy of a place in the paper were to be published. The first essay was "The Bible" by T. J. M.; the second was "The Sabbath" by Eva M. Miller.[289]

It is obvious by the news coverage once more being given the Normal School and especially its new president that Stotler remained a staunch friend of the institution and was an enthusiastic admirer of Hoss. The editor in a "Testimonial to Professor Hoss" copied an article from the January 1872 *Indiana School Journal* which related the reaction of the Indiana University's board of trustees to the president's resignation from that institution. They passed five resolutions stating regret, recognizing his ability, congratulating him, congratulating Kansas, and furnishing copies of the resolutions to Hoss and the Indiana magazine. The fourth resolution read: The Board of Trustees congratulate the people of Kansas upon their success in securing the services of one who is in every way so eminently fitted for the educational head of their Common School System.[290]

Two weeks after the winter term got under way, Hoss delivered a lecture in Humboldt on "Woman—her work and education." He later gave the same speech at the Congregational Church in Emporia as one of the course lectures for the benefit of the poor. Although Stotler was unable to attend, he copied a review from the *Humboldt Union* which referred to Hoss as a good speaker. The subject was an appeal for the opening of all avenues, professional and business, to feminine competition, giving women equal rights in business matters with men. The reviewer called it a moderate, sensible paper. At about the same time, Hoss participated in the State Temperance Convention in Topeka as one of the three members of the organization's executive committee.[291]

The annual meeting of the new Board of Directors held in Topeka on January 11, 1872, was well attended. Only J. W. Horner of Chetopa and Edwin Tucker of Eureka were absent. The board heartily endorsed the recent report of President Hoss which urged not only larger facilities and a return to the model school, but also urged the hiring of a vocal music and drawing teacher. The new executive committee, Riggs, E. P., and Harvey Bancroft, in their report apologized for the difficulty they had experienced in carrying out their duties under the adverse conditions of having acquired their jobs unexpectedly in the middle of the year. After one term, however, the faculty appeared to be well qualified and the school progressing and tranquil. "We are happy to report that the utmost harmony and concord of action has at all times prevailed between the faculty and students."[292]

Soon after the 1872 legislature was organized with Emporians Senator Stotler and Representative Eskridge both serving on their respective ways and means committees, Eskridge introduced an appropriation bill in the amount of $50,000 for a new Normal School building. At the same time, he introduced a resolution to send a committee of three to the Normal School to inquire into its condition, usefulness, and needs—and to report to the house at an early date. Upon its adoption, the speaker appointed former Governor Charles Robinson, Wm. H. Schofield, and T. McIntire to the committee. They visited the institution on January 15 and subsequently made their report through Chairman Robinson. They were favorable towards the work being carried on at the Normal School, but very critical about the crowded conditions under which faculty and students labored. The report was printed and referred to the ways and means committee. The appropriation bill passed that committee with little difficulty, but thereafter, its success was less certain.[293]

Through the efforts of Eskridge, Stotler, Hoss, and various members of the board, arrangements were made for the legislature to visit the Normal enmasse that they might see for themselves the school's need for additional facilities. Eskridge put forth the motion and the house resolved to use Monday, January 29 (Kansas Day), for a trip to Emporia to see the Kansas State Normal School. News of their impending visit did not reach Emporia until Saturday, January 27. Nevertheless, the city council took time to meet and arrange for the visitors to be properly cared for. The Robinson House was contracted to provide dinner, and various prominent citizens offered to show proper attention to the law makers.

The special train which had been furnished free of charge by the Atchison, Topeka and Santa Fe arrived with its hundred or so passengers about ten o'clock on Monday morning. Emporians met the party and escorted them to the Robinson House, and then by carriage to the Normal where school was in session as usual. Eskridge and Stotler with the directors and faculty showed them around the school, encouraging the fullest investigation. After the formal visit, came the hotel dinner and an hour or two to look over the city. At five o'clock in the afternoon, the excursionists boarded the return train to Topeka.[294]

On January 31, the house voted 77 to 8 for the $50,000 for the new Normal building provided the city give $10,000 in bonds for the same. The bill, however, did not pass without some controversy. Colonel Strickler of Junction City offered the most active opposition. He tried to amend the bill by moving the location of the school to Junction City if, in a year, that city would give $100,000 towards the school. In that event, the existing Kansas State Normal building and grounds would be donated to the city of Emporia. Strickler was one of the few house members who did not take advantage of the opportunity to visit the Normal.[295]

On February 9, Stotler sent a special dispatch to his newspaper: "The bill appropriating fifty thousand dollars for the Normal School just passed the Senate. Vote, twenty for, none against." Governor Harvey signed the bill into law on February 12, 1872. (The act in full is in the appendix, p. xxii.)

At about the same time, President Hoss and the faculty announced the modified and extended course of study proposed two years earlier by Kellogg and his faculty and finally adopted by the Board of Directors at their annual meeting, January 11, 1872. To take effect with the beginning of the spring term on April 9, the elementary course would comprise two years of schooling; the full course, four years. Latin was to be a requirement in all three terms of the third year, but German could be substituted for Latin in the fourth year. Greek was offered as an elective. Advanced mathematics courses, also, had become a part of the four year program.[296]

In conjunction with his efforts to upgrade the quality of both the curriculum and the physical environment of the Normal School, President Hoss chose to build for himself and his wife, Harriet, a large, imposing residence on a five-acre tract adjacent to the city on West Twelfth Avenue. The two-story frame house, well braced with iron rods, rested on a stone cellar three feet above ground. Constructed during the fall and winter months of 1871-72, it had ceilings of eleven and ten feet, a 25 foot front and depth of 46 feet. There was a sixteen foot L to the west with a large bay window; a portico on the east; and a veranda across the front. Cornices were supported by ornamental brackets, and the trimmings were of maple. Front windows on both floors, and the bay window, were composed of but two large plates of glass. All windows in the house had blinds. The upper half of the front door was a solid round glass with a ruby colored glass transom above the door.

According to the detailed description in *The Emporia News*, what was termed "one of the most spacious and elegant dwellings in our city" had admirable ornamental work inside and out. The inside of the house contained heavily molded casings, grained woodwork in every room except the kitchen and pantry, handsome grates and mantels in the living, dining, and library rooms on the first floor and in the rooms upstairs. The front staircase had an octagon shaped walnut railing. Plenty of closets, a clothes room, and a bathroom upstairs, and transoms over all of the doors throughout the home added significantly to the comfort of the occupants.[297]

The first social function on record given by President and Mrs. Hoss was for the Normal faculty and students on October 11, 1872. It reportedly was well attended and "the most pleasant affair of the season."[298]

Before any money for the proposed Normal building could be drawn, two conditions set forth in the appropriation bill had to be met. The first one concerned clearing the title to the Normal School site donated by Filley six years earlier. The tract was part of the Indian float section which also comprised the northern portion of the original Emporia townsite, purchased in 1857 by the founding fathers from the estate of Francis A. Hicks, a Wyandotte Indian. In the late summer of 1871, when one Barzillia Gray claimed title to the section, numerous Emporians found themselves challenged in court. In September, the first cases were dismissed by J. H. Watson, Judge of the Lyon County District Court, but a change of venue was requested by the plaintiff because of Judge Watson's interest in the case. Thus it was that the land title in question was before the district court of Shawnee County during the 1872 legislative session.[299]

Prior to the passage of the appropriation bill, Gray and his wife Mary issued to the state of Kansas on January 29, 1872, a quit claim deed which was to become void and of no effect if the 1872 legislature failed to appropriate the sum of $50,000 for improvements upon the site. Such a provisional document, however, was unacceptable, and on February 3 the Grays issued a second quit claim deed relinquishing forever all claim to the site of the Normal School.[300]

The second condition to be met pertained to financial assistance from the city of Emporia in the form of revenue bonds for the minimum sum of $10,000. (Appendix, p. xxii, sec. 3.) At one point while discussing building plans, the Board of Directors approached leading citizens of Emporia in regard to the possibility of the city appropriating as much as $25,000 towards the new building. Those who appeared at the meeting to present their views, however, were opposed to the proposition. The city council subsequently passed unanimously an ordinance authorizing the mayor and the city clerk to issue city bonds in the total sum of $10,000 to be used by the Board of Directors in erecting and furnishing a new building for the Normal School.[301]

Meanwhile, the Normal students lost no time in voicing their gratitude to the Kansas lawmakers. On the same day that the appropriation bill was signed by Governor Harvey, February 12, 1872, the students passed three resolutions thanking the legislature for sending a special committee to find out the wants of the school; for coming themselves in a body to tour the facilities; and for appropriating $50,00 towards alleviating their crowded conditions. They also pledged themselves to personal improvement. Copies of the resolutions were sent to the Lyon County legislators, *The Emporia News,* and the *Emporia Ledger.*[302]

Within a week after the appropriation bill became law, the Board of Directors set about to study various building plans. At a special meeting in Topeka in late February, three builders were on hand to present and explain their individual plans, but the board adjourned until March 8 without making a decision. They agreed, however, to require each architect to present plans to furnish in writing a carefully prepared estimate of the cost of the completed building. They also adopted a resolution stating that it was the unanimous opinion of the board that no building plan should be adopted, the cost of which finished and furnished should exceed the appropriation.[303]

On March 8, 1872, at eight o'clock in the morning, six board members convened in Secretary Bancroft's office in Emporia to consider further the three building plans submitted earlier. Two additional plans were submitted at this time by W. S. Murphy and a Mr. Rawlings. The board recessed until one o'clock when Governor Harvey arrived to conduct the meeting. After further consideration of the plans, the board upon the motion of Riggs recessed until 7:00 p.m., in order that the members might contact some local citizens in regard to increasing the city's appropriation for the building.

That evening after hearing several citizens express their opposition to a proposed increase in the amount of city support for the new building, board members resumed their study of the various plans. Finally, by ballot they chose the plan submitted by E. T. Carr of Leavenworth. They agreed that the building should be constructed of Emporia brick, and the basement, corners, and trim of the principal windows of Cottonwood valley stone. They adopted E. P. Bancroft's resolution that if the lowest responsible bid for construction of the building should exceed by $2000 the architect's estimate, the board would not pay for the plans and specifications furnished by such architect.[304]

The prospect of a new Normal School building generated considerable interest among contractors throughout the state. By April 24, the deadline for submitting bids, nearly thirty proposals had been filed.

The Board of Directors, likewise, showed a great deal of interest. For the first time since being appointed to the Board, as many as eight of the nine members convened for the bid letting. Only Governor Harvey was absent. The construction contract was awarded to McDonald and VanGundy of Independence who submitted the low bid of $49,400 to complete the entire building except for the heating.[305] Inasmuch as the heating proposals had initially been written to include plumbing, the three lowest bidders were invited to resubmit bids for heating only. Not until June 20 did the Board approve the heating contract awarded earlier by the executive committee to H. J. Miller and company of Leavenworth.[306]

In the meantime, the academic program of the Normal continued as usual. At the close of the 1872 winter term, March 27-29, the examination timetable had been publicized far enough in advance that a number of out-of-town visitors were present. One "chance visitor" wrote an interesting letter to the editor in which he reviewed the examinations. Referring to his remarks as "jottings," the reporter's first observation concerned the impossibility of six instructors doing justice to 150 students in the scanty and ill arranged rooms of the Normal. He determined that the new building was coming none too soon. It was a marvel, he said, that the exams could be held as effectively as they were. The students were conscientious—an indication of efficiency in the future teachers. He pronounced the papers on Theory and Mental Philosophy to be full of "good practical common sense." He praised Professor Lamprey for his training and technique. He admitted that he had not witnessed Dilworth, Brewer, or Philbrick at work, but those who had done so pronounced them excellent. The music under Jones was very good, and the visitor was impressed by the announcement of Hoss that no student had been cited during the term for the smallest misdemeanor.

> That we have a Normal School of pupils, faithful, earnest, eager to be fitted for their profession, presided over by a corps of instructors composed of efficient and cultured men and women, is the conclusion of
>
> Yours Truly,
> Spectator[307]

Whether the foregoing review had any bearing upon the decision to have written examinations at the end of the school year is not known, but for whatever reason the examinations at the closing exercises, June 18-20, were written. An address by the Reverend Peter MacVicar, D.D., president of Washburn University, before the Literary Society marked the end of the examinations. He spoke to a big audience in the Presbyterian Church on the refutation of Darwin's theory of the origin of man.

The following day, Friday, was graduation day. President Hoss delivered the Baccalaureate address, the title of which was "The Problem of the Child—or Children. What Shall We Do With Them?" According to some of the visitors, there was a perceptible improvement in the manners and recitations of the students. They declared Hoss to be an able and efficient head of the school. Although there were 190 students during the school year, the only two who qualified for graduation were Mellissa Daniels of Burlington and Samuel H. Davis of Hesper. There nevertheless was a large crowd at the Friday night reception in the Normal building with Jones providing music for the event.[308]

On July 5, Stotler reprinted from the *Chetopa Advance* a lengthy article about the Normal School's end of school activities. Although complimentary of Hoss and the school discipline, the reporter was critical of the written examinations, pronouncing them superficial and a bore to the visitors. He recommended oral exams by an examining board instead of by the faculty. He also was critical of the two "old dilapidated boarding houses" for which the city of Emporia was collecting rent from the students. He believed that a nominal rent should be charged and applied to the repair of the buildings which needed paint, whitewash, and cisterns. The reporter also revealed the following information:

> Miss Brewer submitted to the Board at its recent meeting a plan of personal supervision of the Boarding house providing for a common table for the occupants, both ladies and gentlemen, and a cheap fixed rate for board instead of the present detestable cold-victual regime of self-boarding.

He predicted that there would be at least 150 applications for the fall term. Hoss, he said, was going to lecture throughout the state during his vacation in order to call public attention to the claims of the Normal.

In the same issue of his paper, Stotler felt compelled to reply to some of the remarks from Chetopa. The editor agreed that written exams were a bore to visitors, but they nevertheless were being used in the best schools and were endorsed by the best educators. According to Stotler, Hoss was to visit some 15 counties of the state to lecture and advertise the Normal. As for the boarding houses, Stotler claimed that the city charged only enough rent with which to pay interest on the bonds voted for their construction. He agreed, however, that all repairs and corrections should be made to better the boarding houses and the institution.[309]

At their June 20 meeting, the Board of Directors had instructed the executive committee to procure, if possible, a perpetual lease of the boarding houses from the city of Emporia and to make all needed repairs on the same. The city council, however, had in late winter instructed the property committee to study the practicability of selling the buildings. Eventually, the city decided to lease them to the state for a period of eight years, the state agreeing to keep the buildings in repair and insured for the benefit of the city.[310]

President Hoss was honored at the 1872 spring commencement of Indiana State University by having the Doctor of Laws degree conferred upon him. The prestigious title came at an opportune time, for Hoss was about to begin his summer lectures on education and to present the claims of the Normal. His first visit was to southeast Kansas.[311]

In preparation for the fall term which was scheduled to begin on Wednesday, September 11, the Board of Directors hired S. S. Babcock of Ypsilanti, Michigan to fill the newly-created chair of mathematics. Lamprey had left at the end of June, the chair of languages having been temporarily suspended. Language instruction was to be distributed among the various faculty members until the school could better afford an experienced professor for the department. Students in the newly-leased boarding houses were to pay $1.25 rent per month per student. All who lived there were to board at the public table for $2.75 per week.[312]

On September 11, 103 students enrolled at the Normal, the largest number thus far on opening day. Plans called for the new building to be ready for use by the first of January, and according to newspaper accounts the work schedule was on target. On the twenty-third of September, Champlin and Hughes completed their contract for the stone work which by consensus was declared to be a good job. The mansard roof was under construction with Charles Wheelock superintending the project on which 75 men were at work. McDonald, who had the wood contract, was also making the desks for the new building.[313]

When finished, according to Stotler and other news editors, the Normal would be one of the handsomest buildings in the state. Its rich design, that of Architect E. T. Carr, was selected from ten submitted (minutes of the Board mention only five persons who submitted building plans). Standing immediately in front of the old building, the new one faced the head of Commercial Street. Dimensions were 125' by 76', and in addition to the basement, the building consisted of three stories. Decorating the front of the building were three square topped gables, two square towers of unequal size, through which were the two main entrances, and two ventilating shafts. Each end of the building also had a gable and two ventilating shafts.

The interior design of the building was based upon the experiences of both board and faculty, and the skill of the architect. The basement, which was 11 feet in height, contained two cloak rooms, a large gymnasium, two large rooms connected by folding doors to be used for practical experiments in the natural sciences, a boiler room, fuel room, and the janitor's room. There were five entrances to the basement: two in front, one at either end, and one in the rear. A corridor ten feet wide extended the entire length of the basement. It was intersected by two others in which were the stairs from the front entrances.

The main floor had four entrances, two in front and one at either end, and was divided by corridors the same as was the basement. With a 14 feet high ceiling, the main floor contained six large class or lecture rooms, a reception room, an office, and three closets or cloak rooms for faculty use.

The second floor contained five recitation rooms, an apparatus room, and an audience room capable of seating 250 students at single desks. This room occupied the center of the second floor with a 25 feet high arched ceiling that extended to the roof. All other rooms on this floor had 14 feet high ceilings as did the rooms of the third or upper story where there were two large rooms for the use of literary societies, a library, and a museum.

The principal tower contained a large iron water tank (supplied by a pump in the boiler room) from which water was conducted to all washrooms and the laboratory. Above the tank in the summit of the tower was an outlook, commanding a splendid view of the countryside for many miles.[314]

The president's annual report for the academic year ending June 21, 1872, contained a detailed description of equipment and materials to be furnished for the new structure. Already 217 volumes for the new library had arrived, and more were expected. (A total of 314 volumes were added in 1872.) They consisted of books on education, physical science, English literature, philosophy, music, history, and miscellaneous literature. Hoss recommended that the board set aside a yearly amount for library books.

He declared that: "No investment since my connection with the institution will yield so large a percent of profit as the books will. Students are hungry for them."

Apparatus for physical science, which had been ordered to the amount of the appropriation ($500), was expected to arrive before the end of December. Laboratory worktables for 24 students had a double set of drawers to accommodate two sections or 48 students. Each table would have water, gas, steam, and sand baths. The apparatus had been chosen by Dilworth after he had visited eastern institutions. Students were to make their own simple equipment in the workshop.

Recitation rooms were to be equipped with the best of blackboards, and the gymnasium with rings, wands, dumbbells, and other equipment for gymnastics and calisthenics, suitable for both sexes. There is no record, however, that this latter equipment was ever purchased. In fact, repeated requests by the board for funds with which to floor the gymnasium apparently were ignored by the legislature.[315]

President Hoss in his report spoke of the school discipline as including both kindness and firmness: kindness to encourage the timid and needy; firmness to restrain the wayward. What he considered to be two evils to contend with were (1) the low grade of scholarship with which students entered, and (2) the shortness of their stay in school. Two recommendations made by Hoss were (1) a larger salary for the teacher of music, penmanship, and drawing, and (2) reopening of the model school as soon as practicable.[316]

When the fall term closed on December 19 after three days of oral examinations, Stotler apparently was one of the few spectators on the scene. He maintained that the exams had never been better. He also disclosed that the winter term, which was to begin January 2 for new students and January 9 for others, probably would convene in the new building. Only the heating apparatus remained to be completed.[317]

Irrespective of the publicized intent to open the 1873 winter term in the new building, the move did not take place until late March. The incomplete heating system, which was destined to be a constant source of frustration, apparently was the culprit. Indeed, there was still no heat when the formal opening was held on March 27. According to the board minutes of April 2, the executive committee was ordered to call a meeting of the board as soon as the heating apparatus was completed for the purpose of testing the system. The committee was likewise instructed to procure a competent engineer to make the test in the presence of the board members. On May 6, a test conducted by the engineer from the statehouse in Topeka demonstrated that the boiler was inadequate for its intended job. Miller, the heating contractor, subsequently was contacted by the board and requested to bring his engineer for another test of the apparatus on June 20.[318]

There is no record of Miller testing the heat system, but he was present at the June meeting, offering to make the apparatus effective and provide additional bonds if the board would make payment. The board, however, resolved not to make further payment until the heating system was tested and proved adequate for the purpose intended.

Compounding the solution of the heating problem was the reorganization of the Board of Directors. In January, 1873, members of the board voted to urge the legislature to change their organization so as to have two members appointed each year for a term of three years. They also requested that only the governor and state superintendent be ex-officio members with the president of the Normal as an honorary member. The law as passed, however, permitted the presidents of the state institutions to be ex-officio members. In April, the nine member Board of Directors was replaced by a seven member Board of Regents. This new government board of the Normal was composed of the Reverend George Wood of Severance, Doniphan County; C. B. Butler of Leroy; M. M. Murdock, Wichita; H. C. Cross, Emporia; J. W. Horner, Chetopa; Edwin Tucker, Eureka; and President Hoss. At their organizational meeting on April 2, Butler was elected president; Murdock, vice president; Cross, treasurer; and Hoss, secretary. Butler, Cross, and Hoss were elected to the executive committee.[319]

At their first meeting, the regents' biggest challenge came from one of their members, President Hoss, who reported that a lack of harmony among the faculty was impairing the efficiency of the institution. He suggested that the easiest method of remedy was a reorganization of the staff. To accomplish this end, he proposed that the resignations of all members of the faculty be called for within a certain number of days from date. Hoss then tendered his own resignation to take effect at the close of the current term.

After various board members confirmed the lack of harmony, they resolved that resignations would be accepted within twenty days to take effect at the end of the term, and that faculty members wishing to be reelected were to make application to the board on or before May 1. Hoss was instructed to inform the faculty of the resolutions at their next meeting. In May, the board unanimously reelected Hoss to the presidency of the institution, but they voted to postpone all other elections until the June meeting.[320]

By June, Dilworth had been suspended from teaching because of "violent and offensive language addressed by him to the President of the institution," in the chapel in the presence of students while school was in session. The board approved the executive committee's action and declared the chair of physical science to be vacant. At the same time, they accepted the resignations of the other faculty members, rehiring only T. G. Jones as professor of music, penmanship, and drawing. Presumably, H. B. Norton of Arkansas City, who was elected professor of physical science, had already been substituting for Dilworth. At any rate, the board allowed the sum of $155 to be paid to Norton "for service rendered as a teacher, and for service yet to be rendered. . ." P. J. Carmichael, Emporia's superintendent of schools, was elected professor of mathematics. Not until August did the board fill the principalship of the model school in the person of Rose M. Smith of Sycamore, Illinois, and the position of preceptress in the person of Mrs. Abigail Morse, widow of the Reverend G. C. Morse. By then the board was faced with another resignation. Hoss, who had been offered a professorship in the State University of Indiana, tendered his resignation for the second time to take effect December 25.[321]

Although there had been a festive air to the opening of the new building in March, at which time Hoss addressed a large audience, the formal dedication did not occur until Commencement Day on Thursday, June 19. The occasion was a fitting climax to a full week devoted to the closing exercises of another school year. T. D. Thacher of the *Lawrence Journal* delivered the dedicatory address, and President Hoss gave the baccalaureate address. The 1873 graduates were Clara M. Davis of Marvel, Missouri; and Anna C. Rollins and Hattie G. Vail of Manhattan.[322]

Shortly after the fall semester of 1873 was under way, the executive committee conferred with the attorney general to ascertain the legal rights and powers of the board against Miller and company for warming the building. The committee had been authorized to adopt whatever measures were necessary to secure effective warming of the building, the work to be done by Miller and company at Miller's expense. It is obvious from the Minutes that the heating problems of the new building had become a veritable thorn in the flesh to the Board of Regents, but there is little written record as to how the lack of heat affected students and faculty.[323]

In October, the board considered a successor to Hoss. They studied the qualifications of an interesting group of six applicants: C. R. Smith of Wisconsin; Alfred E. Nolan of Connecticut; C. R. Pomeroy of Iowa; and J. W. Horner, L. B. Kellogg, and J. J. Steadman of Kansas. Pomeroy was the unanimous choice of the board who, at the same meeting, wrote into their records a tribute to Hoss.[324]

Shortly before Hoss completed his last term as president of the Normal, he donated to the institution 100 volumes, many of which were educational documents especially suitable for reference. He also submitted his final annual report for the year ending June 19, 1873, during which time a total of 172 students had been enrolled. In addition to the three who had graduated, there were 22 second year students, 123 first year students, and 24 academic students (those not pledged to teach). Nine states and 28 counties were represented. Twenty-seven applicants during the year had been rejected.[325]

In an effort to upgrade the science courses, the Board of Regents, during the fall term of 1873, ordered special scientific equipment which was the most complete for scientific illustration ever brought into Kansas. Included was a stereopticon with oxy-hydrogen and magnesium light; paintings illustrative of astronomy and geology; and a spectroscope—all of excellent quality.[326]

An apparent attempt to pacify those who had been critical of the end-of-term examinations whether written or oral resulted in the examinations of December 11-18, 1873 being both written and oral. A full schedule indicating subject, teacher, hour, and the mode of examining was published in *The Emporia News,* the orals being held during the final two days of the schedule. Model School examinations had been given the week previous. In a review of the event, the editor expressed his pleasure by declaring that there was "a higher class of scholarship in the Normal than at any former period—that is, there are more good scholars."[327]

During the middle of examination week, the Kansas Normal School Lyceum, a literary society at the school, presented its public exercises in the main hall before a large audience. Professor Carmichael presided over the program which included music, declamation, a formal paper, tableaux, and charades. Hoss closed the evening with what must have been his final address as president. Emporia friends, faculty, and students later gave the departing president an impressive farewell gift of silver, the presentation taking place on the final day of the term, according to Editor Stotler, an hour or two before his paper went to press.[328]

The following week, there appeared in *The Emporia News* a seething review of the Lyceum entertainment. Written by a nameless critic but for the initials J.L.D., the reviewer admitted disappointment in the caliber of the program. There apparently were some rowdy and slapstick numbers to which the writer took offense, and which rendered his twenty-five cent entrance fee a sheer waste.[329]

CHAPTER 9

THE NORMAL IN "SPLENDID WORKING ORDER": 1874

Dr. C. R. Pomeroy and his family, who were to make the Hoss residence their new home, first arrived in Emporia early in December, 1873. Before ever taking over as third president of the Normal School, Pomeroy began to make an impact upon the local community. After the first of many addresses delivered in the Methodist Church, Pomeroy was described by the press as "a gentleman of deep piety, extensive learning, and an agreeable and impressive speaker."[330]

Pomeroy came to Kansas State Normal with outstanding academic qualifications, having earned two degrees from Wesleyan University, Middletown, Connecticut—the A.B. in 1853 and the A.M. in 1856—where he ranked among the top third of his class. In 1874, he was awarded his D.D. degree from Simpson Centenary College. In the intervening years, Pomeroy had studied at Union Theological Seminary, taught Greek, served as principal of several schools, became an ordained minister, and served a pastorate in Batavia, New York.[331]

The winter term of 1874 had no more than gotten underway when Pomeroy, ex-officio member of the Board of Regents, was elected to the executive committee, and not only elected its secretary but also board secretary, offices that he was to hold through 1876. From time to time, he had occasion to speak at the Methodist Church where one of his early appearances resulted in a lengthy review in *The Emporia News*.[332]

In March, H. B. Norton, who had returned the year before to replace Dilworth, found it necessary to resign again, this time because of family illness. The board, however, refused to accept his resignation, granting him a term's leave of absence in the hope that he could return in the autumn. The board chose the Reverend W. E. Copeland to teach for Norton during the spring term.

Norton, sponsor of the Philadelphi—the second of the literary societies which replaced the Normal Literary Union—was honored by that organization at its two-day program of public entertainment, March 13-14. Members passed the following resolution:

> Whereas, since our society was first organized [1865, probably, when the Normal Literary Society began], Prof. Norton has been its firm and fast friend, and we in a great measure owe our success to his untiring efforts:
>
> Resolved, That we do hereby tender him our sincere thanks for the constant kindness and interest he has manifested in our success.
>
> Resolved, That we deeply regret the circumstances which compel the absence of our beloved Professor and esteemed friend.

The Philadelphi program itself was quite a success, netting fifty dollars from the two-night series the group had organized the previous October.[333]

At the close of the 1874 winter session, Stotler wrote that the term had been a good one with every department full. The school was gaining the good will of people all over the state, he said. In his assessment of the new administration, he was enthusiastic:

> President Pomeroy has had charge but one session, yet he has endeared himself to the faculty and students by his quiet, but decidedly firm administration. Faculty and students say he has superior executive ability. He knows how to "keep school."[334]

A week later at the onset of the spring term, Stotler noted that the city was full of Normal students. In May, he urged his readers to visit the Normal where "school is in splendid working order" and where everything "moves in clockwork style." The first public contest between the two literary societies, the Lyceum and the Philadelphi, was held on the evening of May 15, 1874. Included in the competition were debate, orations, declamations, readings, essays, and music. Entries were to be judged upon literary merit which was, according to the publicity, "the palm of the contest." The event, which was free to the public, proved to be good entertainment. The Lyceum won in the opinion of the judges; but according to Stotler, the Philadelphi "did well indeed."[335]

Although the spring term had heretofore been the smaller session of the year, in 1874 it attracted a total of 230 students (155 in the Normal department and 75 in the Model School). At the end of May, President and Mrs. Pomeroy entertained seventeen members of the graduating class and the faculty at a party in their home—the former Hoss home. By the beginning of Commencement week, however, there were but fourteen who had completed the Elementary course. They were eligible to receive the new Bachelor of Elements degree. At the same time, the Board of Regents ruled that those completing the four-year Normal course would be awarded the Bachelor of Didactics degree, and those completing the Scientific course, the Bachelor of Science degree. Not until 1876, however, were there eligible recipients for the latter two degrees.[336]

For the first time, a full week in 1874 was devoted to the Normal's final examinations and graduation festivities. Pomeroy preached the Baccalaureate sermon on Sunday afternoon, June 14. Inasmuch as there were twelve young women among the fourteen graduates, it seems surprising—almost audacious in fact—that he should have chosen as his subject "A Well-Developed Manhood." According to *The Emporia News*, "The president [Pomeroy] claimed the privilege of using the phrase 'young men' in a generic sense and therefore applied his discourse to young men and women."[337]

After written examinations on Monday and Tuesday, Norton, who had returned temporarily to preach for the Unitarian Society of the Congregational Church, gave an address before the two literary societies. Oral examinations were conducted all of Wednesday, followed by what Stotler considered the best Sociable ever held at the Normal. There was no music, no speech, nothing structured—just "promenading and talking." Commencement exercises the next day, however, were very much structured. Dignitaries seated on the platform included faculty, city clergy, present members of the Board of Regents and some former members, and the State Superintendent of Public Instruction. In front of the platform to the left was seated the graduating class. Nearby was the choir and Director Hoagland. Nellie Storrs Newman presided at the organ.

The program opened with a prayer by the Reverend A. M. Averill, and the singing of the University Anthem. Class Salutatorian, Henry Haggard of Emporia, the first of the graduates to speak, chose "Change" as his subject. Interspersed among the fourteen essays were musical numbers. The last to speak was Valedictorian Ella T. Cole of Towanda, whose topic was "Fact and Fancy." Pomeroy gave a brief address, delivered the diplomas, and conferred upon each graduate the Bachelor of Elements degree. Thus ended, in the words of Stotler, one of the most harmonious and prosperous years of the State Normal.[338]

Although some of the faculty left for extended vacations, Pomeroy remained in Emporia throughout the summer, participating in local church meetings, preaching in area churches, and addressing the Normal District Institute held in Emporia. By the end of August, announcements concerning the opening of the fall term appeared in the local newspapers. Apparently, the school would be full. All rooms in the boarding houses were taken, and pleas went out for rooms, furnished and unfurnished.[339]

As the summer of 1874 waned, grave concern was being voiced about reported devastation to crops in the western counties by grasshoppers. As the insects began to spread throughout the state from the north and west, Governor T. A. Osborn called for a special session of the legislature in an attempt to provide some measure of relief to those most affected. For the most part, it was the newly-established counties and the newcomers to the state with nothing but the current crop on which to rely who suffered the most. There was no indication in 1874, however, that the invasion adversely affected the Normal. The opening day enrollment of 200 was larger than in any previous fall term. Stotler voiced the opinion that "It is gratifying to know that the present management of the school has been good enough to more than counter-balance the depression effect of the year's disasters [grasshoppers]." In June, the Board of Regents had decided to expand the Model School, thereby returning to the city school system the borrowed classes of the past year. They created a high school and grammar school department designated as the Model School to be used primarily as a school of observation where Normal students could observe the best methods of teaching and a model system of school government. In addition, a training school consisting of all grades below the grammar level was created wherein Normal students could practice theories of teaching learned in their professional classes. Tuition fees for the high school were set at $7.00 per term; for the grammar school, $5.00; and for the training school, $3.00. Later, to encourage enrollment of the younger primary pupils, Pomeroy advertised their particular tuition fee as $1.00 per term.[340]

According to Pomeroy's first annual report, the new plan for the model and training schools already had resulted in "far better and more satisfactory work [being] accomplished in the professional training teachers. . . ." The aggregate enrollment for the fall term was 236. Included in the figure were 191 enrolled in the Normal course; 20 in the high school and grammar department; and 25 in the training school. Pomeroy confessed that the chief embarrassment of the term had been the inadequate number of teachers to meet the demands of the school. Classes had been too large; recitations too short; and some studies that should have been taught were dispensed with entirely. In spite of the overload, however, Pomeroy maintained that the faculty had performed faithfully and harmoniously.[341]

Although the current plateau was but a fleeting period of success in the long span of history, it seems essential to examine in some detail the organization of the Normal during 1874-75 in order to understand more fully the extent of the misfortunes that followed. By the fall of 1874, improvements which had been recommended by former President Hoss and even his predecessor, L. B. Kellogg, were finally implemented, partly because steady growth in enrollment had given the regents every reason to be optimistic about the school's future, but mainly because at long last there were enough advanced students enrolled to warrant the expanded program.

Seven members comprised the Normal School faculty in September of 1874. In the Normal proper, three courses consisted of a preparatory year and two additional years. Graduates of this program were deemed competent to teach in common schools or in primary departments of city graded schools. Second was the Normal course which embraced the elementary course of two years and two additional years. Graduates of this four-year program were eligible to teach in any high school or grammar school in the state. Third was the scientific course which was equivalent to the Normal course, but which substituted higher mathematics and more natural science classes for the languages of the Normal course.

The purpose of the high school grammar school department, or the Model School, in addition to being a school of observation, was to provide a thorough academic education to fit students for either business or college. The department included those academic students not pledged to teach, who previously had been in the Normal proper. Four years were required to complete the course. The training school was designed to be a thoroughly organized common school with students ranging from primary grade one to grammar school level.[342]

The primary department of the training school initially failed to attract as many pupils as could be accommodated, and late in September, Pomeroy advertised that there was room for several primary students at one dollar per term for tuition and books. A month later, Stotler espoused the cause by writing that the Normal School had a small primary department "being delightfully trained by Miss Gilbert." He added that "there should be more six year olds up there. Hours are short and the instruction very superior."

The only hint at this time that the future of the Normal might not yet be secure came from Cottonwood Falls in a letter to the editor in which the anonymous correspondent suggested that the Normal Schools of Leavenworth and Concordia (established in 1870 and 1874 respectively) be consolidated with Emporia (at Emporia), and the Kansas University and the Agricultural College be consolidated since the former had the building and the latter, the endowment. These suggestions were being made, supposedly, because of the expectation that the 1875 legislature would demand retrenchment. Another hint of unrest came from a Shawnee County Reform candidate for public office who, in a political speech at Dover, attacked the State Normal School, declaring that the institution cost the state $150,000 and had graduated but five students. In a rebuttal of the inflammatory speech, Stotler corrected many erroneous statements. The cost to the state, several thousand less than claimed, had for the most part been for buildings which were a permanent investment. The number of graduates quoted, of course, was a complete falsehood. By the fall of 1874, a total of thirty-nine students had graduated from the Normal.[343]

Late in the term, Norton and others at the Normal who were interested in promoting the natural sciences organized the Agassiz club. Its first public meeting was on December 11, 1874, the first event of the closing of the term exercises. In addition to a lecture "The Progress of Antiquarian Research," scientific papers were read. Membership in the club was open to anyone who was willing to work "to promote the spread of scientific knowledge" and to build a first class museum of natural history, the two-fold purpose of the new organization.[344]

The fall term, "one of unprecedented progress and success," closed on

December 16 after the written and oral examinations and the traditional term sociable. At the same time, advertisements and accompanying stories appearing in Stotler's newspaper were permeated with confidence toward continued growth in enrollment during the winter term beginning January 6, 1875. Tuition and textbooks for Normal department students again would be free; incidental fees remained at $2.00; high school tuition, $7.00; and grammar school, $5.00. A dollar charge, however, had been added for the use of textbooks. Special attention was given the training school for which tuition had been decreased to one dollar per term plus fifty cents for use of books. There were to be two rooms for primary instruction, each under an experienced and accomplished teacher who would devote careful attention to morals, manners, and physical education. Claims were made by the editor that the instructors were thorough and that facilities for instruction were better at the Normal than anywhere west of the Mississippi.[345]

CHAPTER 10

RESILIENCE AFTER A LEGISLATIVE SHOCK: 1875

At the beginning of 1875, state officials reported that the previous autumn a total of 15,000 Kansans had been rendered destitute by the grasshopper invasion. Nevertheless, the Normal School opened on January 6 with an increase in enrollment. In December, the Board of Regents had authorized its executive committee to hire a teacher of languages to be paid from the contingency fund until the new position could be funded by state appropriations. Mrs. C. R. Pomeroy was chosen for the job. Although her credentials do not seem to appear in any extant record, she was referred to at the time as "a most cultivated and experienced teacher." By the end of 1875, the Normal faculty had grown to nine full time teachers and two assistants.[346] Seeds of problems to come were contained in Governor Thomas A. Osborn's annual message to the 1875 legislature. One of his concerns was the fact that neither the university's nor the Normal's endowment lands had yet been sold. By voicing approval of the Agricultural College for having sold 50,000 acres, thereby assuring that school a yearly income of $20,000 or so, Osborn underscored his disapproval of the fact that the Normal lands remained unsold. He also suggested that the legislature might well be able to cut appropriations to the state schools in order to assist the impoverished farms in purchasing seed for spring planting.

In an editorial, Stotler attempted to ward off any undesirable effects of the Governor's message by defending the Board of Regents' policy towards the Normal endowment. Those lands were located away from the railroad and the track of immigration. They would be worth more later, he reasoned. "Why squander a valuable endowment to save a few years of appropriation?" Stotler wrote that since the Normal had a larger enrollment than any other state school—254 students for the winter term of 1875—and was doing its allotted work with "splendid success," the legislature surely would govern themselves accordingly.[347]

The legislature, nonetheless, slashed the appropriations of both the Normal and the university. The combined cut of $5000 was made after an extended fight over appropriations. Stotler himself spent three days in Topeka during the struggle. In a follow up review of the legislation, he condemned an unidentified Labette County legislator for calling the Normal an aristocratic institution where the rich attended school. Stotler wrote: "Our Normal students would have smiled to hear him. Nine-tenths of them are working their way through school." The same legislator was critical of the Normal for employing a teacher of languages—an argument that appealed to the farmer legislators who were asked if they were going to lavish their money upon rich sons and daughters and "dead languages."[348]

Almost immediately, the Board of Regents convened in Emporia to wrestle with the problem of rearranging salaries in the face of their twenty percent cut in appropriations. (They had requested $11,800 for salaries but were allotted only $9,440.) Present at the meeting, held on March 9 at the Normal School office, were C. B. Butler, M. M. Murdock, J. H. Crichton, H. C. Cross, and President Pomeroy. Regents Edwin Tucker and G.W. Wood, soon to be replaced by A. Sellers, were absent. Following is a table showing the decisions made at that meeting:[349]

TABLE 1.Board of Regents Salary Decisions, 1875.

Faculty	Salary Requested		Salary Adjusted
President	$2500		$2200
Prof.　　　Natural Sciences	1600		1400
	1600		1400
Prof. Mathematics	1600		1200
Prof. Ancient & Mod. Languages	1100		900
	800	(combined)	750

Preceptress	800		
Music Teacher	1100		900
Drawing & Penmanship	700		700
Princ. Training School			
Ass't. " "			

On March 26, at the close of the term, Stotler wrote "The Grasshopper Versus the Schoolmaster," a semi-humorous editorial that for the most part described the situation. "The locusts have made themselves felt in our school matters as elsewhere. They are wreaking revenge upon the pedagogues who have in all past times impaled them upon pins. . . ." Stotler revealed that the *Kansas School Journal* "gave up the ghost early in the winter;" that various state institutions were working with reduced subsidies; and that public and private schools had "all taken in sail." As for the Normal School, he reported that the president's salary had been reduced 12 percent; the two professors 12½ percent; and the two lady teachers, 18.5 percent. "Mrs. Pomeroy has been added to the faculty at $1200—in languages." For whatever reason, he ignored the fate of the other three faculty positions. He closed the editorial prophetically, stating that he presumed "many learned men will soon 'light out' for fresh fields and pastures new," but that by the fall of 1875, the state would be driving ahead as if nothing had occurred—and the schoolmasters would have found some way by which to avenge the grasshopper.[350]

No more than three weeks elapsed before the first portion of Stotler's prophecy came to pass. A half column of his newspaper was devoted to the disclosure that H. B. Norton had been elected to a position at San Jose State Normal in California. The erudite professor was to leave Kansas at the end of the school year (in June). His leaving, Stotler surmised, was partly due to the "idiotic" action of the legislature. In summarizing Norton's qualifications and accomplishments, the editor was very complimentary. He lamented Norton's departure as a loss to Kansas and a gain for California.[351]

Because his new job, which would involve much institute work, was to commence the end of June, Norton found it necessary to leave for California before the end of the school year. Two days before he departed on June 10, he and Mrs. Norton were honored by faculty, students, and friends at a farewell party. As evidenced by the multiple headlines given the story in *The Emporia News*, the event was one of the more important social occasions in the early history of the school.

Prof. and Mrs. Norton's Farewell:
A Fine Audience

A valuable Gold Watch and Chain
Presented by His Friends

An Album from the Students

Speech by Prof. Carmichael
And Reply of Prof. Norton

By eight o'clock in the evening, the parlor of the Normal School and other rooms were filled with the town's best citizens. The Nortons devoted an hour to receiving and conversing with their friends. At nine o'clock, all gathered in the auditorium for presentation ceremonies. Prof. Carmichael called the audience to order and gave the presentation address. Mrs. Nellie Storrs Newman, a graduate of the Normal, handed to Norton a gold watch, the inside casing of which read: "Presented to Prof. H. B. Norton by Friends in Emporia, Kansas, June 8th, 1875." Then Miss Effie Partch of the 1875 graduating class and a newly-elected teacher at the Normal, stepped forward and presented Norton an album containing photographs of the class of 1875.[352]

Norton in his reply reminisced about his coming to Emporia ten years before. For the first time, he revealed that he had ridden as far as Lawrence upon a construction train. He gave tribute to Kellogg "for the seed planted from which the current plant grew." He acknowledged Eskridge as "a founder to whose legislative tact and skill the Normal owes its existence." He paid tribute to the late G. C. Morse, to Stotler and Preston Plumb, and spoke of his gratitude for having been given the opportunity to be a part of the institution.[353]

In the late spring, the Normal School also had been the setting for a different kind of gathering. Twenty-four male applicants from various locations within the third congressional district met to be examined for the first West Point cadet appointment ever allotted to the area. The competitive examination, given on Saturday, May 29, 1875, was administered by a committee of three: President Pomeroy and F. B. Hunt,

Chase County superintendent of schools, were the educational examiners; L. D. Jacobs, M.D., was medical examiner. Applicants were required to be able bodied, between 17 and 23 years of age, at least five feet tall, and well versed in English studies. The one making the highest grade would become a cadet, receiving one ration and $500 per annum. Charles M. Truitt of Emporia won the appointment.[354]

Commencement week, June 13-16, 1875, was special on two counts. Eighteen graduates—the largest number to date—received diplomas, and the occasion marked the tenth anniversary of the institution. Beginning on Sunday with Pomeroy's annual sermon, activities included an address to the literary societies by L. B. Kellogg, oral examinations, and the end of the year sociable. Graduation itself, however, was the event that stood out. By nine o'clock on Wednesday morning, June 16, the Normal building was thronged with students and visitors who more than filled the auditorium, which was decorated for the occasion. "Near each corner there hung from the ceiling a large design in evergreen, comprising a wreath, anchor, cross, and shield, and from the center a massive bell of leaves and flowers with a bouquet [sic] of roses for its clapper."[355]

The class motto, "Granum protecimus; finis opus coronet," was displayed in large letters in a half circle upon the wall at the head of the room. Faculty members and distinguished visitors occupied seats upon the rostrum where at the right end were chairs for the graduates. Behind them was a piano and a large choir that opened the program by singing "Happy and Blest." After the opening prayer, they continued with "Hail, Festal Day." The two top students of the class were S. Cornelia Slack of Hartford, Iowa, and Joseph H. Hill, Osage City. Carmichael assisted Pomeroy in presenting diplomas and conferring the Bachelor of Elements degree upon the ten young women and eight men.[356]

During the summer months, the old stone Normal building was refurbished in order to accommodate the Model School. Other concerns of the Board of Regents were the hiring of teachers (see footnote #345), and the ever present problem of an inadequate heating system. Pomeroy in his first annual report had ignored the problem, but in 1875 he suggested that for the sake of economy and better efficiency both buildings should be heated with one boiler. Another of his concerns was the lack of lighting. Thus far, the new building had been lighted only with kerosene lamps for social events and public gatherings. Not only was that light insufficient, but conflagration was a constant danger. There was neither any means of extinguishing a fire nor any insurance on the structure. Pomeroy requested that it be lighted with gas.

No longer were the two boarding houses adequate for the growing enrollment. In August of 1875, Pomeroy requested that anyone having a furnished or unfurnished room to rent to students should send him the address, type of accommodation, and terms. Simultaneously, Stotler pointed out that good crops and the "brightening up of business matters" would help the Normal and the other state schools. In an earlier editorial, he had recommended the Normal as "a fit place for learning to teach."[357]

One hundred new students arrived for entrance examinations prior to the opening of the fall term on September 8. While there is no known record of the total number of first day students, the president's report compiled later in the semester gave the total as 302. Members of the Lyceum wasted no time that fall in preparing for what was to be their most ambitious production to date. They produced what was billed as a popular drama with "appropriate music and scenic effects." Proceeds went into the organization's organ fund. The drama, presented on October 22 in Bancroft Hall, was much better than the average troupes that visited Emporia, according to Stotler. The Prologue was a tableau of soldiers around a campfire at Valley Forge. The main performance was "The Spirit of '76 or The Coming Woman," a prophetic drama in three sets—the supposed time period, 1876. The Epilogue was a tableau of projected 1976 "Women's Rights" in which at least one professor (Carmichael) and Judge J. Buck were scrubbing and washing dishes while the mother of the household read the newspaper and smoked a cigar. Unattended children were playing marbles in the parlor and pulling each other's hair.[358]

About a month later, a sinister real life melodrama took place at the Normal with no advance billing whatsoever. Fortunately, it was stopped after the first act before any real damage occurred. On a Sunday afternoon, November 14, at five o'clock, John Eskridge who lived northeast of the Normal saw a light in the basement windows of the school building. Running to the scene, he discovered a fire kindled of sticks and kerosene in the coal room. As it had not made much headway, he was able to extinguish it immediately. Local headlines read "A Villainous Incendiary Tries to Burn the Normal School." The janitor, who lived in a downtown boarding house, was not at school when the fire occurred. The building, moreover, was kept locked on Sundays. What could have developed into a tragedy ended as a mystery, one which was never solved. The building was uninsured; thus, as a precautionary measure, the city council authorized the mayor to appoint a special watchman for the Normal.[359]

The closing exercises of the fall term lasted from Thursday, December 9 through Wednesday, December 15. Written examinations occupied the first three days while oral examinations interspersed with music and calisthenics occupied the final two days. It was these latter exercises which attracted the most spectators. In fact, on the morning of December 15, an unusual procession occurred on Commercial Street. Delegates to the State Grange meeting then in session recessed at nine o'clock, and upon Pomeroy's invitation marched to the Normal to witness the exercises. After a cordial welcome, they listened to some singing by the glee club, observed calisthenics by a large class of young ladies, and toured the buildings before returning to their hall to resume their meetings.[360]

In summarizing the week's events, Stotler admitted that he had been unable to witness the examinations. He had learned from others, however, that they were most satisfactory. In fact, the students apparently worked harder than usual, for the scholarship average was raised from 70 to 80. He announced that a new society called the Sumner had been formed to supersede the Philadelphi. Considering the newness of the organization, their first public performance on the night of December 13 had been a credit to the group. Stotler declared the end of term Sociable on the following evening to have been a "very pleasant affair." Both teachers and students, he reported, were there working together to make it a success.[361]

As anticipated, the Normal School was all but overflowing with students when the winter term opened on January 5, 1876. Both buildings were in use. Two weeks into the new term, enrollment was reported to be 335 students, 150 of whom were new students necessitating many large classes in the lower grades. For instance, Carmichael's Arithmetic B with seventy-five students was the largest class; Mrs. Pomeroy's Latin B with five students was the smallest. There seemed to be a burst of new energy in all areas of the Normal except, perhaps, in the societies. The Agassiz club had been considering only one meeting a term, a schedule that did not please all its members. Thus the club president, C. C. Delap, announced early in the term that two lecture meetings were scheduled for January 23 and 24. Professor B. F. Mudge of Manhattan, former state geologist, spoke on "Geology of Kansas," and "The Coal Formations in Kansas." Tickets for the series were twenty-five cents, and each lecture drew a large, appreciative audience, largely students. The Lyceum Society, then in its fourth year, was burdened by its organ debt to the point that the organization had asked local businessmen to come to their assistance. Nevertheless, in conjunction with the new Sumner Society which claimed some of the best talent at the Normal, the Lyceum was planning to have a contest sometime in February.[362]

The Board of Regents fully expected the new legislature to provide ample funds for the growing Normal School. In October, members had drawn up what they considered to be an essential appropriation request. The salary figure of $14,400 was for eleven teachers including the president, one training school assistant, and a janitor-engineer. A request of $6,970 for maintenance and supplies brought the total to $21,3700.00. Included in the maintenance figure was a request of $1000 for lighting the new Normal building, and $2500 for installing steps and walks.[363]

Unfortunately, the 1876 legislature had difficulty with consensus from the very beginning. Getting organized took them several days, three of which were devoted to choosing a speaker. Eskridge, newly-elected representative from Lyon County, was one of three nominees for the position. Finally, he was defeated. On January 25, members of the Ways and Means committees of both houses visited Emporia for a first hand inspection of the Normal School. In the forenoon, Eskridge escorted the legislators on their inspection tour. They toured the buildings, spoke to the students, and "expressed themselves as well pleased with all they saw." That afternoon the legislators were hosted by Emporians at a downtown hotel.[364]

On February 11, the long awaited contest between the Lyceum and the Sumner societies took place. The crowd was large, but not particularly polite. The local reporter who reviewed the event complained that during the essay competition there was a great deal of disturbance by people coming into the room late. Pomeroy, whom the students had chosen to be chairman for the evening, rose at one point to reprimand those whose loud applause was accompanied by the loud stomping of feet. Acknowledging that he realized non-students were among the crowd, he nevertheless declared that such behavior was intolerable.

After the essays, and the debate on the question of whether "the position of the Roman Catholics is compatible with our public institutions," the hour grew so late and the audience so restless that Pomeroy suggested adjourning for the evening and hearing orations at a later date. A debate over adjourning ensued, and the matter was put to a vote. The crowd voted to remain, but before the orations began, Pomeroy dismissed those who wished to leave. Although many left, a sizable crowd remained. The report of the judges, one of whom was L. B. Kellogg, named Miss R. Davis of the Sumner Society winner of the essay contest; A. Stubbs, president of the Sumner, winner of the orators; and the negative team of Sumner, J. H. Hill and Miss Davis, winners in debate.[365]

Two weeks later, the Normal School administration was suddenly thwarted in all of its endeavors by the totally unexpected action, or rather non-action of the legislature who voted to postpone indefinitely any consideration of the appropriation bills for the state Normal Schools. *The Emporia News* in an unprecedented story in headlines summarized the situation thus:

Black Friday
Normal Schools at a Discount
In the Kansas Legislature
600 or 700 Normal Students
Out in the Cold
Kansas Takes a Step Backward
In Education
200,000 Children to be Neglected
A Bold Stroke at the Common Schools
'Buncombe' Economy and Local Jealousy
Do Their Work
Central and Southern Kansas 'Scooped.'
Institutions in the Kaw Valley
Get More Than They Ask For[366]

No one seemed able to pinpoint any logical reason for the legislative action, but one fact was clear. The legislature had killed the Normal Schools. The Concordia Normal School, said to have been established by fraud and declared to have no legal existence, was the first to fall. Established in 1874 under the act of 1870 which called for a Normal School in Northern Kansas, the Concordia Normal, considered by many to be a local school, not a state institution, was not funded by the legislature until 1875. The Leavenworth Normal, which predated the Concordia school, was established in 1870 at the time the above mentioned law went into effect.[367]

Although Representative Eskridge introduced a new appropriation bill for the Emporia school, it was defeated. In the meantime, the 1876 legislators had appropriated money to the agricultural college for buildings, and to the state university to strengthen its programs and to establish a normal department. Eventually, they addressed themselves specifically to the Normal School problem. In a miscellaneous appropriation bill, they made final appropriations of $2,297.50 to the Concordia and Leavenworth Normals to cover current expenses of the first quarter ending March 1, 1876, and $4,200 to the Emporia Normal for expenses through March 22:

> Provided, That these appropriations to the Leavenworth Normal School, the Concordia Normal School, and Emporia Normal School shall be received in full for all claims against the State, and that said schools cease to be maintained at the expense of the State, and that under no circumstances shall the regents of said institutions incur any liability or create any debt beyond this appropriation, and the State shall not be liable for any expense in excess of this appropriation; and that the Leavenworth and Concordia Normal Schools cease to be State institutions.[368]

Newspapers throughout the state registered surprise and dismay at the legislature's treatment of the Normal School movement. The Lawrence and Topeka editors especially voiced support for the Normal School system. Leavenworth papers understandably espoused the cause of the Leavenworth Normal, but the Atchison *Champion* declared that the Leavenworth school was just like Atchison's high school except that Atchison citizens supported their school instead of the state doing so. The editor believed that Emporia had the only real bonafide Normal School. Stotler in *The Emporia News* devoted two columns in behalf of Normal School education in general. He did a masterful job of remaining objective throughout the article.[369]

There has been much speculation as to why the 1876 legislature took such drastic action, but to this day the reasoning behind the action remains obscure. It was thought by some that three Normal Schools were more than the state could support, but special interest groups were so strong that the only way lawmakers could curtail one or more of the schools was to cut off financial aid to all of them. Some believed that proponents of the Emporia school were trying to develop it into a university, and that the only way to correct the situation was to cut off the funds. Others thought that political animosity and jealousy, rather than reason, motivated the legislators. Undoubtedly, there was some truth in all of the foregoing speculation.

A study of the *House Journal* for 1876 reveals that at least one bill to locate yet another Normal School was rejected by the committee on public institutions. Members of that committee believed that one university, one agricultural school, and one Normal School were enough.[370] S. N. Wood, chairman of the retrenchment and reform committee, protested the law of 1870 which had resulted in two Northern Kansas Normal Schools [Leavenworth and Concordia]. Wood maintained that if two schools could be organized under that law, one hundred could be. Already Leavenworth and Concordia were asking appropriations of $18,000 annually. Wood's committee urged immediate repeal of the 1870 law, but no action was taken.[371]

Much bitterness ensued among the 1876 lawmakers as a result of an unfortunate incident that occurred early in the session. Charles S. Aldrich, legislator from Smith County, had written a newsy letter to his home newspaper, the *Pioneer*, in which he described the struggle of choosing the speaker of the House. In the letter, Aldrich characterized the three candidates, stating that Eskridge may smile and smile, but he was a villain still. A copy of the letter found its way to the House floor where it was read, causing an uproar among the members. A motion to expel Aldrich finally was amended to require only an appropriate apology. He willingly apologized, an act that was written into the record. Ultimately, Aldrich was forced to resign from his chairmanship of the railroad committee, for his committee members refused to sit so long as he was chairman. Eventually a whole new committee was formed, but the damage had been done. Aldrich and his friend, S. N. Wood, remained enemies of Eskridge who had been a member of the original railroad committee. Under such circumstances, it is not surprising that Eskridge's substitute appropriation bill for the Emporia Normal failed to pass.[372]

Whatever the true intent of the legislature, the Board of Regents refused to let the Emporia school die. Even before the board had developed a plan of action, President Pomeroy and at least one of the other regents were insisting that the Normal would continue classes in spite of legislative attempts to strangle it. "She still lives, and will live!" declared Pomeroy. On hand in Emporia to lend moral support and to commiserate with the school administration, students, and townspeople during the first days after the legislature's "shameful action," were 200 Kansans who gathered for the statewide Methodist conference. Their visits to the Normal and their universal expressions of regret over the lack of appropriations surely must have been a boon to those who had decisions to make.[373]

On March 15, at a special meeting of the regents called by the executive committee, the board decided to use the entire appropriation of $4200 for salaries after deducting $43 for coal. Teachers and janitor were to be paid on the basis of last year's salaries, pro rata, and the board was to recommend that the next legislature pay the balance due on the basis of appropriations requested for the current year.

Apparently, there was consensus among the regents that the denial of appropriations was but a temporary situation, and that if the school could struggle through the current year, a more rational legislature in 1877 would meet the school's needs. In any case, the concern of the regents at the March meeting was to see that school was kept through June in order that the large number of seniors could graduate on schedule. At an evening meeting, the board went on record as having no means for carrying on the school, being unable to make promises for the future, but deeming it desirable to continue school and to graduate the present senior class. They voted to authorize the executive committee to invite the current Normal teachers to remain until the close of the school year, agreeing to pay them, pro rata, on the basis of present salaries any money that might remain after meeting necessary current expenses. They also voted that the principal of the training school be invited to remain, and that she be allowed the receipts of her department, $3.00 per pupil, after current expenses for the old building were met. The board resolved also that for the spring term a tuition fee of $5.00 be charged for the preparatory students and $7.00 for more advanced students in addition to a $1.00 incidental fee for all.[374]

Almost immediately, the winter term drew to a close, and from all indications the faculty intended to follow Pomeroy's example of sticking by the school and taking willingly whatever pay he could get from the foregoing arrangement without expecting or asking for more. At the close of the term exercises, March 16-22, the sociable on the final evening attracted the most attention. Because a large number of students— presumably discouraged at having to pay tuition fees—were leaving, there were an unusual number of both students and townspeople present to bid reluctant goodbyes. Included in the entertainment was the training school's choral reading group. It is a tribute to Miss Gilbert's ability as a teacher that patrons of the Model School contributed financially in order to retain her.[375]

More than one hundred students attended the opening day of the spring term on Wednesday, April 5, 1876, and expectations were that the number would soon increase to 125. Three weeks later, in "Leaves from a 'Student's Notebook,'" enrollment was reported to be "not far from 130."[376]

No time was lost in planning events of interest for both students and townspeople. Two days after the spring term had opened, the Agassiz Club held its first meeting of the term at which a spirited debate took place upon the question "That the most reasonable interpretation of science is based upon the theory of evolution."[377]

Although April 1 had been designated as Arbor Day by Governor Osborn, weather had not cooperated.[378] On April 27, however, students at the Normal participated in planting at least 125 "buds of promise" in the shape of ash, elder, and cherry seedlings which had been selected by a student committee. At President Pomeroy's request, students lined up around the area to hear an oration by I. T. Way in honor of the occasion. "The clay soil and unpropitious conditions with which the trees must contend if they were to grow was likened to the obstacles in the way of the Normal students since the 'Moguls' at Topeka had failed to make an appropriation." Following the oration was an original poem sung by students to the tune of "Auld Lang Syne." Professor Kellogg was asked to speak. His advice was practical, suggesting a fortnightly celebration for the following three months in order to loosen the soil around the trees.[379]

During the summer, it became apparent that President Pomeroy's popularity was waning, for his detractors were becoming vocal. The first public awareness of a problem came in the form of the Normal Institute ruckus. Early in May, President Pomeroy had requested the local newspapers to announce that a six weeks' Normal Institute would be held in the Normal School building from July 5 to August 16. The Institute would cover all studies required to be taught in the common schools of Kansas, including United States history, Bookkeeping, Constitution of the United States, Botany, Geology, and Entomology. There were also to be a series of lectures upon the Theory and Art of Teaching.

Two weeks later in *The Emporia Ledger* over the name of A. D. Chambers, county superintendent of schools, was a notice of a normal institute to be held early in July in Emporia's city school building under the direction of the County Board of Examiners.

A week later, in "A Card to the Public," President Pomeroy withdrew his previous announcement of an Institute under his direction, stating that he believed "One Institute in this place is all that the interests of education demand, and that a rival contest of the character here involved would be every way undesirable and unworthy of education." Pomeroy also explained that he had solicited Superintendent Chamber's joint action, and that it was Professor P. J. Carmichael who actually submitted the notice using Chamber's name. The latter information prompted a reply from Carmichael who accused Pomeroy of insinuating that he had used Chamber's name without permission to do so. Eventually, Chambers declared that he had no problem with either Pomeroy or Carmichael; but the damage had been done.[380]

At about the same time as the Carmichael, Pomeroy, and Chamber exchange, another verbal battle involving S. N. Wood broke out. Initially, Wood's vindictiveness was aimed primarily at Eskridge, his enemy in the legislature. There were those who believed Wood and his friend Aldrich were at least partially responsible for the Normal's loss of legislative support simply because Eskridge was laboring for the Normal. Moreover, Stotler and *The Emporia News* apparently had little respect for Wood. In an article under the caption of "That Skunk Again," Stotler maintained that Sam Wood had gone way back to the fight for the University and brought out the legend of the Normal School. Wood maintained that the Board of Regents had departed far from the laws of 1863 and 64. Some of the charges he had made in the 1876 legislature were that the school was run by a ring; that Pomeroy drove out Norton and hired his own wife; that Pomeroy was running the school for his own benefit; that the poorest teachers come from the Normal; that half the students should be in common school; and that the last time the school was a Normal was under Kellogg and Norton.[381]

At the same time, H. W. McCune, editor of *The Emporia Ledger*, was critical of the Board of Regents' decision to allow Pomeroy to operate the Normal School during what was generally believed to be a temporary situation, the Board expecting the next legislature to be more compassionate and generous than the one of 1876 had been. Pomeroy answered the criticism by pointing out that such a denouncement served only to the further detriment of the Normal School.[382]

Eventually, McCune attacked Pomeroy personally by declaring him to have become exceedingly obnoxious, not only to some of the teachers and students, but to the larger portion of Emporians. The editor concluded by asserting that Pomeroy had lost much of his power for usefulness as president and that "his immediate and unconditional dismissal would be generally accepted as the surest pledge for the future prosperity of the school."[383]

During what escalated into a series of complaints from McCune regarding the dismissal of teachers, and the matter of Mrs. Pomeroy remaining on the faculty, *The Ledger* published an account of the president being burned in effigy by "a gang of Normal students." The following week, however, a notice by students maintained that only two young men were guilty of the deed, one of whom had been expelled earlier for misconduct. McCune denounced the deed as rowdyism unbefitting the students, stating that he was glad they were almost unanimous in their denunciation of the act.[384] Nevertheless, he continued his attack upon Pomeroy, accusing him of having reduced the teachers' salaries in order to hire his wife to teach languages at a salary of $1200.

It is interesting that such an accusation arose over the Chair of Languages when the teaching of languages had been a part of the curriculum since 1872 when President Hoss and the board initiated the two year elementary course, a four year full course, and a third option of a language course. Indeed, even earlier languages, though optional, had been offered. During the Kellogg era, according to the Catalog of 1870, Latin was taught for two terms the first year; German, the third term of the first year and the first term of the second year; French, the second and third terms of the second year; and Greek, the first and second terms of the third year. This program had been referred to as the Classical Department. Its development was slow, probably because of the high turnover of students. Most of them were not enrolled long enough to pursue the elective course. Those who could, however, availed themselves of the opportunity. One such case was that of Mary A. Williams, a Normal graduate of 1869 who married a classmate, Charles T. Cavaness, and returned in 1871-72 to pursue languages as a post graduate student.[385]

As early as December 14, 1871, a Chair of Languages had been established. According to the Board minutes of that date, "On motion of E. S. Stover, the Chair of Languages was established as a permanent one in the institution, and that the action of the Executive Committee in calling M. C. Lamprey, A.M., to fill that position was endorsed and approved by the Board and the salary of the position fixed at $1600 per annum."

According to the Minutes of June 20, 1872, however, a Chair of Mathematics was established and the Chair of Languages temporarily suspended, presumably because the Board members believed they could not afford both while the building program was in progress.

In spite of the various complaints being voiced by Pomeroy's detractors, school at the Normal apparently was continuing as usual under the guidance of the beleaguered president. Nearly a week of festivities had been planned leading up to Commencement for eighteen students on Tuesday, June 13, 1876. Following two days of written examinations, came the annual sermon delivered in Normal Hall on Sunday, the 11th. Next day came more written examinations followed by literary exercises that evening. Heavy rains on Tuesday postponed commencement until Wednesday morning the 14th, when thirteen graduates from the three-year elementary course and five from the four-year Normal course received diplomas. The morning program included oration, essay, and song.[386]

The Board of Regents at their regular meeting of June 13 drew up and adopted five resolutions to be followed as the basis for conducting the State Normal School until further legislative action. At the close of the commencement exercises, Pomeroy announced the discharge of all teachers except himself who had been given authority to employ any others he thought necessary. This apparently was the first public indication of the scheme to keep the Normal open for fall and winter terms.[387]

In the June 23 issue of *The Emporia News*, there appeared letters to the editor by both Eskridge and Pomeroy, in an attempt to correct some of the false accusations that had appeared for months in *The Ledger*. Eskridge took Wood to task for the part he had played in the non-funding of the Normal School, and Pomeroy gave a lengthy and reasonable explanation regarding the plan for continuing the school until the new legislature met. Contrary to Wood's claim that Pomeroy had driven Norton away, Pomeroy revealed that Norton had left of his own choosing, primarily because of his wife's precarious health. He had applied for the California job before the legislature cut off appropriations; and upon Norton's request, Pomeroy himself had written a letter of recommendation.

The following week, Stotler, who had been away for some time because of family illness in the East, published an editorial on "The Faculty Difficulty." He inferred that the problem seemed to be personal and mainly one-sided. In so far as he had been able, the president had remained silent—he had not gone into the boarding houses or into the streets for "his side." The other paper in town and the public tongue had enabled the "war" to continue. Stotler maintained that he was writing not for one side or the other, but "with a hope of preventing such disgraceful affairs in the future." According to Stotler, his information had not come from Pomeroy's friends. The fight upon the president, which was made by two members of the faculty, was uncalled for, vicious and harmful to the school and all concerned. It was carried on unnecessarily by personal ambition and urged on by sectarianism. "Instead of being assisted, the president had been ridiculed and sneered at in the classes, and his efforts weakened by these subordinates whenever an occasion could be found. He has been watched with the eye of a hawk, his words and actions have been purposely misconstrued, and his name has been bandied about the houses as though he was a criminal." Stotler maintained that "the same interest, to a great extent, which has backed these two in their senseless war upon him [the president] made it 'so hot' for a former president of the school, a good and competent man, that he resigned. They are trying the same game again." In his words, Stotler put it strong because the disease needed strong treatment. He pointed out the irony of the situation: that whatever failure or disaster the "war" had brought upon the school would be laid at the president's door. He would be held responsible by the public and the regents, while those to blame for the evil consequences would escape the censure they deserve. Stotler believed that any problem should be taken to the Board, then to the Governor, if not relieved.

On July 7, Stotler pleaded for a cessation of hostilities in his editorial "That Fight Again." A student who had intended to return in the fall changed his mind because of the personal persuasion of one of the two teachers involved. Earlier a prominent student had left, saying his mind had been "filled so full of the poison against the president that he could do no good in the school." According to Stotler, Pomeroy's "course in this fight has made him friends." He had been high-minded and gone about his business.[388]

At least two ministers answered Stotler's claim that sectarianism was helping to feed the flames of controversy. The Reverend J.H. Clary of the First Presbyterian Church wrote a denial that Presbyterians were in any way involved despite the fact that his son was the only minister's son enrolled at the Normal. The Reverend O.J. Shannon of the Congregational Church wrote in defense of Mrs. Abigail Morse and Professor Carmichael, the two purported agitators. He took Stotler to task for what he had written about the matter. In the meantime, Pomeroy came out with a pamphlet concerning the faculty problem, the account being too long for the newspapers.[389]

In late July, S.C. Delap, who had replaced Norton, left for Pennsylvania to take a position in the State Normal of that state. Carmichael left for his new home in Nevada City, California to become the superintendent of schools there; and Mrs. Morse was appointed to teach in the Emporia school system. With Pomeroy's making public a letter from the State Superintendent's office declaring the recent diplomas of the Normal to be valid, the atmosphere seemed to clear and all energy became focused upon a new school year.[390]

By mid-August, a Normal School ad concerning the fall term appeared in *The Emporia News*. Stotler's editorial called attention to the ad. He listed the Board of Regents as Edwin Tucher, Greenwood County; Murdock, Sedgwick ; J.H. Crichton, Labette; C.B. Butler, Coffee; A. Sellers, Wabaunsee; and H.C. Cross, Lyon; stating "In brief they decided it was best to 'hold the fort' until the decision of the next legislature could be had." Stotler did not hesitate to recommend the school. To counteract the strong efforts being made to break up the school, Stotler declared that all of its friends needed a united front. The school must rise above the interests of individuals.

According to the ad, the fall term of 14 weeks was to be the longest term of the year. It would be especially advantageous for those students whose attendance was to be limited. The term was to begin on September 6 and end on December 13. Books could be purchased at cost or rented for two cents per week. Tuition for advanced students was $7.00 and $5.00 for the prep-year. The incidental fee was to be $2.00.[391]

The 1876 fall term opened with 60 students, but it was expected to increase to 75 and employ a full faculty. Pomeroy was determined to re-open the model department and engaged Ella Murdock, a recent Normal graduate, as teacher.[392] Indicative of the seriousness of the summer squabbles is the fact that since March of 1876, when the appropriations were cancelled, enrollment at a high of 340 in the winter term had decreased by nearly two thirds in the spring term when 125 were enrolled. While the lack of appropriations and the initiation of tuition fees were largely responsible for the first decrease, undoubtedly the further decrease in the fall term was brought on by the lack of harmony among the faculty and the resulting bad publicity within the community and elsewhere.

By the end of September, however, the emotional climate at the Normal seemed to have changed dramatically. A student wrote in *The Emporia News* that in spite of attempts to crush the Normal or rather its president, the school "flourishes." The president, the student thought, deserves a word of compliment for his firmness and persistence in the face of all opposition. There hasn't been a better faculty than now though we loved and still love those that are gone. "That the president is avaricious and mercenary, we question very much. The next legislature may discharge the president—if they do it will be a great error. He stands higher in our estimation than ever before—this is doubtless the sentiment of all the students and they're not new ones by any means."

According to a report to the State Superintendent of Public Instruction, the 1876 fall term of the Normal ended with an enrollment of 107 students in all departments. "In many respects the term, in its educational work, has been one of the most satisfactory and successful in the history of the Normal.[393]

Teachers for the fall term of 1876 were Professor T.M. Harris, a well-qualified young man; Mrs. Pomeroy; Rebecca Buchanan; Lucy Peebles; and Ella Murdock of the Model School. Stotler attended some of the closing exercises in December and lamented the fact that a larger number of students had not availed themselves of the excellent advantages offered for a solid and beneficial education. He deemed Mrs. Pomeroy's rhetoric class examination the finest he had witnessed at the Normal, due not only to the teacher's ability but to the hard work and devotion of every member of the class. The term social was one of the most largely attended and successful ones ever held in the new building; entertainment included a literary contest, singing by Miss Peebles' students, and Miss Peebles herself.[394]

As early as November, information concerning the winter term of January 3, 1877, was forthcoming. Tuition would remain the same, but there was a promise of a refund to all Normal students at the close of the term if appropriations commencing with the fiscal year should be granted by the legislature. The cost of students' board with private families would be from three to four dollars per week. Furnished rooms in the boarding hall for ladies would be three and a half dollars per month. Students were to apply to President Pomeroy.[395]

While the students were home for the holidays, many having taken advantage of excursion rates given by the Santa Fe and the MK&T railroads, area newspapers began to laud the progress of the Normal, hoping that the next legislature would renew appropriations for the struggling school.[396]

As stated in the Board Minutes of November 16, 1876, the amount requested of the 1877 legislature was $13,580: $10,400 for teachers' salaries; $900 for a janitor and engineer; and $2280 for miscellaneous. When the legislature met, that body allowed a total of $880 for the Normal.[397] Also passed was an Act to reorganize the State Normal School at Emporia and to provide for the sale of its land. The Act provided that the school was to be governed by a six member Board of Regents, appointed by the governor and confirmed by the senate. Three were to be appointed for two years, and three for four years. Instruction at the Normal was to be confined to the various branches of an English education and the method and art of teaching. It was to be the duty of the Board of Regents to sell or cause to be sold the lands belonging to the Normal at not less than three dollars per acre; "and no appropriation shall be made for this school in the future." This Act became law upon its being published in *The Commonwealth* on March 13, 1877.

Barely a week elapsed, after the devastating news that the Normal was not to be funded by the State, before a special meeting of the Board of Regents was called. They adopted the proposition submitted by President Pomeroy that the 1877 summer term ending in June should be conducted like the past fall and winter terms, that the present faculty be re-elected, and that the president, if he desires it, be permitted to occupy the Normal building as residence and to have the use of adjacent land.

A significant piece of business at this special meeting concerned the Normal School endowment of land. A committee of two, J.H. Crichton and J.J. Wright, were ordered to report at the regular June meeting regarding the amount of Normal lands sold; the condition of the funds derived from lands already sold; and any other matter germane to the subject. The Board also resolved that E.P. Bancroft, the land agent, be required to deposit all money he had received for any sales into the State Treasury as provided by law.[398]

By way of background, as early as 1866, the Board had voted to make provisions for sale of the land. The executive committee employed a suitable person, H.D. Preston, to appraise the land preparatory to selling it in the smallest legal sub divisions of forty acres, and to make a full description of the same. In 1867, the Board declared Preston's report satisfactory and paid him $450 for his services. The Board voted in 1869 that none of the lands be sold for less than three dollars per acre. The following year it was decided that disposal of the lands should be left to the discretion of the executive committee, whether to hold or to sell, whichever they deemed best. Not until 1872 was the executive committee instructed to place the lands on the market. At the time, E.P. Bancroft was secretary of the Board. On May 6 of the following year, the Board authorized the executive committee to employ him as agent for the sale of Normal lands if he could be hired on satisfactory terms. Not until November 16, 1876, was the land matter again mentioned in the Board Minutes, then only to re-affirm Bancroft as land commissioner, the details to be arranged with him by the executive committee.

Crichton and Wright reported to the Board in June of 1877, as ordered. They had received from the State auditor a complete list of lands set aside as Normal lands. The auditor's records showed no sale nor disposal of those lands except for one quarter section sold to one Patrick Hall for $1,280 and the patent issued by the Governor as provided by law. They found, however, that the patent had been issued upon the certificate of E.P. Bancroft, whereas the law directed that it was to be issued only upon the certificate of the secretary and treasurer of the Board of Directors. Therefore, the committee notified the auditor and the Register of Deeds office that hereafter no patents were to be issued until a certificate was filed as the law directed.

In April, the committee had called upon Bancroft "who had been acting as agent for the sale of the Normal lands under appointment by the Board of 1872" [sic], and asked for his report. According to the report, Bancroft had sold 1293 acres by contract including 160 acres patented. He received as principal $2148.90 and interest of $621.33 for a total of $2270.23 plus $58.45 interest. The committee received and receipted the total of $2828.68. The committee determined that Bancroft still owed the school fund $208.37 in interest (based on six percent [interest] from the time of receipt until time of payment). Bancroft, however, thought he should not be charged any more than the $58.45 already paid. The committee then submitted the matter to the Board.

According to Bancroft's report, one contract of sale was forfeited for non-payment of interest and another contract had interest due. Bancroft was directed to notify all parties in default to pay immediately to the secretary of the Board, or a penalty would be assessed. All money due should be paid at once to the secretary. The committee further ordered Bancroft not to make any more sales until the meeting of the Board.

The committee deposited money in the two national banks of Emporia, time deposits for three months subject to the order of the Board. As for Bancroft, the committee found his mode of conducting the land agency highly unsatisfactory. He had recklessly violated the law, and his failure to report his transactions to the Board was inexcusable. Moreover, the committee considered re-appraisal to ascertain if more lands had been sold than reported, but thought it best to wait for the Board's instructions.

Upon digesting the lengthy report of the Land Committee, the Board passed a total of thirteen regulations. First on list was the determination that when the time deposits expired, the principal from the sale of lands be paid to the State Treasurer as required by law. All lands sold hereafter were to be sold upon a down payment of ten percent of the principal, and ten percent interest payable semi-annually on the balance of the principal; the balance of the principal to be due in ten years, or sooner if the purchaser desired.

The Board ordered that the appointment of E.P. Bancroft as Agent be revoked. In his stead, Van R. Holmes was appointed Agent. He was required to execute a Bond for $10,000 to be approved by the president of the Board. The lands were to be re-appraised; Holmes and Crichton were named as the committee of appraisement. Crichton was instructed to prepare printed blank contracts for sale of lands. The treasurer, secretary, and land agent were ordered to procure the necessary books for their use in conducting land sales, and their bonds were to be approved by the Board president. Crichton and Wright in their report had recommended $10,000 for the agent and $6,000 for the secretary.

The Board ordered that $500 of the money on hand be paid by the treasurer of teachers for services for the present term. They determined that hereafter school terms were to consist of twelve weeks each, and that the course of study be changed. Entomology and English Literature were to be introduced in the Elementary Course. They also determined that seven elementary students were eligible to be awarded diplomas.

By judicious management in the sale of lands, the committee believed that the Normal School could be made a permanent institution with an endowment large enough to be self-sustaining, and one of the most substantial institutions in the State. As we now know, due to the dedication, excellence and hard work of the leaders described in these pages, the prediction of the Normal becoming a permanent and substantial educational institution has more than been achieved.

Gwen Zimmerman's ambitious initial plan for this history was for it to cover the first 60 years of Emporia State University. Her work, however, ended here.

NOTES

[1] Wichita State University was founded after the scope of this volume, in 1886.

[2]C.S. Griffin, "The University of Kansas and the Years of Frustration, 1854-1864," *The Kansas Historical Quarterly* (Topeka: Kansas State Historical Society), v. 32, (Spring, 1966), p. 3. The writer is greatly indebted to Mr. Griffin's well-documented article which provided road signs for facilitating the ensuing story. Griffin is author of a comprehensive history, *The University of Kansas* (Lawrence: The University Press of Kansas, 1974).

[3]Daniel W. Wilder, *The Annals of Kansas*, New Edition, 1541-1885, v. 1 (Topeka, KS: T. Dwight Thacher, Kansas Publishing House, 1886), p. 52.

[4]*The Statutes of the Territory of Kansas; Passed at the First Session of the Legislative Assembly, One Thousand Eight Hundred and Fifty-five* (Shawnee Manual Labor School, Kansas Territory, John T. Brady, Public Printer, 1855), pp. 931-936.

[5]Wilder, *Annals*, v. 1. All four constitutions drawn up in Kansas before statehood finally was achieved are reprinted in their entirety therein. Article VII of the Topeka Constitution concerns education. See Section 4, p. 98.

[6]*Ibid.*, Section 4 of the Ordinance, p. 191.

[7]*Ibid.*, Article VII, Section 7, pp. 224-225.

[8]*Ibid.*, Second part of Ordinance, p. 217.

[9]*Ibid.*, Article VI, Section 7, p. 270.

[10]*Ibid.*, Article XV, Section 8, p. 274.

[11]Griffin, *KHQ*, v. 32, pp. 18-19. See also Don W. Wilson, "Charles Robinson: An Educational and Intellectual Leader," Ibid., v. 41 (Summer, 1975), p. 135. Wilson is author of *Governor Charles Robinson of Kansas* (The University Press of Kansas, 1975). *House Journal of the Legislative Assembly of the State of Kansas*, Begun and Held at Topeka, on Tuesday, March 26, 1861 (Lawrence, KS: Printed at the Republican Book & Job Office, John Speer, State Printer, 1861), pp. 355 and 510.

In all probability, absentee legislators defeated the Manhattan bill (#65). An examination of both the May 9 votes when the House first passed the bill, and the

May 29 votes when the House tried to override the governor's veto, shows that eight legislators were absent on the 29th, six of whom had voted in the affirmative on the 9th. The other two, both Douglas County representatives, cast negative votes on the 9th but were not necessarily steadfast. (See Footnote #17.) In fact, it seems likely that had all eight absentees voted on May 29, at least six would have voted for Manhattan, thus assuring the necessary two-thirds majority.

[12]*The Emporia News*, May 18, 1861. All three representatives from Breckinridge County, A.K. Hawkes of Hartford; G.H. Rees, Americus; and R.W. Cloud voted consistently against Manhattan, although Rees was on leave May 9. (See *House Journal*, 1861, pp. 355 and 510.) The Emporia paper, however, gave credit to Senator Bancroft to which he was not entitled. In 1861, Bancroft actually voted in favor of Manhattan's Bluemont College as the university site. In fact, Senators Sleeper and Bancroft cancelled each other's votes regarding the location of the university, the penitentiary, and the capital. See the *Senate Journal of the Legislative Assembly of the State of Kansas, 1861* (Lawrence, KS: Printed at the Republican Book & Job Office, Speer & Moore, Public Printers, 1861), pp. 292-293.

[13]*The Emporia News*, March 30, 1861.

[14]Griffin, *KHQ*, v. 32, pp. 17-19.

[15]*The Emporia News*, October 19, 1861. Interestingly, more than ten years later, Stotler maintained that "Topeka must lose the Capitol." His reasons given sounded much like those he gave in 1861 for support of Lawrence in the struggle over the Capitol. On June 7, 1872, Stotler wrote in *The Emporia News* that Topeka was becoming too far east and north in the state so far as population is concerned. He added solemnly that Emporia was a likely spot for the Capitol.

[16]*Ibid.*, October 24, 1861.

[17]*Ibid.*, November 2, 1861.

[18]Mr. Stotler was correct in stating that Shawnee County's four representatives and one senator had unanimously supported Manhattan's first bid for the university. However, he not only was mistaken about the motive behind the Lawrence opposition to Manhattan, but he also was mistaken in the unanimity of the Lawrence vote. According to the record, the Douglas County delegation was less enthusiastic about saving the university for themselves than was Governor Robinson. Although the county's eight representatives had initially opposed Manhattan by a vote of 6 to 2, the vote to override, two opposed, and three were absent. One of the absentees had favored Manhattan on May 9. By contrast all eight supported Leavenworth for the penitentiary, and six voted for the capital

bill, the other two being absent. See Wilder, *Annals*, v. 1, pp. 314-316. *House Journal*, 1861, pp. 350-352, 355, 422, and 510. *Senate Journal*, 1861, pp. 292-293.

[19]Griffin, *KHQ*, v. 32, p. 20.

[20]Wilder, *Annals*, v. 1, p. 345.

[21]*State of Kansas Senate Journal, 1862* (Lawrence, KS: Steam Printing Press of the State Journal, 1863), pp. 155 and 191-192. See also *Senate Journal*, 1861, p. 292.

In order to understand what went wrong for Manhattan in 1862, it is necessary to examine the 1861 votes of five controversial senators, none of whom were in the Senate for the final vote on March 3, 1862. The five men were Bancroft, J.F. Broadhead of Mound City; O.B. Gunn, Wyandotte; James A. Phillips, Paola, and S.N. Wood, Council Grove. In 1861, all of them except Broadhead had voted in favor of Manhattan as the university site. But by the time the issue came before the Senate in 1862, the picture had changed. As early as January 29, Senator Wood was replaced by C.S. Lambdin of Plymouth; and on February 21, Senator Phillips, who resigned, was replaced by Thomas Roberts. (See Ibid., 1862, p. 128 or *Annals*, v. 1, p. 344.)

When the bill came before the Senate on February 27, the two replacements, Lambdin and Roberts, voted against Manhattan. Further hurting Manhattan's chances was Bancroft's decision to switch from his 1861 position and vote against Manhattan. Broadhead remained consistent by voting against. Senator Gunn also remained consistent. His was the only "yes" vote among the aforementioned senators in the February 27 defeat.

By the time that reconsideration of the Manhattan bill became an issue, the three remaining controversial senators had been ousted. Rankin replaced Bancroft and Horatio Knowles, Broadhead. No replacement had been named for Gunn whose chair remained vacant. On March 3, all replacements except Roberts voted in favor of reconsidering the Manhattan bill; but concerning the bill itself, only Knowles, who the previous year had opposed Manhattan in the House, voted in favor. Ironically, Gunn was the only one of the senators in question to have voted consistently in favor of Manhattan. Had a replacement of like persuasion been there to vote, quite possibly the vote would have been a tie instead of 11 to 12 defeat.

[22]January 11, 1862.

[23]March 22, 1862; James C. Carey, *Kansas State University: The Quest for Identity* (Lawrence: The Regents Press of Kansas, 1977), p. 13. Carey, in condensing the beginnings of Kansas State University, generalized to the point of implying that it was largely the $15,000 endowment offer by Lawrence lobbyists that cost Manhattan the university; whereas in reality the endowment offer played no significant part in the legislative struggle until 1863 when Lawrence managed to

wrest the university from Emporia. By then, Manhattan all but had the agricultural college.

[24]*The Emporia News*, January 24, 1863. The Governor's speech appears on page 1 and is published in its entirety.

[25]Griffin, *KHQ*, v. 32, p. 26.

[26]*The Emporia News*, February 14, 1863. See also Ibid., October 19, 1861, for a note that C. V. Eskridge and Watson [should be William] Foster had been nominated as representatives from the county. Also in Ibid., February 6, 1864, Stotler mentions having recently seen Professor Foster, late of Lyon County, later of Douglas County, and latest of Leavenworth, who had wanted to be legislator in November, 1861 to get for "us" the university "because Emporia, above all points, was the place for it." Within a year Foster denounced Emporia as an unfit place for the institution. By 1863, Foster had become a representative from Douglas County.

[27]*Ibid.*, February 21, 1863. There was much confusion about the final vote. Stotler corrected his earlier statement that the vote in favor of Lawrence was 38 to 35. See *Ibid.*, February 14, 1863; also Griffin, *KHQ*, v. 32, p. 28. The *State of Kansas House Journal*, 1863 (Lawrence, KS: Steam Printing Press of the State Journal, 1863), p. 230, has the final vote as 39 to 32; but according to the names of those who voted, the recorded votes were 38 to 32.

Note: Everett Fish and Kathyrn Kayser, unpublished thesis, *An Outline of the History of the Kansas State Teachers College of Emporia, 1865-1934*, p. 4, gives the vote as 38 to 35. (Their source was *The Emporia News*, February 14, 1863.) This thesis is very valuable as a guide to the early history of the Normal School.

[28]*General Laws of the State of Kansas*, Passed at the Third Session of the Legislature, Commenced at the Capital January 13, 1863 (Lawrence, KS: "Kansas State Journal," Steam Press Print, 1863), "An Act to locate the State University," Secs. 2 and 4, pp. 115-116.

By 1869, mistakes were creeping into the often repeated account of the whole university struggle. One error placed the Lawrence requirement for obtaining the university at $16,000 in cash within 30 days. This error originated in the *Topeka Daily Commonwealth* and was reprinted in *The Emporia News*, June 11, 1869. See also Fish and Kayser Thesis, v. 2, p. 13.

[29]Wilder, *Annals*, v. 1, p. 373. See also Wilson, *KHQ*, v. 41, p. 137; *Public Documents, 1863*, p. 8. The Treasurer's report indicates that the $15,000 endowment for Kansas University was received on October 29, 1863. *The Emporia News*, November 7, 1863 carried verbatim Governor Carney's November 2 proclamation declaring that the university was located at Lawrence. In the same

issue, Stotler voiced the only indication this writer has found that some Emporians throughout the summer may have continued to hope for the university. Stotler wrote:

> Some of our people have expressed the opinion that Lawrence had not fulfilled the requirements of the University Act and that we would yet get that institution by their default, as the law located it here provided Lawrence failed to do what was required of her. By the following proclamation of Governor Carney, it will be seen that the question is forever settled, and the institution located at Lawrence.

[30]Wilder, v. 2, p. 624, for an appendage to an appropriations report. See also Griffin, *KHQ*, v. 32, pp. 30-32. *The Emporia News*, January 23, 1864 published Governor Carney's address in full.

[31]Griffin, *KHQ*, v. 32, pp. 27-28.

[32]*House Journal*, 1863, p. 227.

[33]*Ibid.*, pp. 237-238.

[34]*Ibid.*, p. 292.

[35]*Ibid.*, pp. 294, 305, and 311. *Topeka Daily State Record*, March 2, 1863, v. 3, no. 41, p. 1. This paper published the daily legislative business. It appears to be the only official record of the vote on the Normal School bill. The vote is not recorded in the *House Journal* although announcements of the bill's passage in the Senate, its being sent to the Governor and his subsequent signature, are all duly recorded on pages 362, 364, and 367. The only logical clue found thus far for this glaring omission is a parenthetical note in *The Emporia News*, January 16, 1864, written by the Topeka correspondent who reported upon a House resolution requesting that copies of all previous laws and legislative journals be furnished each legislator. According to the correspondent, the 1863 *House Journal* had not been published, the manuscript having been burned in the Lawrence massacre [Quantrill's raid], August 21, 1863.

Until evidence to the contrary is forthcoming, this writer conjectures that the *House Journal*, 1863, as it appears in our libraries today, is a compilation of sundry notes, minutes, memories, or diaries, and not necessarily complete. It undoubtedly was assembled sometime after the other requested materials were distributed to the 1864 legislature. (See *House Journal, 1864*, p. 45 for notice that only the *Senate Journal* for 1863 was available for distribution to the legislators.) Nor is the 1863 *House Journal* entirely accurate. For instance, the State Normal bill when introduced by Eskridge carried the number 255, but when its passage by the Senate was announced on March 2 in the House, the bill had become number

150 in spite of the fact that another bill #150 pertaining to county boundaries had passed the House during the same session. (See *House Journal*, 1863, pp. 338 and 340.)

The above conjecture is further substantiated by the following item found under miscellaneous appropriations: "Freeman Bell, for copying House Journals destroyed at Lawrence, seventy dollars and thirty cents." See *The Laws of the State of Kansas*, Passed at the Fourth Session of the Legislature, Commenced on Tuesday, January 12, 1864 (Lawrence, KS: Printed at the Kansas Daily Tribune Book and Job Office. John Speer, Printer to the State, 1864), p. 13.

[36]*Senate Journal*, 1863, pp. 280, 301, 307. Although there were no negative votes cast in the Senate, it appears that unanimity was lacking at least in spirit. According to the *Journal*, p. 307, "Pending the vote, Mr. Lowe was excused from voting." The reason for the excuse is probably lost forever, but D.P. Lowe of Mound City, Linn County, was present that day and voted on other legislation that came before the Senate.

[37]Goodnow, state superintendent of public instruction, was from Manhattan. Both Fick, business associate of Eskridge, and Crandall, doorkeeper of the 1863 legislature, were Emporians.

An error appears in the official information at the end of the published Act in the March 7 *Emporia News*. The date on which the bill was first introduced in the House is given as January 30, but the bill was not introduced until February 19. In the same paper, Stotler announced that the bill had passed the House with 49 affirmative votes and the Senate with 23. His House figure differs from that in the *Topeka Daily Record*. (See Footnote #34.)

[38]It seems rather unlikely to this writer that Eskridge, the man responsible for the 1863 law authorizing Lyon County to issue bonds for the building of a schoolhouse—a law generalized the following year to include every school district in Kansas—had not at least some general knowledge of theNormal School concept. Eskridge had been in Kansas since 1855, actively engaged in politics, the newspaper business, and merchandising.

Indeed, most Emporians may have known more about Normal Schools than later generations have credited them with knowing. At any rate, theNormal School bill was formulated, and even before the university question was settled, a large ad for a Normal School appeared in *The Emporia News*, January 24, 1863. One Simon Bucher on Eagle Creek in Lyon County had opened a school for the benefit of those who had no school at home. He had furnished a room with every necessity and was of the opinion he could give full satisfaction to those who patronized him.

> All persons who wish to qualify themselves to teach a common
> district school would do well to attend this school, as scholars
> will be thoroughly drilled in articulation and spelling. . . .

Instruction in vocal & instrumental music—if desired. . . . Tuition of $1.20 per month; board $2.00 per week.

(*Our Land—A History of Lyon County*, a bicentennial publication, 1976, Emporia State Press, p. 110, states that the first school in the Elmendaro Community was located in the Simon Bucher home in 1860.)

[39]*The Emporia News*, June 11, 1869. A reprint from the *Topeka Daily Commonwealth*. Just prior to adjournment of the Senate in March, 1870, when Lt. Gov. Eskridge completed his term of office, a lengthy tribute to Eskridge and a biographical sketch appeared in the *Topeka Daily Commonwealth*, written by the Topeka correspondent of the *Atchison Champion and Press*. It was reprinted in *The Emporia News* on March 11, 1870. The tribute refutes the Eskridge of the Legend.

> We are intimately acquainted with him, Eskridge, and have had every opportunity of watching and knowing his private moral character. We have never heard him utter an oath, or even a profane word, or speak in a manner unbecoming gentlemen. He is a man of great moral worth.

[40]*Kansas Historical Collections*, Vol. VI, 1897-1900, p. 114. Ten years earlier, Isaac T. Goodnow had been credited with first suggesting the idea of a Normal School. See *A History of the State Normal School of Kansas for the First Twenty-Five Years*, Emporia, Kansas, 1889, p. 134. This valuable book represents the best efforts of faculty and students who compiled a vivid record of the beginning years despite the sad fact that most official records had been lost by fire. President Taylor supervised the undertaking.

[41]This letter was found in the Alumni Association files and is now a part of the Normaliana collection of the William Allen White Library. It was sent to President Thomas W. Butcher by ex-President Taylor with the accompanying note:

> Decatur Ill., Sept. 8, 1920
> Dear Pres. Butcher, In looking over some files, I find this letter from Dr. Goodnow, the most outstanding supt. of Public Instruction in the early years of the organization of the public schools of Kansas. This data is largely incorporated in the Quarter-Centennial History of the State Normal, but you may care to file it in the archives. Someday it may prove valuable.
> All well. Regards to family,
> Sincerely yours,
> A.R. Taylor

In this connection it is also interesting that in no record uncovered to date does Eskridge credit either himself or anyone else with the idea of a Normal School — not even in his history edition of *The Emporia Daily Republican*, January 1, 1884.

Of interest also is the fact that in his diary, the original of which is in the Kansas State Historical Society, Goodnow does not even mention the Normal School bill nor its passage. While that seems almost like negligence on his part, inasmuch as he was state superintendent of public instruction at the time, Goodnow was deeply engrossed with legislation pertaining to the agricultural college during February of 1863 as evidenced by reading a transcript of the diary. Whatever involvement he had with the Normal School at that time must have been too casual to warrant a notation. He does note, however, on February 18 (the day before the introduction of the Normal School bill) "Eskridge's proposition to divide college endowment! No go!" From this entry one can only deduce that Eskridge, seeking to endow his as yet uncreated Normal School, had sought a portion of the agricultural college lands. Apparently no hard feelings resulted from his unsuccessful effort, for on April 6, when he arrived in Emporia, Goodnow wrote: "Put up horses at Hotel, ourselves at Eskridge's." Goodnow Collection, Isaac T. Goodnow Diary Transcription, 1863, Manuscript Department, Kansas State Historical Society, Topeka.

[42]J. Scott McCormick, "The Development and Growth of the Kansas State Teachers College of Emporia, 1865-1925" (bound manuscript in Normaliana Collection, White Library), January 23, 1925, pp. 11-12. Fish and Kayser in their Thesis, v. 1, pp. 11-12, repeat the legend told by McCormick, whose source is listed as the stenographic notes taken on the occasion of Taylor's speech at President Hill's inaugural. (These notes have not been located by this writer to date.) Fish and Kayser credit Taylor rather than McCormick although they apparently used the latter study.

Actually, Taylor spoke on Thursday evening, November 15, 1906 just prior to installation ceremonies the following morning. According to *The Emporia Gazette*, November 16, 1906 and the *State Normal Bulletin*, November 22, 1906, Albert Taylor Hall was full to overflowing for what both papers called a highly entertaining speech on the history of the school. Neither paper, however, quoted from the text. Only the *Normal Alumnus*, November, 1906 seems to have quoted excerpts from Taylor's text. It is interesting that no part of the legend itself was chosen for the *Alumnus* although the magazine used other portions of the speech included in McCormick.

See also "Semi-Centennial Address, June 1915," by Dr. A.R. Taylor, President, 1882-1901, *Kansas State Normal School Emporia, Fiftieth Anniversary Number*, February, 1918 (W.R. Smith, State Printer, Topeka, 1918), p. 23; also the *Sunflower*, 1904 (Kansas State Normal School), p. 15. The student version of the legend does not refer to Eskridge by name but refers to "the promoter member of the legislature." The student version ignores Goodnow's role. (No subsequent issues of the *Sunflower* were published after 1904 until 1910 when the name was adopted officially.)

[43]"The Founding of the State Normal School," an address by Lyman B. Kellogg at Founders' Day celebration, February 15, 1910, *Kansas Historical Collections*, Vol. XII, 1911-1912, pp. 95-96. This appears to be the only record of Kellogg relating any semblance of the legend. Judge Bailey, a part time Emporian who had emigrated from Massachusetts, certainly would have been capable of suggesting the Normal School and writing the historic bill. Moreover, he was a family friend of Kellogg's first wife, Abbie G. Homer. She had come from Massachusetts to Kansas to teach school upon Bailey's recommendation. Thus Kellogg was in an excellent position to learn firsthand about Bailey's role in the matter. (See the *Emporia Gazette*, June 18, 1927, "Early Days at the Emporia Normal" by L.B. Kellogg, Part IX. This series of memoirs had been written in 1915 and was published posthumously, Kellogg having died in 1918.) Bailey's biographer merely stated that Bailey "helped to get the State Normal School established." See preface to Bailey's *Border Ruffian Troubles in Kansas*, Charles R. Green, editor (Lyndon, KS, July 1899).

[44]*Emporia Gazette*, August 17, 1927, "An Old Debt" by W.A. White, reprinted in the *Alumni News*, October, 1927. See also clippings about Eskridge, Lyon County Museum. White's editorial was a tribute to Mrs. C.V. (Mary) Eskridge whose body was brought from California to Emporia for burial with that of her daughter Mattie (Mrs. John M. Steele) who had died out there ten years earlier. (Both women were interred in Maplewood Cemetery.) White urged both oldsters and newcomers to attend the memorial services, "for only through her can we express our gratitude to her husband for the splendid service he rendered." Eskridge himself had died on July 15, 1900 from a self-inflicted gunshot wound near the end of a long and painful bout with cancer of the liver. Large crowds attended his funeral. See *The Emporia Daily Republican*, July 16, 17, 18, and August 7, 1900; also the *Emporia Gazette*, July 16, 17, and 21, 1900.

[45]*The Emporia News*, March 14, April 4 and 11, June 20, and August 22, 1863.

[46]*Ibid.*, May 9, 1863.

[47]*Ibid.*, September 5, 1863.

[48]According to the transcript of his diary, Goodnow was at this time enroute home from an extended visit to Chicago and other eastern points. On August 17, he "took late cars" for Quincy and spent that night at the Quincy House. See also *Kansas Public Documents, 1863*, "Report of the Commissioners Appointed to Locate the StateNormal School, with Accompanying Papers," pp. 3-6. This report to Governor Carney is signed only by Fick and Crandall, witnessed by Eskridge who under oath declared them to be a majority of the commission. Two other official documents accompany the report: the actual land transaction between Fick and his wife who agreed to convey the land to the State of Kansas for the

sum of $500, the Ficks to provide a warranty deed in exchange for the check; and the sworn affidavit showing that the deed was duly recorded on August 24 with the Lyon County Register of Deeds, F.G. Hunt. (See also the Thesis, v. 2, p. 12, for a copy of the official report. Goodnow's name mistakenly appears therein as one who signed the report.)

Stotler in *The Emporia News*, April 11, 1863, announced that Superintendent Goodnow had spent most of that week in Emporia attending the Teachers' Institute and "for the purpose of looking up, in company with the other commissioners, a site for the State Normal School." In his 1889 letter to President Taylor, Goodnow said the commission had met on April 9, 1863.

Also, entries in the Goodnow Diary for 1863 indicate that on Wednesday evening, April 8, after delivering a lecture on education at the Congregational Church [Emporia], Goodnow was involved in a "discussion on site for Normal School." The following day (April 9), a portion of the entry reads "Commissioners meeting to locate State N.S." (Goodnow Diary Transcription, Goodnow Collection, Manuscript Division, Kansas State Historical Society, Topeka.)

[49]Throughout that summer and autumn, *The Emporia News* carried accounts of troops on the Kansas-Missouri border. See issues for July 9 and 16, August 13, October 8 and 15, 1864. In the September 24 issue was the announcement that Jacob Stotler had sold out to Jonathan Hunt and joined the Kansas forces in Paola. The October 29 issue contained a dispatch from Stotler in which he mentions many ministers from the area [Emporia] being among the troops. Two Emporians listed were the Reverend Solomon Brown (Christian Church) and the Reverend G.C. Morse (Congregational). In the same paper was another dispatch under the dateline of Fort Scott, October 26, 1864: "Price has been defeated at Mine Creek, Linn County. Generals Marmaduke and Caball and 500 prisoners captured. Kansas is safe."

[50]Senator F.P. Fitzwilliam of Leavenworth County cast the lone dissenting vote against the Organization Act which had carried by 70 to 0 in the House. The appropriation bill passed 42 to 15 in the House and 13 to 0 in the Senate, although at least seventeen senators voted on other legislation that day. See *Senate Journal of the Legislative Assembly of the State of Kansas, 1864* (Lawrence, KS: John Speer, Public Printer, 1865), pp. 212 and 408.

Stotler in his February 27, 1864 issue of *The Emporia News* had been pessimistic about the appropriation bill passing. In fact, he had stated flatly that it had no chance of passing "as the immortal! 48 of the House and 16 of the Senate are resolved that no local measure shall be adopted unless it is asked for by one of their own number." The so-called fraud and anti-fraud parties of 1864 to which Stotler referred had resulted from the legislature's premature election of Governor Carney as the next United States senator from Kansas. Carney soon resigned from that position.

[51]Morse, a dedicated friend to public education, and his wife Abigail, had opened a short-lived academy in Emporia before the town could boast of more than a dozen houses. Both were well-educated New Englanders who had come to Emporia as newlyweds in 1857. Morse, a graduate of Dartmouth and Andover Seminary, chose Emporia as the place to begin his missionary sojourn. In the thirteen years before his untimely death, he not only established the Congregational Church in Emporia, but those in some of the outlying communities as well. Morse and his wife homesteaded their farm southeast of Emporia; he served as Lyon County superintendent of schools and was a director of the Normal until his death from a farm accident in 1870 at the age of forty-three.

Why Morse's name has never figured in the Legend is curious, but the most logical explanation seems to lie in the fact of his early death. Then, too, he lived away from Emporia for the most part during the last two years of his life after accepting a pastoral call to Grasshopper Falls in Jefferson County (known as Valley Falls after 1875). There is but little evidence in family accounts that Morse was instrumental in locating the Normal School. His obituary in *The Emporia News*, July 15, 1870, made no mention at all of the Normal, but he was eulogized nevertheless: "In educational matters he was always foremost. . . . By visiting, writing, and talking, he created an interest in the common schools. . . ."

This writer feels compelled to point out that in the Morse genealogical file in the Lyon County Museum is a typewritten obituary of G.C. Morse attributed to *The Emporia News*, July 15, 1870, which contains the following statement: "Mr. Morse suggested and the legislature acting on his suggestion located the State Normal School at Emporia." But this statement does not appear in the published obituary. A similar claim, however, does appear in a feature story about Morse, written by a student, Betty Breukelman, for Emporia's centennial year. See *The Emporia Times*, June 27, 1957.

More than forty years after Morse's death, his widow in 1912 wrote a brief biography of the Reverend in which she stated that after the Normal was located, "he [Morse] was the one to whom the people of Emporia looked to lead in its establishment." She also stated that at his death "All the people of Emporia united in building a monument of native stone which marks his grave in Maplewood Cemetery." (Manuscript in the G.C. Morse-Abigail Morse genealogy file, Lyon County Museum.) It is because of Abigail herself, however, that the Morse name has become immortalized on the Emporia State University campus. The Morse Hall Dormitory complex and Morse Drive are named for Abigail who, after being widowed, taught for three years at the Normal and served as preceptress in the ladies' boarding house before becoming affiliated with Emporia High School.

[52]According to the Fish-Kayser Thesis and the 1889 History of the Normal, it was Superintendent Goodnow who, in his December, 1863 annual report, called for the immediate beginning of the Normal School. An inspection of the report, however, shows no such call. Instead, Goodnow declared that "How soon this

[the Normal School] can be made a living institution will depend upon legislation and the benevolence of individuals." See *Kansas Public Documents, 1863* for Goodnow's report, pp. 30-31.

Not until March 12, 1864 did *The Emporia News* publish anything about the report. In addition to quoting from the superintendent's school statistics, Stotler wrote: We hope soon to be able to say that the Normal School is in session. The appropriation given us this winter will hire teachers for a good portion of the year, and soon Kansas will furnish her own teachers, independent of foreign competition.

[53]*Ibid.*, August 27, 1864. In their thesis, Fish and Kayser reprinted the newspaper announcement in their source book, v. 2, p. 13. They also copied from Taylor's 1899 Kansas Historical Society address (p. 14). Unfortunately, they based their manuscript upon the latter source which is in error. (See v. 1, p. 10.) Taylor says that four members were appointed on August 19, 1864 and two others, Brockway and Rogers, on the same date in 1865 (*Kansas Historical Collections*, Vol. VI, p. 115). Where Taylor found such erroneous information remains a mystery, but the December 31, 1864 issue of *The Emporia News* published portions of the minutes from the first Board of Directors meeting which was attended by six of the nine members (by proxy or in person). Included were the names of Brockway and Rogers.

[54]*Ibid.*, December 31, 1864. See also a transcription of Minutes of the Board of Directors of the Kansas State Normal School, W.A. White Library, Normaliana Collection. The original minutes are in the Normaliana vault.

[55]*Ibid.*, July 2, 1864. The Eskridge resolution passed "almost unanimously."

[56]*Ibid.*, December 31, 1864. One reason that no one seems to know just when Morse went east on his search is that there were no issues of the Emporia paper published after December 3 until December 24 when a mere "half sheet" was printed. According to a notice in that diminutive issue, the supply of paper had arrived too late on Friday night to print a full issue by Saturday. The same notice informed subscribers that the two previous issues [December 10 and 17] could not be printed for want of paper because of an embargo on the Hannibal and St. Joseph Railroad.

[57]*Pioneer Days in Kansas* by Richard Cordley, D.D. (New York, Boston, Chicago: The Pilgrim Press, 1903), pp. 14-18. Cordley, a Congregational minister, had been a seminar classmate of Morse. They and two other classmates, P.S. Storrs and R.D. Parker, migrated to Kansas in 1857 as missionaries, and were thereafter known as the Andover band. Cordley, who located in Lawrence, preached for a time in Emporia during the 1870s.

[58]*A History of the State Normal School of Kansas for the First Twenty-Five Years, 1889*, p. 14, states that George Howland, later superintendent of the Chicago schools, was the first man approached by Morse for the job. Fish and Kayser in their thesis cite this secondary source. (See v. 2, p. 19.) The origin of this information is not known.

[59]*The Emporia Gazette*, June 9, 1927, "Early Days at the Emporia Normal," Part I, by Judge Kellogg.

[60]*Ibid.*, Part II, June 10, 1927.

[61]*Ibid.*

[62]*Ibid.*, Part III, June 11, 1927.

[63]*A History of the State Normal School of Kansas First the First Twenty-Five Years*, p. 14. See also thesis, v. 2, p. 19.

[64]Thesis, v. 1, p. 13. Probably most of the recent publications that have perpetuated this error have been based either upon this Thesis or the 1889 *History*. See *Qualities of Greatness*, An Anniversary Publication of the Kansas State Teachers College—Emporia, edited by Roy Durham, associate professor of social sciences, p. 2. Dr. Orville Watson Mosher, author of the vignette "Lyman B. Kellogg" writes that Kellogg, full of enthusiasm, "began teaching the very next day after his arrival." See also the genealogical files of the Kellogg family, Lyon County Museum. Many newspaper clippings retell an inaccurate story of L.B. Kellogg's arrival. Especially have these stories been prevalent around Founder's Day (February 15) all through the history of the school.

[65]January 21, 1865.

[66]*The Emporia Gazette*, "Early Days at the Normal," Part IV, June 13, 1927.

[67]*Ibid.* William Allen White first mentioned the manner of his mother's arrival at the time of her death. See the May 7, 1924 issue for his editorial "Mary A. White," which later was reprinted in his book, *Forty Years on Main Street* (New York, Toronto: Farrar & Rinehart, Inc., 1937), p. 7. In *The Autobiography of William Allen White* (New York: MacMillan Company, 1946), p. 8, White also wrote of his mother's sharing that ride with Kellogg. According to White, Kellogg remembered well the young woman passenger. "He always said she was a proud little piece, sitting on the box with the driver."

Dr. Everett Rich, professor emeritus of E.S.U. has captured the drama of that stage ride for modern day students and general readers in a poignant essay, "Emporia and the Teachers College," which was reproduced in the centennial

Founders Day Convocation program, February 16, 1965. Rich's essay is reprinted here in full:

It was almost 10 o'clock on a Thursday night in January, 1865, when the Emporia stage stopped at a Lawrence hotel to take on its last passenger. The stage, known as a jerky, was designed for a driver and four passengers. Already eight passengers and a driver were crowded into the three seats, so that the new passenger looked on his prospects with some misgivings. But the driver, checking his waybill, found everything in order, and a man in the back said, "you may come with us. There are three of us here already, but you may sit on my lap for a while anyway." The young man climbed in, took his seat upon the knee of Jonathan H. Hunt, editor of the Emporia News, and began the last lap of his journey to Emporia where he was to open the new Kansas State Normal School.

That journey, a ninety mile trip, took all Thursday night and all Friday until after dark, a distance one may now travel by the Santa Fe railway in ninety minutes; and in keeping with the other pioneer condition, Lyman B. Kellogg, the new college president, attended a public meeting the next day which was to prepare against a threatened Indian raid. Nevertheless, raid or no raid, the Emporia News appeared on schedule that Saturday and noted that "distinguished arrivals" had arrived by last night's stage. Among these were Professor Kellogg, Editor Hunt, two county officials and one or two "honorables." The name of one of the passengers was missing, an Irish girl who was coming to Kansas to attend the new Normal School. Her name was Mary Ann Hatten, who became the mother of William Allen White.

On the Friday night when Lyman Kellogg and Mary Ann Hatten arrived in Emporia, all Kansas had not a single foot of railway, no electrical lights, no telephone, no gas ranges, no paved streets. In fact, the road the Emporia stage traveled from Lawrence was scarcely more than a trail across the prairies. Emporia was not yet ten years old: and within the past decade their boyhood homes in Americus the dark shadow, as from a summer cloud, on the hill where Emporia now stands. The shadow was a herd of roaming buffalos.

Yet Emporia had about 500 people in 1865 and looked forward to becoming a thriving metropolis. She did not have then, as she has not had frequently since then, enough jobs for all students who had to work their way through college; and Mary Ann Hatten, failing to find a job to work her way, went on to Council Grove where she secured a school for the spring term. Lyman Kellogg, meanwhile, found himself president of a college that existed only on paper. Borrowing from chairs from the first Congressional Church, he opened the school in the upper room of the Emporia public school building on February 15. He was the only teacher and he had 18 students.

Both the city of Emporia and the Teacher's College have passed the 100th anniversary of their founding. Emporia, a country town, became the best known small town in America largely because it was the home of Kansas' most distinguished citizen, William Allen White. The college, likewise, became known as one of the first institutions of its type in America, not through the efforts of one person but many. It even had the dubious distinction of being the largest teachers college in America at one time, but its reputation has always rested upon the quality of its instruction rather than its size.

The relationship of a college and its town is somewhat like the relationship of two individuals. At the worst, one dominates the other; at its best, the two complement each other. In Emporia the relationship has been wholesome. Both the Teachers College and Emporia have maintained their own personalities though vitally interested in the welfare of each other.

Dr. Everett Rich.

[68]*The Emporia News*, January 14, 1865.

[69]*Ibid*. January 21, 1865.

[70]*Ibid*.

[71]*Ibid*. See p. iii of Appendix for Sec. VI of Organizational Act.

[72]*Ibid*. January 28, 1865. Under the caption of "Prof. Kellogg," Hunt wrote "We believe from our acquaintance with him, he is well qualified as a teacher." Hunt also had "a very high appreciation of his social and mental qualities." In the Thesis, v. 2, p. 19, Hunt is given credit for the articles arousing interest among Emporians in the Normal School, but most of them were written and signed by C. G. Morse.

[73]*The Emporia News*, February 11, 1865. See p. vi of Appendix for facsimile of the advertisement.

[74]H.D. McCarty, editor (Leavenworth, February 1865), pp. 47-49.

[75]*History of the State Normal School*, "The Original Eighteen" by Mrs. George Plumb (Ellen M. Cowles), p. 92.

[76]"Early Days" Parts IV and V, *Emporia Gazette*, June 13 and 14, 1927.

[77]See Appendix, p. xii. The *Kansas Educational Journal*, March 1865 (Leavenworth), H.D. McCarty, editor, p. 67; also *The Laws of the State of Kansas, 1865*, Topeka, Kansas: S.D. MacDonald & Co., printers to the State, 1865, p.127.

There is no reference to the above appropriation bill in either the Fish and Kayser thesis or the 1889 *History* except that in the latter work in a Table of Receipts on page 143 there is a figure of $3,000 which presumably represents the sum of the 1864 and the 1865 appropriations. Kellogg mentioned the 1865 act in his dedicatory address of January 2, 1867, when he reviewed the brief history of the school: "A further appropriation of $2,000 was added to the $1,000 already in the hands of the Board."

Half a century later in his memoirs, he wrote thus of the appropriations act: Mr. Eskridge and Mr. Stotler both assured Mr. Morse that if the Normal School could get into actual operation by February 15, the date then agreed upon for the opening of the school, they could get through a small appropriation for salaries. The appropriation actually made was $3,000 (sic). (*The Emporia Gazette*, "Early Days," Part VI, June 15, 1927).

[78]*Ibid.*, Part VI, June 15,1927.

[79]*Ibid.* , June 10, 1927, Part II; June 16, 1927, Part VII. In the latter issue, Kellogg mistakenly remembered February 15, 1865, as a Monday. It was, however, a Wednesday.

[80]*The Emporia News*, January 12, 1867. Kellogg's address was published in full on page 1. See also *The Kansas Educational Journal*, May, 1867 (P. McVicar, editor), pp. 1-5, for extracts from the same address, including the paragraph describing the first day. Under the title "Kansas Normal School,", the article also contained parts of the address by President Horner of Baker University, delivered at the dedication of the Normal, all of which gave an imposing account of the fledgling institution.

The authors of the 1889 *History of the State Normal School of Kansas*, pp.14-45, cited Kellogg's 1870 report as their source for the description of the first day of school. They must have been acquainted, however, with Kellogg's "Dedicatory Address," for they added the anecdote about the Indian visiting the school—a detail that is not mentioned in either *The Educational Journal* or the 1870 report. Insofar as their writer can determine, the Indian episode was mentioned by Kellogg only in the 1867 address and fifty years later in his series of recollection. See *The Emporia Gazette*, June 16, 1927, Part VII.

Another detail missing from early accounts except Kellogg's 1867 dedicatory speech and his later memoirs (*The Emporia Gazette*, June 13, 1927, Part IV) is the color of the county treasurer's chair, borrowed for the use of the teacher. In both accounts, Kellogg said that the chair was painted yellow. In all probability, Kellogg, himself, eliminated that detail in most subsequent reports; and others, likewise, considered it too trivial to mention. Also see *Biennial Directory of the City of Emporia* (Topeka, Kansas State Record Book and Job Printing House, 1870), p.193. Kellogg, who wrote the article about the Normal School, described the yellow chair but ignored the Indian visitor.

Although it is general knowledge among those familiar with the early history of Emporia State University that the borrowed settees were from the Congregational Church, Kellogg did not reveal the fact in any of his early public documents. Not until his recollections or memoirs were printed was there any known record of Kellogg having identified the "neighboring church" as the Congregational. (*The Emporia Gazette*, Part VII, June 16, 1927.) The only reference to the specific church that this writer has found in early day records is in the 1889 *History of the State Normal School* in the account of "The Original Eighteen" by Mrs. Plumb. On page 91, she refers to "the upper room of the old Constitution Street school-house, at that time the pride and boast of Emporia, seated with the settees borrowed from the First Congregational Church..."

In the same discourse, page 92, Mrs. Plumb remembered the bare glass windows:

> ...windows, through which the Kansas sunshine poured in
> blinding quantities, so that even the strongest eyes quailed
> before it, forcing us to adjourn until we could make, and hang
> some curtains. Blue Holland they were, made by the girls, hung
> by the boys, and superintended by the principal himself.

The Emporia News, February 18, 1865, contained the cryptic note that the next Sabbath services of the Congregational Church were to be held in the Normal Schoolroom. There also was a brief mention of high water from the storms having stalled all mail, resulting in a lack of late news for the paper. Presumably, when the waters receded allowing travel once again, the Normal School furniture was delivered. At any rate, in the March 4 issue of the paper, Editor Hunt stated that the Normal School which now numbered about thirty students had "all the paraphernalia for the comfort and convenience of the student..."

One perplexing error in recent years has resulted from either the misreading of Kellogg's description or from an error in calculation. In the Thesis, Vol. I, Chapter II, p.14, the narrative concerns the historic first day. The writers, however, state that there were fifteen pupils on the first day in Lexington, Mass., and seventeen at the Illinois Normal. The correct numbers, of course, are three and nineteen respectively. The authors' source, the 1870 five-year report, is accurate. See Thesis, Vol. II, p.21.

[81]February 18, 1865.

[82]*Kansas State Normal School Reports of Regents, 1865-1912*, (Normaliana Collection, W.A. White Library, Emporia State University), "Report of the Principal of the Kansas State Normal School to the Board of Directors, for the Year 1865," pp.1-3.

Note: In his recollections, Kellogg mistakenly included Mary Jane Watson and Ellen Plumb among the first day students. (*The Emporia Gazette*, June 17, 1927, Part VIII). Just when they enrolled cannot be pinpointed, but since they participated as students in a Teachers' Institute at the Normal School early in May, 1865, they must have matriculated sometime before then. (*The Emporia News*, May 13 and 20, 1865.)

Miss Watson appeared on the program of an educational meeting in the Methodist Church, March 25, 1865, at which Principal Kellogg lectured on Normal Schools. Miss Watson and Bettie Maddock, both of whom are listed as students in Kellogg's 1865 Report, presented readings from Tennyson and Longfellow. It seems reasonable to assume that they were students prior to this particular meeting. (*Ibid.*, March 25 and April 1, 1865.)

[83]*The Emporia News*, March 11 and April 1, 1865.

[84]*Ibid.*, March 4, 1865.

[85]*Ibid.*, April 1, 1865.

[86]*Ibid.*, April 8 and 15, May 13 and 20, 1865.

[87]*Ibid.*, May 20, 1865.

[88]*Ibid.*

[89]*Ibid.*, June 17 and 24, 185.

[90]July 8, 1865.

[91]*Ibid.*, "Note Along the Way," July 1, 1865.

[92]*Ibid.*, July 15, 1865.

[93]*Ibid.*, March 18, 1865. Rankin, however, did not attend the June meetings.

[94]Minutes of the Board of Directors, Kansas State Normal School, Nomaliana Collection (Vault) , W.A. White Library, Emporia State University.

[95]*The Emporia News*, July 22, 1865, and "Report of the Principal of the Kansas State Normal School to the Board of Directors, 1865," pp. 2-3. Lavina Fawcett was destined to be the first "Normalite" to die while still a student. On December 3, she died at her home near Emporia. A student resolution of sympathy was published in the December 9, 1865 issue of *The Emporia News*.

[96]*The Emporia News*, July 22 and August 12, 1865. See also *A History of the State Normal School of Kansas for the First Twenty-Five Years, 1889*, p. 91, for Ellen Cowles Plumb's account of that trip. On page 16 of "General Sketch" in the same *History*, the author mistakenly located the 1865 summer meeting at Leavenworth, probably because the association president was from Leavenworth. On the same page, the author alludes to a newspaper account that has not been identified. It is not from *The Emporia News*.

[97]*The Emporia News*, August 12, 1865. The rather detailed account of the meeting consisted of extracts of a news story from the *Atchison Daily Champion*. According to the account, Morse on behalf of the Normal introduced the following resolution:

> That recognizing the importance of a special preparation for the most successful labors of the teacher, we recommend our State Normal School to the attention and confidence of the friends of education and the fostering care of the State.

See also the *Kansas Educational Journal*, Vol. II, No. 8, August, 1865, pp. 228-246, for proceedings of the state teachers meeting.

[98]*Ibid.*, July 22, September 9 and 16, 1865. When Norton came to Emporia, either Jacob Stotler or his partner, David Gilmore, reported his arrival. When Kellogg came, the editor was Jonathan Hunt. For descriptions of Norton, see "Sketches of Faculty," pp. 50-52, *History of the State Normal School*, 1889; "Early Years," Part VIII, *The Emporia Gazette*, June 17, 1927; also Thesis, v. 1, pp. 20-21, and *Memorials of Henry Bruce Norton*, published by the State Normal School of San Jose, California, December 1885; Normaliana Collection, W.A. White Library, E.S.U.

[99]*The Emporia News*, September 9 and 16, 1865. What appears to be a typographical error is in the "Report of the Principal of the Kansas State Normal School" for 1865. Therein, the opening date of the second term is given as Wednesday, September 14, whereas Wednesday actually was on the thirteenth. (See "Calendar" in the advertisement, page viii of the appendix.)

[100]Seventy-eight students had been admitted by December.

[101]*The Emporia News*, October 14 and 21, 1865.

[102]"Report of the Principal of the Kansas State Normal School to the Board of Directors For the Year, 1865," p. 4. This report was published in pamphlet form by *The Emporia News*. On December 30, 1865, the editor apologized for his late paper, stating that the printing of Kellogg's report and other jobs which could not be postponed had delayed the paper until late Saturday. Copies of the report were mailed the following week to exchange papers, according to *The Emporia News*, January 6, 1866.

[103]See Appendix, p. iv, Secs. 8 and 9.

[104]*Ibid.*, p. iii, Secs. 5 and 6; also "Admission," and "Expenses," p. vi. Tuition for non-teachers would have amounted to $9.50 for the 19 weeks' term. Board of Directors' minutes, February 27, 1865.

[105]*Ibid.*, "Admission," p. viii, and Minutes, June 27, 1865. See also Report of the Principal for 1865, p. 4. The required declaration of the students' intent to teach probably was not a specific pledge at the outset, but rather developed into such sometime prior to the beginning of the second term. At any rate, not until September 9 did the word "pledge" appear. The earliest copy of the pledge found thus far is that included in Kellogg's 1865 report.

[106]*Ibid.*

[107]*The Emporia News*, December 23, 1865. Although much of the lengthy discourse sounds as if it had been written by G.C. Morse, there is no signature nor initial to identify the article as there had been in Morse's early writings. It presumably was written by either Stotler or Gilmore, both of whom had apparently attended the closing exercises and written a resume of the examinations. This particular newspaper article was deemed so important to Kellogg that he appended it to his 1865 official report. A handwritten note across the bottom of the last page of the report at E.S.U. (see footnote #101) reads, "Written by P.B. Plumb & published as Editorial matter in the News [Emporia]." Inasmuch as there is no indication in the article itself—nor in the newspaper— that such was the case, the above notation probably is the source of the claim made in the 1889 *History*, p. 16, that Plumb wrote a portion of the article.

[108]Report of the Principal for 1865, pp. 9-10. At the time, there was not yet a model school because of the lack of space. Nor had the boarding house, promised since the school opened, yet come into being. Each subject, important to the life of the Normal, is discussed in detail elsewhere in this narrative.

[109]*The Emporia News*, December 2 and 23, 1865. In the earlier issue, the editor mentioned a forty-acre tract adjoining town on the west which had been purchased by ten persons with a view of offering half of it as a site for the Normal.

He also said there was talk of a twenty-acre tract north of town at the head of Commercial Street—"but with little prospect of success." His personal choice was the west tract which was beyond West Street and south of Sixth Avenue, land long since owned by the Santa Fe Railroad. See the 1889 *History*, "Lands," pp. 106-108, for a more detailed account of the change of site.

[110]*The Emporia News*, January 20, 1866. See also the *State of Kansas Senate Journal, 1866*, p. 516.

[111]"Plant Funds: Investment in Plant, Land, and Buildings, June 30, 1977," a transcript from records in the office of Administrative Affairs, Normaliana Collection, W.A. White Library. Heading the list of land tracts that make up the present 207-acre campus is the Filley tract, designated as the original campus, a donation. It actually is listed as containing 19.36 acres, a little less than the prescribed twenty. For more information about Filley, see the 1889 *History*, p. 107.

[112]See the 1889 *History*, p. 108, for a full copy of the "Act to Change the Location of the State Normal School, at Emporia," approved January 15, 1866.

By June 14, 1866, when the Fick tract was deeded back to the former owners, Henry and Sarah Fick were no longer husband and wife. Henry had deserted her and moved to Arkansas, and in the autumn of 1865, Sarah obtained a divorce. (*The Emporia News*, August 12 and September 23, 1865.) Consequently, Sarah's name does not appear in the 1866 transaction.

According to Lyon County records, the transfer of the original Normal School site to its former owner was executed by John R. Swallow, state auditor, acting on the authority of Section Two of the "Act to Change the Location of the State Normal School at Emporia." Henry W. Fick of Pope County, Arkansas, paid $500 to Swallow for return of the twenty-acre tract. Swallow, on behalf of the State of Kansas, signed and affixed the state seal. Witnesses to the transaction were J.W. Thomas and A.J. Huntoon.

In all probability, the puzzle of the $500 exchange will remain forever unsolved. In spite of the fact that the 1863 law creating the Kansas State Normal specified clearly that the twenty-acre site be donated to the state, $500 nevertheless was paid in 1863 to Mr. and Mrs. Fick for the land. (See footnote #47.) Nearly three years later, Fick, in order to reclaim his land, paid back the same amount. Commissioners Fick and Crandall in their report to Governor Carney in August, 1863, had declared that the chosen site was a donation to the state. (See *Public Documents*, 1863, Chapter VII, "The State Normal School," pp. 3-4.)

No record at either the county or state level has been found of any appropriated money being used for the transaction. The only likely explanation seems to be that local enthusiasts for the Normal School paid the sum of $500 to

Fick for his tract in order to donate it to the state for the school, and that they likewise were reimbursed when Fick bought back the acreage.

[113]*The Emporia News*, January 13, 20, and 27; February 10 and 17, 1866. See also *Senate Journal*, 1866, pp. 240-241. Senator Eskridge saw the appropriation bill through the senate. Rules were suspended and a vote taken on February 6. The bill passed 24-0. Known as "An Act to Aid the State Normal School," it was signed by Governor Crawford on February 7 and became law upon its publication in the *Leavenworth Daily Conservative*. It subsequently was published in *The Emporia News*, February 17, 1866, and appears herein, appendix, p. xi. Section three is particularly interesting in its stipulation that the appropriation for the building be considered a loan to be repaid to the state whenever the endowment lands produced sufficient income.

[114]Minutes of the Board of Directors, February 8, 1866. Kellogg in his 1867 Dedicatory Address referred to Lescher as a Lawrence architect. (*The Emporia News*, January 12, 1867.)

[115]*The Emporia News*, April 21, 1866. Hammond personally did the carpentry work and was contractor for the whole job. Howe and Griffith did the stonework and the Messrs. Love of Lawrence the plastering. (*The Emporia News*, January 5, 1867.)

[116]Minutes of the Board of Directors, January 10, 1867 and *The Emporia News*, January 12, 1867. (The executive committee report was signed on January 7, 1867.) For brief progress reports regarding construction of the Normal School building, see *The Emporia News*, June 23, July 7, August 4 and 18, and October 6, 1866. See also the 1889 *History*, pp. 109-111; Thesis, v. 1, p. 26, and v. 2, pp. 40-41; and *The Emporia News*, January 5, 1867.

[117]The Board of Visitors in 1866 included the Reverend H.D. Fisher, Judge Andrew Akin, and S.S. Prouty, all appointed in accordance with the law. Akin and Prouty visited the Normal on December 5. Presumably Fisher had visited at some earlier time. Their report to State Superintendent Goodnow to become a part of his annual report. (*The Emporia News*, December 8, 1866.)

The visitors' report was very favorable towards the Normal School, and it is significant that they recommended to the legislature a sufficient appropriation to the Normal School to finish the building, fence and embellish the grounds, provide furniture and apparatus, reference books, a cabinet organ, and support for the faculty.

[118]*The Emporia News*, December 15, 1866.

[119]*Ibid.*, October 14 and December 9, 1865. First officers of the Society were James Hurst, president; Addie Roe, vice-president; William Price, secretary; Coke Watson, treasurer; Kellogg, Mary Jane Watson, and Ella Spencer, executive committee.

[120]*Ibid.*, February 24, March 3, 10, 17, and 24, 1866. Much of the success of the Literary Union's first money making project can be attributed to the publicity provided by *The Emporia News*. Stotler, who on March 20 again became sole owner of the *News* after buying David Gilmore's interest, remained enthusiastic about the program after the event, stating that it had been up to the anticipations of the audience and that such an occasion was good for performers and the community.

Kellogg's enthusiasm also flavored the newspaper publicity. Above his signature appeared the following declaration: "The Society will be obliged to all friends who pay for more tickets than they take." (March 17, 1866.) Tickets were fifty cents and net receipts, $150.

[121]*Ibid.*, March 31 and May 12, 1866. The poem was published in the March 31 issue, a typewritten transcript of which is deposited in the Normaliana Collection at the William Allen White Library. Stotler announced on May 12 that the *Prairie Beacon and Valley Blade* of Paris, Illinois, had copied the poem.

[122]*The Emporia News*, May 26, 1866.

[123]*Ibid.*, June 23, 1866. After the examinations, State Superintendent Goodnow was on hand to address the students about some of the causes for teacher failures. A timely debate on reconstruction in addition to music was the Normal Literary Union's entertainment. Only the singing failed to be up to par, probably, according to the review, because of the illness of the leading singers and the general exhaustion of the students. The closing event was a student reception referred to by the editor as "a crowded Sociable."

The second Anniversary Address, "What Shall We Teach?" by H.B. Norton was deemed worthy enough for publication by the school's Board of Directors; consequently, the full text appeared on page one of *The Emporia News*, July 21, 1866. The Reverend G.C. Morse wrote an enthusiastic review of the second anniversary address for *The Leavenworth Daily Conservative* which was gratefully printed even though it was longer than desired. (*The Emporia News*, July 7, 1866.)

Note: Discrepancies regarding the second anniversary speaker appear in *The History of the State Normal School of Kansas for the First Twenty-Five Years*, 1889. In a graph on page 144, I.T. Goodnow is listed as anniversary speaker for 1866 instead of Norton. On Page 17, the narrative lists both men as speakers. By the same token, the graph omits the 1865 speaker entirely, but on page 15, the narrative correctly names Judge Brewer as the first anniversary speaker in 1865.

These inconsistencies occurred, apparently, because different persons (according to the preface) were responsible for certain portions of the book.

[124]*The Emporia News*, June 23, 1866.

[125]*Ibid.*, December 15, 1866, p. 1. (The Principal's Report.)

[126]*Ibid.*, July 14, 1866. Norton's paper "What Shall We Teach" was published in two installments in the September and November issues of 1866. Peter McVicar of Topeka was editor of the magazine. He also was the teachers' union nominee for state superintendent, the candidate to be selected at the state Republican convention, September 5. He subsequently succeeded Goodnow in that position.

[127]*Ibid.*

[128]*Ibid.*, August 4, September 1 and 8, 1866.

[129]*Ibid.*, August 18, September 1, 8, and 22, 1866.

[130]*Ibid.*, June 24, 1865. The first public organizational meeting was scheduled for 2:00 p.m., in the county clerk's office, Saturday, June 24.

[131]*Ibid.*, July 8, 1865.

[132]*Ibid.*, July 29, 1865. Temporary trustees were John Hammond, C.V. Eskridge, G.C. Morse, G.D. Humphrey, and L.D. Bailey. Selected to draw up articles of corporation were R.M. Ruggles, T. McIntire, and J.C. Fraker; to draw up rules or by-laws were Eskridge, Morse, and Edward Borton. The committee to solicit stockholders included Morse; W.A. Ela of Burlington; J.R. Swallow, Topeka; Bailey, Clint; Jesse Carter and R. Howe, Lyon County. Among the initial 48 stockholders were many from elsewhere in the state.

[133]*Ibid.*, August 12, 1865. Permanent officers for the first year were G.D. Humphrey, president; Jacob Stotler, secretary; R.B. Hurst, treasurer; G.C. Morse, C.A. Britton, John Hammond, and W.T. Soden, directors. The location of the building lot was not settled at the August 8 meeting, and an August 22 meeting was called for that express purpose.

[134]*Ibid.*, August 26, 1865. The adopted building plan was that of a three story 38' X 60' structure with a 19' X 24' ell of a story and a half.
   In the 1865 Board of Visitors' report, Judge Bailey stated that "some six to eight thousand dollars have been raised for that object [a boarding house large enough to accommodate 100 students], the greater portion being contributed by the citizens of Lyon County, but very liberal amounts by leading friends of

education in different sections of the State." (From extracts published in *The Emporia News*, March 17, 1866, p. l.)

[135]*Ibid.*, October 14, 1865.

[136]*Ibid.*, December 9 and 16, 1865, and January 20, 1866. The stonework went to the lowest bidder. Hammond was the only one to bid on carpentry, but his bid was accepted because it was considered to be a reasonable figure. (It is interesting that Kellogg in his 1865 Principal's report which was written prior to the letting of bids gave the probable cost of the boarding house as $12,000.)

[137]*Ibid.*, February 3, 10, 17, 1866. A comparison of the seventeen signatures with the earlier list of the first 48 stockholders indicates that all but four of the signers were charter members of the organization, most of whom owned a single share of stock. Perhaps the most significant name among them was that R.B. Hurst, treasurer of the company.

[138]*Ibid.*, February 23 and March 24, 1866.

[139]*Ibid.*, April 28, May 5 and 26, 1866. The citizens' meeting was to have been in the Congregational Church on the night of April 30. It was rescheduled for May 1. The stockholders' meeting for the purpose of adopting a plan for the contemplated building was scheduled for the afternoon of May 7.
   An error appears in what is otherwise an accurate summary of the boarding house venture in the 1889 *History of the State Normal School of Kansas*, pp. 121-122. J.N. Wilkinson, who according to the preface compiled the information, wrote that "It is said of a meeting of stockholders called April 28, 1866 that 'the crowd consisted of four men and a boy, and the meeting adjourned without transacting any business.'" Not only did Wilkinson take the liberty of altering the quotation, but he mistakenly assumed that the meeting in question was that of the stockholders. Apparently, he was unaware that in the April 28 newspaper two notices of meetings appeared. One was the stockholders' meeting for May 7 in the afternoon; the other was a called meeting of Emporia's citizens for the night of April 30. The above quotation (in part) appeared in the May 5 newspaper before the stockholders had met.

[140]*Ibid.*, June 2, 1866.

[141]*Ibid.*, August 18 and November 24, 1866. Although ground had been broken on May 31, 1866, it was 1869 before the location was mentioned in newspaper accounts or any known official reports, and by then it had become a hotel. The project was on the southwest corner of Sixth Avenue and Merchant Street where the Kansas Power and Electric building now stands. (*Ibid.*, January 1, 1869.) Lyon County records show that on May 13, 1867, a deed to that property was

registered in the name of the State Normal School Boarding House Association. Although that was the first deed to that particular lot, the boarding house apparently was not the first structure to be built on the site. In the first city directory can be found the following information:

> The first house erected exclusively for a private residence was built (literally) by E.P. Bancroft, on the corner now occupied by the Roninson House [L.N. Robinson purchased Hunt's hotel in 1869] and may still be seen by the curious, occupied as a stable, on the same street a block further south. (*Biennial Directory of the City of Emporia, 1870.*)

[142]*Ibid.*, November 24 and December 1, 1866. Six months before Hunt actually expanded (*Ibid.*, June 21, 1867) the Emporia House operated by J.J. Campbell became Emporia's new hotel. (*Ibid.*, January 5, 1867).

[143]*Ibid.*, December 8 and 15, 1866. Visitors appointed for 1866 were the Reverend H.D. Fisher, Judge Andrew Akin, and S.S. Prouty. The latter two men visited the Normal on December 5. Their official report to the state superintendent was included in his annual report and was also published in the December 15 issue of *The Emporia News*. Kellogg's report may be found there also.

[144]*Ibid.*, July 26, 1867. For other progress reports on the boarding house, see issue for February 15, April 26, and October 18, 1867. In late April, the building was apparently progressing, for in a news story about a Kansas earthquake, the local editor stated the "Workmen on the Normal School Boarding House ran down their ladders."

[145]*Ibid.*, August 23, September 20, and November 8, 1867.

[146]*Ibid.*, May 15, 1868.

[147]*Ibid.*, May 29 and June 12, 1868. According to the Lyon County Register of Deeds records, Jonathan Hung filed a deed on June 22, 1868, to the property at Sixth and Merchant, and on the same date, the Normal School Boarding House Association filed a deed to lots 93 and 95 on Exchange Street, between Sixth and Seventh Avenues on the west side of the street.

[148]*Ibid.*, April 17, May 1, and June 12, 1868. According to the Emporia Director, 1870, John Wood, a carpenter, lived in a boarding house at 125 Commercial Street.

Morse left in the middle of his second year as county superintendent of schools. What prompted him to leave Emporia where he had worked diligently and successfully for his church and for public education over a span of ten years or more is not of public record. If he had any problem with his church congregation, his last Sunday in the pulpit did not reflect it. According to the news editor, there were eight or ten admissions to the Congregational Church that Sunday [April 12]. The editor, probably Stotler, paid tribute to Morse's contribution to the Normal.

> For its efficient organization and good accomplishments, our State Normal School owes as much if not more to him than to any other man. We are glad he'll retain his position on the Normal School's Board of Directors. (April 17, 1868.)

Morse also retained his farm southeast of Emporia (off East Logan Avenue) where the family continued to live.

[149]August 21, 1868.

[150]*The Emporia News*, January 1, 1869. Whether the Normal's first boarding house actually was coeducational is not clear. The original proposal in June of 1865 had been to erect a ladies boarding house, but thereafter no reference to gender was made in connection with the project. That well may have been because during the initial term most of the students were women whereas by 1868 the enrollment of men and women was nearly equal (78 females and 75 males). The announcement of the opening of the spring term of 1869 revealed that rooms for ladies were still available at the boarding house. (*Ibid.*, April 2, 1869.)

[151]*Ibid.*, February 15, 1867; April 8 and June 17, 1870.

[152]*Ibid.*, January 1 and September 17, 1869. See also the issue for October 22, 1869. Stotler announced that a new first class boarding house [public] would be opened immediately at Sixth and Mechanic. E.B. Peyton had sold his large stone residence at that address to a newcomer named Daniel Knox who would operate the establishment. According to Stotler, boarding places had been scarce since spring.

[153]*Ibid.*, December 3, 1869, page 1. Kellogg's proposal, which was never implemented, marks the first instance of a request for state owned or subsidized house at the Kansas State Normal School. More than fifty years were to elapse before the State provided housing.

[154]*Ibid.*

[155] *Ibid.*, April 15, 1870.

[156]*Ibid.*, December 10 and 24, 1869; June 3, 1870. Stotler's latest partner in *The Emporia News* was W.W. Williams, a graduate of Hillsdale College in Michigan, recently of Marshaltown, Iowa, where he had charge of a seminary. According to

Stotler, the job had become too big for one man to handle and he had sold one-half interest to Williams. (December 10, 1869.)

Regarding ownership of the Normal boarding house, none of the early records hint of wrongdoing on the part of John Wood. Both the 1889 *History* and the Fish and Kayser Thesis treat the matter without a hint of anything unscrupulous having occurred. But in *The Alumni News* of the Kansas State Teachers College, Emporia, October 1962 (the hundredth anniversary issue), p. 23, appears the statement that "the plan to use the hotel as student housing was stymied by some unscrupulous business tactics." To date, the source for such an allegation has not been found.

Lyon County records in the Register of Deeds office show that the property remained in the name of the boarding house association until John Wood sold the property to a private party. On February 26, 1866, Wood provided the buyer with two deeds. One was from the Normal School Boarding House Association signed by himself, John Wood, as president. (For seventeen years he presumably had been the sole member of the association.) The other deed was signed by himself as a private homeowner. The Emporia City Directory for 1877 listed John Wood as living in a residence between Sixth and Seventh on Exchange Street and conducting his business as carpenter and joiner between Fourth and Fifth on Commercial Street.

In order to have clear title to the property, Wood had appeared before the Lyon County probate judge to explain how he had acquired the property. The affidavit, filed for the record on August 15, 1882, had been subscribed and sworn to three days earlier. Lending credence to the affidavit is the interesting fact that the probate judge had been one of the directors with Wood at the time Wood bought up the stock. His name was L.B. Kellogg. The affidavit of John Wood is copied here in full.

> John Wood being duly sworn on oath says that he is the owner and ever since July 22, 1868 has been the owner and in the actual, open, notorious and exclusive possession of Lots 93 and 95 Exchange Street in the city of Emporia, Lyon County, Kansas. That his said ownership and title to said real estate was derived and resulted from the facts therein stated, to wit:
>
> On or about May 1, 1867, Jonas Maurer, Joseph Moon, E.R. Holderman, Jessie Carter, this affiant Wood and 88 other citizens of Kansas associated themselves together as a joint stock company under the name and style of the State Normal School Boarding House Association. And as such association and in the said name, acquired by purchase from one Jonathan Hunt and wife the said real estate on or about June 22, 1868, receiving from said Hunt and wife a Warranty Deed therefor which was on said 22nd day of June 1868 duly filed for record and recorded in Book K. of Deeds in the office of the Register of Deeds of Lyon County, Kansas, at page 47.

Thereafter and during the summer and fall of 1868 this affiant Wood purchased from his co-associates and members of the said Normal School Boarding House Association each and every certificate of stock issued by said Normal School Boarding House Association and all the right title and interest of each and every of his co-associates and members of said association in and to all the property of said association, and now has in his possession all of the said certificates of stock duly assigned and delivered to him. And thereby this affiant Wood became and is now the sole and only member of said Normal School Boarding House Association and as such sole and only member of said association is the sole and only owner of said Lots 93 and 95 Exchange Street. House Association were fully paid and discharged for during the year 1868, by this affiant and his co-associates and members of said association.

(signed) John Wood
Subscribed and sworn to before me this 12th day of August A.D. 1882.
(signed) L. B. Kellogg, Probate Judge
(Misc. Records, Vol. 13, p. 507; Lyon county Register of Deeds Office.)

[157]*The Emporia News*, October 6, 1866. The Board of Visitors reported seventy-five students in attendance. (See Footnote #142.)

[158]*Ibid.*, September 8, December 1 and 15, 1866. The actual wedding of Abbie Homer and L.B. Kellogg was a surprise event, but the ever vigilant Stotler had intended to forewarn his readers of the possibility only to be foiled in his attempt. After the wedding, Stotler wrote:

Prof. Kellogg cut us out of an item handsomely. We had the following in type intending to take folks by surprise when lo! the Prof. surprised us by coming in ahead of time: '. . . that there is to be a consolidation of a portion of the Normal School faculty Christmas Eve. Who knows?' That's what we call cheating the printer. (December 22, 1866 issues.)

[159]*Ibid.*, December 22, 1866. Abbie Homer Kellogg taught for at least one term in 1867, probably until pregnancy prompted her retirement. (Their first son Vernon was born in December, 1867.) According to the January 10, 1867 Minutes of the Board of Directors, "Necessity requiring it [that is, the growth of the school], your committee appointed Miss A.G. Homer (now Mrs. Kellogg) of Westfield, Mass., Normal School as an assistant teacher." According to the Minutes of June 28, the Board authorized the executive committee to hire two new teachers; one to head the projected model school and the other, an assistant teacher presumably to replace Mrs. Kellogg. If there was any question about the propriety of husband

and wife teaching together, no evidence to that effect has come to light. Nepotism, apparently, was not yet an issue.

Nowhere has a description of the romance been found except in Kellogg's memoirs. Fifty years later, Kellogg referred to the marriage as the most important thing that happened to him while he was teaching at the Normal School. According to the memoirs, Miss Homer had left her home in Massachusetts to teach school in Stillman Valley, Illinois, which happened to be the home district of Henry B. Norton. Later, upon the recommendation of Norton and Judge L.D. Bailey who had known her family in Massachusetts, Miss Homer came to Kansas to teach school. She was teaching at the Rinker Ford schoolhouse and boarding with the David Plumb family when Kellogg first met her. He was rooming at the Norton home where Miss Homer often visited on the weekends. ("Early Days at the Emporia Normal," Part IX, *The Emporia Gazette*, June 18, 1927. See also Footnote #42.) The marriage was a brief one, for Mrs. Kellogg died on May 15, 1873 of tuberculosis. (1889 *History of the State ormal School*, p. 38.)

[160]*The Emporia News*, January 5 and 12, 1867. According to the Minutes of the Board of Directors, January 10, 1867, there soon were eighty-two students.

[161]*Ibid.*, January 5, 1867.

Although not a school-affiliated organization, the Silver Cornet Band participated in so many of the early school-sponsored events (beginning with the Kellogg wedding) that a brief look into its origin is in order.

Organized in July or August, 1866, the band consisted of twelve Emporians* who by subscription or other means managed to raise enough money to order second hand silver instruments, used only four months and "as good as new." Although the sum raised was insufficient to purchase the instruments outright, members borrowed the balance, primarily from themselves, using the instruments as collateral. After six weeks of practice, the band serenaded the editor of *The Emporia News*, who liked what he heard according to his news item "The First Call."

Shortly afterwards, the band hired M.J. Stimson of Ottawa for a period of three months to teach and direct them. By November, they were planning their first "grand concert" to pay off their debt. The concert, played in the Methodist Church on a Saturday night (November 24), was attended by nearly three hundred persons. [Emporia's population at the time was scarcely more than six hundred.] Net receipts were $121.50, barely enough to pay half their indebtedness; thus a second benefit was played in mid-January.

M.J. Stimson, a baritone singer as well as an instrumental specialist, was retained for a second three-months period. While in Emporia, he gave private lessons in voice and instrumental music, formed a children's singing class, and taught for at least one term at the Normal School. (*Ibid.*, August 18, September 22, October 20 and 27, November 3 and 17, December 1 and 22, 1866; and January 19, 1867.)

*The twelve band members were George Wait, J.C. Hall, A.R. Bancroft, Thomas Mantor, Max Fawcett, J.R. Hall, E.R. Trask, Samuel Hall, H.V. Bundrem, John Bay, J.T. Pierson, and H.C. Clark.

[162]*Ibid.*, January 19, 1867.

[163]February 2, 1867.

[164]Minutes of the Board of Directors, January 10, 1867. That meeting which took place in Topeka was attended by five of the nine members. They were Governor S.J. Crawford, C.V. Eskridge, William Spriggs, James Rogers, and G.C. Morse. The executive committee (Eskridge, Morse, and Rogers) originally had recommended $2,000 for fencing, making a total of $15,000; but the board reduced the fencing item by half, reducing the total to $14,000.

The Emporia News, January 12, 1867, published the executive committee's full report in which an appropriation of $15,000 was recommended. The subsequent board action was not included, however, causing Stotler to err when, in the same issue, he addressed himself to the legislators urging them to care for the needs of the school and revealing that there would be a request for a $15,000 appropriation during the current session.

[165]*The Emporia News*, February 2, 15, and 22, 1867. In the first issue, Stotler stated that the prospects for a Normal School appropriation were "very flattering." His optimism was mainly hinged to Kellogg's January 29th lecture before the legislature regarding the education of teachers. In the latter issue, Stotler credited the appropriation to the Emporia area legislators who had urged the bill's passage. From the district were Senator Perry B. Maxson and Representatives Preston Plumb, James Jaquith, and G.R. Harper.

NOTE: In the February 22 issue, Stotler made an editorial error by stating that the senate had passed the $14,500 appropriation bill for the Normal. Elsewhere in the same issue, however, he corrects himself, declaring that the amount was $14,000 according to the law as passed. A copy of the appropriation bill in full appears in the 1889 *History*, p. 111.

[166]*Ibid.*, May 24 and 31, 1867. Eskridge and Morse planned the landscaping. Norton was superintendent of construction, and John Hammond installed the fencing.

[167]*Ibid.*, March 29, May 24 and 31, and July 5, 1867. Apparently, the Normal Literary Union program was not presented as initially advertised, but rather in two segments. On May 24, the main feature of the N.L.U. program was a debate as to whether women possessed superior governing qualities, the negative taken by a team of three men and the affirmative by three women. The latter won.

On the evening of June 27, the N.L.U.'s Penetralia Exhibition was a part of the commencement festivities. According to the local paper, the audience room of the Normal was crowded to "utmost capacity" to hear the lengthy program. What is not clear is whether admission was charged for either of the above programs. No mention of an admission fee or receipts taken in was made in connection with either program.

The original program, planned to end the winter term, had been given much advance publicity in *The Emporia News* beginning with a February 8 notice to "Get the 50 cent pieces ready." There was to have been choral and quartet singing directed by Prof. Norton; a ten-member cast presenting "The Taming of the Shrew" with Prof. Kellogg directing and playing the part of Petruchio; a series of tableaux prepared by Mrs. Kellogg and students; and another socio-political poem "Into the Promised Land" by Norton (*Ibid.*, March 8, 15, and 22, 1867.). As finally presented at the end of June, the program included the chorus and quartet, the latter consisting of both Prof. and Mrs. Norton, Miss Alice Norton, and Prof. Kellogg. Extracts from "Taming of the Shrew" were presented and a poem, "Southward Ho!" was read by the author, Norton. Whether the title had been changed or an entirely new poem written is not known. (The above poem appears in full on page 13 of *Memorials of Henry Brace Norton*.) No mention of Tableaux appeared in the July 5 review, and it is doubtful if any were presented. By this time, Mrs. Kellogg apparently had ceased teaching, Miss Ellen M. Cowles (Mrs. George Plumb) finishing the term for her ("The Original Eighteen," p. 93, 1889 *History*).

[168]*Ibid.*, March 8, 1867. Kellogg requested that "State Papers Please copy."

[169]*Ibid.*, April 19, May 10, and December 6, 1867. According to the latter issue, Elder Solomon Brown was league president. Brown established the Christian Church in Emporia in 1857.

[170]*Ibid.*, October 25, 1867. Construction of the sidewalk was to be done by J.C. Fraker.

[171]*Ibid.*, April, 19 and 26, 1867. According to the latter issue, the April 24 earthquake was recorded in the Lawrence and Leavenworth papers, their accounts being similar to those experienced locally. See footnote #143 for the reaction of construction workers to the quake.

[172]*The Emporia News*, July 5, 1867; 1889 *History*, pp. 53 and 56. Ellen Plumb, daughter of David Plumb and sister of Preston B. and George Plumb, had attended school in Marysville, Ohio, prior to moving to Emporia. Upon her graduation from the Kansas State Normal, she taught in Leavenworth briefly before returning to teach from 1868-1870 in the newly instituted Model School

and K.S.N. She abandoned teaching to open a bookstore in Emporia, a business venture that proved successful for her. She died in 1913.

Mary Jane Watson, daughter of Judge John H. Watson of Emporia, had taught school in Ohio prior to coming to Emporia. She opened the town's first school on October 14, 1858. After graduating from the Normal, Miss Watson taught language and history there for three years before moving to the city schools where she taught another twelve years. She operated a boarding house on North Mechanic Street until 1888 when she married Dr. Short of Trenton, Missouri. She subsequently moved to that city but after her husband's death she returned to Emporia where she died in 1908.

According to the "Old Timer's Column" of *The Emporia Gazette"* April 8, 1927, a memorial to the first graduates was established by their nieces in the Memorial Union soon after the first phase of the building was constructed. Dedicated as the Plumb-Watson Memorial Room, but commonly called the Pioneer Room, it was a second floor reception room "just off the hall to the south with a view of campus and other buildings." The room, furnished in the style of the 1860s, contained the framed diplomas of the two women, and a portrait of them in their graduation dresses. A picture of Emporia in 1859 and another of Miss Watson's boarded in front of her home (about 1880) also hung in the room.

Apparently, this well-intentioned Memorial was short lived, for by 1930 the room no longer existed. By then, the second phase of the Union Building had been finished and the second floor rooms originally built for visiting alumni, had become permanent living quarters for some of the single faculty women. The diplomas, no longer in the frames, and the portrait are in the Normaliana Collection at the Wm. A. White Library. Other furnishings were reclaimed by family members.

[173] *The Emporia News,* July 5, 1867.

[174]*Ibid.*

[175]*Ibid.* p. 2. For a newspaper that seldom devoted much space to headlines, this feature story carried an impressive four line head which read
Kansas Normal School
Closing of the 7th Term
Commencement Exercises
The First Graduating Class
[176]*Ibid.,* July 5, 1867; "General Sketch," P. 19, 1889 *History.* The Reverend S. E. Mac Burney offered the opening prayer. Ellen Plumb spoke on "Success in Life," and Mary Jane Watson on "The Christian Statesman." The commencement invitation which, according to the June 28 issue of *The Emporia News* was extended by the Executive committee of the Board of Directors and printed by *The Emporia News* to be circulated statewide. The invitation has been re-printed in full in the 1889 History and in the Thesis, v. 1, p. 27.

[177]*The Emporia News*, July 12, 1868. H. B. Norton wrote the Emporia editor that Kellogg read a paper on the metric system and reported on the status of the Normal School. (The former was subsequently published in the *Kansas Education Journal,* December – January, 1868, p. 186-88). Miss Watson read an essay and a student, Alice Norton, sang a solo. [Miss Norton was no relation to H. B. Norton.] In the same issue of *The Emporia News* appeared in reprint from the *Leavenworth Conservative* stating that if the Normal continued its rate of improvement it soon would be second to none in the nation.

The Board of Directors were the ones responsible for bringing the 1868 Teacher convention to Emporia. At their annual meeting in June, they had agreed to invite the state teachers to hold their next annual get together in Emporia "in connection with the anniversary exercises of the Normal School." (Minutes, June 28, 1867).

[178]*The Emporia News*, October 4, 1867. In the September 6 issue, Stotler had announced that he was beginning to set up the October issue of the *Kansas Educational Journal,* having contracted to print it for one year. He described his new type and recommended that local businesses advertise in the magazine and that citizens subscribe to it. On September 27, Stotler apologized for a mere "half sheet" of news, caused by illness of an employee and a rush of job work. By the following week, however, the journal was ready. Kellogg and Norton's first journal was the September issue although it came out in early October. The 1889 *History*, p. 60, states that the two became editors in May, 1867. Actually, however, they were not named editors until July.

[179]Although there is no mention of the Teachers' Institute in the June 28 Minutes of the Board of Directors, the official announcement in the August 2 issue of *The Emporia News* states the following:

> The Board of Directors at the annual meeting (June 28)
> 'Resolved, That the Faculty of the Normal School be requested
> to join with the State and County Superintendents of Public
> Instruction in the conduct of a State Normal Training Institute at
> Emporia during the first week of the next school year.'

A follow-up story after the event reiterated the earlier statement that the idea of the institute had originated with the Board of Directors in June and was endorsed by the State Teachers Association in July. Patterned after the Illinois Normal Institute which drew no more than a dozen members the first year but had since grown to include three hundred, the Kansas State Institute had a tenuous beginning when heavy rains on Monday, September 9, delayed the arrival of those from afar. Clearing skies, however, enabled a good-sized audience to assemble at the Methodist Church where that evening Kellogg lectured on "The Degeneracy and Regeneracy of American Politics." His prime concern was that the science of government and an analysis of the national and state constitutions be added to the examinations of every teacher and to the course of study in every school. (*The Emporia News*, September 20, 1867.)

Tuesday marked the beginning of the drill work for the institute. The schedule, made up of short lesson periods of thirty minutes each, consisted of arithmetic, reading, penmanship, and theory and art of teaching by Kellogg; geography, grammar, natural science, and singing, Norton; phonics and free gymnastics, Mrs. J.H. Gorham. (*Ibid.*)

On Tuesday evening, Norton lectured on "The Teacher of the Twentieth Century." There was a sociable on Wednesday evening, and on Thursday evening State Superintendent Peter McVicar lectured on "School Government." The institute closed at noon on Friday, September 13. (*Ibid.*)

[180]*Ibid.*, September 6 and 13, 1867. Participating in the institute were McVicar, Professors J.E. Platte of the Agricultural College and J.M. Ranking, Ottumwa; A.D. Chambers, president of Hartford Collegiate Institute; Mrs. M.E. Carpenter, Lawrence High School; superintendent of Schools E.F. Heisler, Wyandotte County; M.E. Hunt, Chase County; G.C. Morse, Lyon County; and Kellogg, Norton, and Mrs. Janette H. Gorham of the Normal School. Mrs. Gorham was new to the community, having only recently arrived from Illinois Normal University. (Note: Professor Platte was on a two weeks' leave of absence from the Agricultural College in order to attend the Normal.)

[181]*Ibid.*, September 13, 1867. After the November elections, Major Martin Anderson replaced Treasurer Spriggs. Peter McVicar had replaced Goodnow as state superintendent of public instruction a year earlier. Governor Crawford submitted all six appointments to the 1868 legislature for approval, but for some undetermined reason the senate failed to approve the reappointment of Eskridge. Subsequently, Crawford appointed Samuel A. Kingman of Atchison, chief justice of the state supreme court and president of the newly formed state historical society. The senate approved Kingman's appointment, but he apparently did not serve. In the March 13, 1868 issue of *The Emporia News* was the brief notice: "Glad to state that appointment of Judge Kingman as one of the Directors of the State Normal School has been recalled and that Mr. Eskridge retains his position on the Board." (See also the 1868 *Senate Journal*, pp. 609 and 649; Wilder, Vol. I, pp. 449 and 454.)

[182]*The Emporia News*, September 20, 1867. By this time, the course of study as advertised included a lengthy array of subjects: arithmetic, algebra, geometry, trigonometry, astronomy, natural philosophy; reading, spelling, writing, rhetoric composition, literature; geography, history, chemistry, physiology, botany, geology, zoology; singing, drawing, and the theory and art of teaching. (*Ibid.*, August 16, 1867.) Although there was no mention of physical exercise, that, too, was a part of the daily program.

[183]*Ibid.*, August 16, 1867.

> I hereby appoint _____, who is a person of good moral character, of the required age, who intends to become a teacher, and who is otherwise fitted to be a student in the Normal School as a delegate to said school from this District.
>
> (Signed) Representative of _____
>
> District

[184]*Ibid.*, September 20 and December 6, 1867. The latter issue contained the Principal's Third Annual Report which was published in full.

[185]*Ibid.*, August 16, 1867.

[186]*Ibid.*, December 6, 1867. The teacher hired to head the Model School was Mary R. Pitman. Arriving for the winter term, she remained but a short time before resigning to return to new York at the end of the first term.

The teacher initially hired to organize the Model School but released from her contract before ever beginning the assignment was Harriet M. Case of Illinois Normal University. She became a teacher in her alma mater where J.N. Wilkinson, president of K.S.N. from 1901-1906, was one of her pupils. (*Kodak*, 1898, Kansas State Normal School Yearbook, p. 156, Normaliana Collection.)

The December 27 issue of the paper listed those students attending the Model School. Both grades were included in the end-of-term public examinations of December 20. (*Ibid.*, December 13, 1867.)

[187]Other needs included a musical instrument, either a piano or organ; bookcases or cabinets to replace the inadequate ones from the district school; more insurance on the building; additional painting and graining; and improvement of grounds. Nothing yet had been done about the latter.

The Executive Committee report, published in the January 17, 1868 issue of *The Emporia News* and subsequently endorsed by the Board at their January 30, 1868 meeting, included an appropriation request to the legislature for most of the items except for the musical instrument. It was purchased the following year from proceeds earned by the Normal Literary Union. Amounts requested were:

Books, maps, and encyclopedia set	$250
Catalogs	250
Stoves	75
Chandelier in assembly room and Lamps in halls and rooms .	60

Insurance   75

. . . .

Lightning rods   30

. . . .

How quickly some of the above items were forthcoming is not known, but the first school catalog bore the date of 1868, having been published early in 1869 at the Emporia News Book and Job office.

[188]Minutes, January 30, 1868; *The Emporia News*, December 27, 1867 and January 3, 1868. The Congregationalists had a Christmas tree, sold items at a bazaar, served supper, and provided music by a brass band, realizing a $200 profit from the venture. The Methodists reportedly netted more than $1000 for their parsonage fund from the New Year's Eve extravaganza. It included music from the Normal's singing class, and a sumptuous variety of holiday foods including oysters prepared by a local restaurateur. Cakes left over from the feast were auctioned off for as much as $200 per cake. Others brought $100 such as the one bought by Stotler. Eskridge was one of several who paid $50 for one.

[189]August 23, 1867. The articles upon which Stotler based his article "Kansas Public Institutions" was from the *Hiawatha Sentinel*.

[190]*The Emporia News*, January 3, 1868.

[191]*Ibid.*, January 17, 1868, from the report of the executive committee published therein. Because Kellogg had been offered an opportunity to move to Missouri, the Board raised his salary to $2000. Norton's was $1800; Gorham and Pitman, $900 each. For classifying, describing, and appraising the Normal School lands, H.D. Preston of Osage County was to be paid $427. Ironically by this time, there were more students than ever before, but a greater majority had signed the teacher pledge, and thus were attending tuition free. For an explanation of the Normal's indebtedness, see Footnote #112.

[192]The *Kansas Educational Journal*, Vol. IV, December-January, 1867-68, p. 204; *The Emporia News*, February 21, 1868. In the Journal, editors Kellogg and Norton replied to the White Cloud editor's claim that the state's institutions were of no benefit. According to the Emporia paper, it was Editor Joe Lane of the *Chief* who made the scurrilous attack under the headline "Economy and Misconstruction." Stotler's able answer was called "Misrepresentation."

[193]*The Emporia News*, February 7, 1868. The Board of Directors' meeting was especially well attended but two members present. Governor Crawford presided. Representative Preston B. Plumb, Kellogg, and Norton also attended.

At the Hall of Representatives, Kellogg lectured on Politics in the Schoolroom. Norton spoke in behalf of the Normal School. Afterwards, in a letter to Stotler, Eskridge remarked that "prospects of the Normal were never better."

[194]*Senate Journal of the Legislative Assembly of the State of Kansas Begun and Held at Topeka on Tuesday, January 14, 1868*. Published by Authority, Lawrence, Kansas, John Speer, Printer to the State, 1868, pp. 285, 319-322.

Chairman Dodge assured the senate that committee members, impressed by the far reaching importance of the question, had devoted more than the ordinary amount of consideration to the matter before coming to the following conclusions:

1. That the Legislature could have inaugurated no more ruinous policy financially than to distribute the various state institutions into different and distant localities beyond the immediate watchful vigilance of the people's representatives.
2. That by so doing, the state had largely deprived itself of the direct supervisory control which was necessary in order to insure that those entrusted with distributing appropriations do so with economy, system, and purity.
3. It places the state treasury in the control of strong and powerful combinations of interest so as to render powerless any successful resistance to their demands for appropriations, and to the amount asked for.
4. That the state in its present embarrassed financial condition could not meet the demands for money and still preserve its credit at home or abroad; that it would be to the advantage of the state to relinquish its interest entirely in most of its institutions distantly located from the Capitol, to be relieved from further obligations to support them and institute a new policy of building them up at the capital or other designated points gradually, and as necessity demanded and finances of the state would admit.

Senator Sharp stated that he and Maxson favored the bill's rejection for the following reasons:

1. The state already had invested large sums of money in the purchase of locations for erection of the various institutions in the different areas of the state and in the erection of suitable and permanent buildings.
2. The state had also acquired valuable real estate by donation in consideration of locating and building said institutions in the places now located and in useful operation.
3. It would be an act of bad faith on the part of the state towards the various localities if the legislature were to remove the institutions

198

from those places which had donated valuable property, the title to which was now in the state.

4. The state had expended large sums of money in equipping these various institutions now in successful operation, and the only appropriation needed hereafter would be for current expenses for support and maintenance whereas if they should be concentrated in one place, the whole labor of the state and the money already expended would be a dead loss.

[195]*Ibid.*, pp. 378 and 542. Bill #101 if it had passed, most certainly would have been a death warrant for the Normal. Much credit has to be given to Maxon and Sharp for their astute minority report. Especially was the Normal indebted to Sharp for postponing action on the bill. The Normal's cause surely must have been aided, too, by the presence of Representative Preston B. Plumb on the Judiciary committee and Representative J.D. Jaquith of Americus on the Education committee. Senator Maxson of the local district chaired the latter committee.

Nor were the pens of Kellogg and Norton idle. In their April 1868 issue of the *Kansas Educational Journal*, pp. 274-275, appeared an editorial about consolidation in which the editors discussed the pros and cons of the matter, while at the same time voicing their belief that Normal Schools should be independent of colleges or universities. Anticipating that the question would be revived in the next legislature, they planned to present "certain testimonials which will have weight with every candid mind."

[196]*The Emporia News*, March 13, 1868.

[197]*Ibid.*, March 20, 1868. An interesting point made by Chief Clerk Morton in his letter was that he wished Miss Emma Hunt to be assured that the error was not in her department. Miss Hunt, a former K.S.N. student, had been chief enrolling clerk for the House of Representatives the past session. Her picture appeared in *Harper's Bazaar* as the first woman to hold the job. Following adjournment of the session, she taught the spring term at Rinker school, northeast of Emporia, where she had forty pupils. (*Ibid.*, April 10 and May 22, 1868.) Later, Miss Hunt held the position of chief clerk for the state senate.

[198]*Ibid.*, March 20, April 3, May 22, June 12, and July 3, 1868. Tickets to the literary event were fifty cents and net proceeds about $100. Tickets to the floral festival were twenty-five cents; ice cream and cake were sold for ten cents extra. Total profits from the latter event was $125. The new organ though priced at $350 was purchased for $250. Of Peloubet make, it was purchased from Foster and Yelverton of Lawrence. The organ had taken a premium award at the Kansas State Fair in the fall of 1867. Presumably, the difference between the above earnings and the cost of the organ was made up through some other school fund. If additional fund projects were held, they were not publicized.

[199]The words of the song first appeared in *The Emporia News*, June 19 and again on the 26th, 1868, as part of the advertisement of the commencement and anniversary program. See Appendix XV.

  According to information in the 1889 *History*, p. 62 of the 1888-89 annual catalog which is appended to the *History*, all four of the graduates taught school. Miss Ela taught for a period of three years at Grasshopper Falls, Lawrence, and Chetopa, before marrying a Mr. Howell and moving to Arkansas City. She died there March 19, 1888. Alice Norton taught five years in Emporia, Manhattan, Chanute, and Lawrence before marrying a Mr. Ingersoll and moving to Denver, Colorado. Josephine L. Patty taught thirteen years: one year at Waushara; Paola where she was associate principal for a year; Emporia city schools, eight years; and Golden, Colorado, three years. She married J.M. Manahan in Golden but died a few months later, in March 1882.

[200]*The Emporia News*, July 3, 1868.

[201]*Ibid.*, June 26 and July 3, 1868. This time it was Norton to whom the visitors were to report in order that he might direct them to their hosts' homes. The following list of prominent male visitors appeared in the latter issue of the newspaper: Richard Edwards, Normal, Illinois; General Fraser, president of Kansas University; Joseph Denison, president of the Agricultural College; H.D. McCarty, principal of Leavenworth High School; Judge L.D. Bailey; D.L. Bradford, principal of Atchison High School; Judge D.J. Brewer, Leavenworth; Professors R.D. McCartney, Grasshopper Falls; Professor J.E. Platt, Agricultural College; W.G. Williams, Marysville; R.W. Putnam, Leavenworth; Professor Palmer, Wyandotte; Reverend J.S. Brown, Lawrence; Professor R.B. Dilworth, Paola; Professor L.B. Pierce, Manhattan; and Professor I.J. Banister, Paola. According to the news article, nineteen Kansas counties were represented at the Teachers' meeting.

[202]*Ibid.*, July 3, 1868.

[203]*Ibid.* McVicar was absent from all of the week's activities. He was in Washington, D.C. in regard to the Indian lands and the late treaty with the Osage Indians. His concern was over a potential loss of school lands. The treaty already agreed to by the Osage Nation and at the time being considered by the Congress would convey 8,000,000 acres of land to one railroad corporation with no provision for reserving the 16th and 36th sections for common schools.

[204]*The Emporia News*, July 10, 1868. Three of the newspapers which Stotler quoted were the *Burlington Patriot*, *Chase County Banner*, and the *Kansas Farmer*.

  Ibid., September 11, 1868; *Kansas Educational Journal*, Vol. V, Nos. 4 and 5, August, 1868, pp. 93-95; and September 1868, pp. 142-43. Supt. McVicar reportedly was not interested in serving another term; thus the Association selected Norton as their candidate. In September, however, McVicar apparently changed his mind. Norton, who originally agreed to run only because he understood McVicar would not do so, now said that since he believed McVicar was really the Association's first choice, he, Norton, upon learning that McVicar would indeed run if nominated, "cheerfully" withdrew his name from the race.

Ibid., July 31, 1868. Mrs. Gorham had gone to visit her parents in Nebraska and became a robbery victim in Omaha, losing both money and luggage. When the thief was apprehended, a portion of her money was recovered, but not the trunk. Principal Kellogg and his family, meanwhile, left by wagon for El Dorado to visit his brother, but enroute the party experienced a breakdown which forced them to spend the night on the prairie beyond Cottonwood Falls in what the local editor referred to as a "supperless bivouac." In his humorous account of the vacationing faculty, Stotler added that Norton, though eager for a journey, was remaining quietly at home—afraid to venture out. He was waiting for the Governor to send an escort.

Note: Kellogg's brother, H.D. Kellogg, M.D., a graduate of Rush Medical School in Chicago and an experienced physician, had arrived in Emporia in the spring of 1867 to practice medicine. After a few months, however, he decided to locate in El Dorado where a doctor was desperately needed. (*Ibid.*, April 19 and 26; August 9, 1867.)

[205]*The Emporia News*, March 6 and August 14, 1868.

[206]*Ibid.*, April 10, July 3, August 14 and 28, 1868; 1889 *History*, pp. 52-53.

[207]*Ibid.*, March 20, 1868; Thesis, v. 1, pp. 27-28; v. 2, p. 45. An error which needs to be corrected appears in both volumes of the Theses. Authors Fish and Kayser wrote that a primary department was added to the Model School on April 8, 1868. Their source was the March 20, 1868 issue of *The Emporia News* wherein the executive committee of the Normal Board announced their plan to organize such a department. Authors of the Thesis, however, mistakenly dated the newspaper article as that of April 8, whereas there was no issue on that date. Had they read further, they would have learned of Miss Pitman's resignation (*Ibid.*, April 10, 1868), the subsequent hiring of Miss Plumb, and the fact that the Model School out of necessity had been suspended for some months. (*Ibid.*, July 3, 1868.) The next reference to a primary department came on April 2, 1869, when an article in *The Emporia News* declared that such a department would be started if a sufficient number applied. Children from the ages of five to seven or eight years who had not attended much school were eligible. There is no evidence, however, that a primary department materialized in 1869.

[208]*The Emporia News*, January 1, 1869, from the Board of Visitors' Report published therein.

[209]*Ibid.*, December 18, 1868; 1889 *History*, pp. 20 and 21. The latter volume contradicts itself on the two pages cited. On page 20, the correct number of four faculty members for 1868 is given, but on page 21 appears the inaccurate statement that by 1868 the faculty consisted of seven people plus four seniors teaching in the Model School. Undoubtedly the source of the error was the Normal catalog for the year ending December 31, 1868. Therein, seven teachers are listed: Kellogg, Norton, Gorham, Stimson, Pitman, Plumb, and Watson. They were not, however, teaching at the same time. Stimson taught music only one term; Pitman taught the Model School for one term, being replaced in the fall by Plumb. Watson, who subsequently was hired as a permanent teacher, was merely assisting Norton for the term that Kellogg was on leave.

[210]See Footnote #228 for a slight discrepancy between the Principal's Report and the catalog in regard to the numbers of preparatory and model school students for 1868.

[211]A copy of the 1868 Catalog is among the holdings of the Lyon County Historical Museum and the State Historical Library, Topeka. A reprint is in the Normaliana Collection, E.S.U. Complimentary copies must have been forwarded to Stotler's exchange newspapers, for on March 5, 1869, Stotler ran an article from the *Leavenworth Commercial* acknowledging that the editor had received the Normal School Catalog which "speaks volumes for the success of the school and the good business taste of the *Emporia News*."

[212]Minutes of the Board of Directors, January 30, 1868 and January 20, 1869; *The Emporia News*, January 29, 1869; and 1889 *History*, pp. 22-23. An error appears in the letter volume which mistakenly gives the date of 1870 as the year Kellogg became an honorary member of the Board.

[213]*The Emporia News*, June 22, 1861. Governor Robinson appointed a committee of three to locate the lands. E.P. Bancroft, state senator from Emporia, was on the committee. Others were H.B. Denman, Leavenworth; and S.E. Hoffman of Woodson County.

[214]*Ibid.*, March 7, 1863 and November 22, 1867. The latter issue contained an advertisement for 37,760 acres of Normal lands for sale, signed by the executive committee. The earlier issue, which included the official publication of the Normal School law, stated that "the endowment of the institution, in land, is 59 sections." Before the Normal bill became law, however, Stotler had written that probably all but the salt springs would be included in the endowment, giving the school sixty sections of land. See *ibid.*, February 28, 1863.

In his 1868 message to the legislature, Governor S.J. Crawford stated that the State Normal School had a land grant of 37,760 acres.

[215]*Senate Journal, 1869*, pp. 246, 267-268, 284, 619, 651, and 666. The Act itself was no more specific than the Board's request had been.

> Whereas, It appears by the Act establishing the State Normal School, that all the salt lands belonging to the State were set apart for its "perpetual endowment" save and except the salt springs, and the section of land upon which each of the said salt springs are located, and one additional section; and
>
> Whereas, For the purpose of more clearly designating the lands belonging to said School, and the section of land reserved and belonging to the State:
>
> Be it enacted by the Legislature of the State of Kansas:
>
> Section 1. That the "one additional section" of the said salt lands referred to in section three of the act to which this is supplemental, be and the same is hereby granted to the State Normal School as a further endowment, upon the same terms, conditions and restrictions applicable to lands heretofore granted to said School, reserving to the State exclusively the sections of land upon which each of the twelve salt springs are designated.

[216]*Transactions of the Kansas State Historical Society*, 1897-1900, edited by Geo. W. Martin, secretary, Vol. VI (Topeka, W.Y. Morgan, state printer 1900), "History of Normal School Work in Kansas," a paper by Albert R. Taylor read before the Kansas State Historical Society at 23rd annual meeting, January 17, 1899, pp. 114-121.

On page 114 of the paper, Taylor claimed that of the seventy-two sections of salt lands received under the enabling act of congress to be used as the legislature shall direct, forty-eight sections had been

> set apart and reserved as a permanent endowment for the support and maintenance of the Normal School established and located by this 1863 Act. The law of 1869 added twelve more sections to the endowment, and the law of 1886 the remaining twelve sections, making a total of seventy-two sections thus set apart.

Taylor may well have been influenced in his interpretation by an almost forgotten report of the Board of Commissioners on Public Institutions in 1873. The commissioners, in their report on the Normal School (page 18), quoted Section three of the 1863 Act establishing the Normal followed by their own declaration that

> It will be seen by the above that the State reserved two sections out of every six, making the donation from this source to the Normal School to amount to forty-eight sections.

They also quoted the 1869 Act which added the "one additional section" to the Normal School endowment asserting that

This would make an additional twelve sections added to the original forty-eight sections, making a total grant of 38,400 acres. . . .

NOTE: The above board came into being by Section twelve of a March 6, 1873 law regarding the appointment of regents and trustees for the state institutions. Section twelve of this general law called for a commission of three citizens in no way connected with any of the state institutions to be appointed by the Governor for a term of three years and to be confirmed by the Senate. Their duties were to visit the various institutions at least twice each year to inspect and investigate the wellbeing of each institution, and to report their findings in writing to the Governor.

The life of this board proved to be of short duration. An attempt early in 1874 to abolish it was foiled, but the next year it was phased out by a law repealing Section twelve. Proof of the commission's labors may be found in the *First and Second Reports of the Board of Commissioners on Public Institutions, 1873 and 1874* (Topeka, Kansas, George W. Martin, Public Printer).

According to the 1889 *History*, p. 141, there was no record that the commission ever visited Emporia, but *The Emporia News*, December 19, 1873, stated that the Board of Commissioners consisting of J.C. Wilson, Atchison; Captain Charles Puffer, Burlington; and C.S. Broadbent of Wellington visited Emporia on December 17. Stotler, who was paid a visit by the three, wrote the following:

> They have been over the ground thoroughly and their report, which will be made about the time the legislature meets, will attract much interest.

[217] Eight years earlier, in 1878, the land committee of the Board of Directors, comprised of J.H. Crichton and J.J. Wright, had recommended in a written report to the Board that

> The next session of the Legislature be requested to grant the "Salt spring Sections," twelve (`12) in number, included in the original grant to the state, to the Normal School and set apart for its use as the lands we now have are set apart . . . By this being done, it would be quite an increase to our fund, as most of the lands are good included in said twelve (12) Sections.

The committee also was aware that the particular lands in question were not valuable to the state, and the Board was informed of that fact.

> The Salt springs spoken of in them [the twelve sections] are in most instances a "Myth." The springs are of no earthly value for mineral purposes, and said lands will never be fit for anything to state or others persons but for agricultural or grazing. We cannot urge too strongly that at least an attempt should be made at once to secure these Sections. (Minutes, October 18, 1878.)

[218] Appendix, p. I, Sections 3 and 4; p. xi, Sections 3 and 4; and p. xvi, Sections 3 and 4.

[219] Minutes, June 10, 1866 and June 28, 1867. See Appendix, p. xvii and xviii for copy of the 1866 Land Sales law. Section 1 designates the minimum price per acre at $1.25. (The Thesis, v. 1, p. 25 mistakenly states that the lands were not to be sold for less than one dollar per acre.)

H.D. Preston's report to the Board on June 28, 1867, probably was oral. At any rate, according to a resolution introduced by Eskridge, the appraiser was to be paid $450 for his services upon filing a statement in detail of time, persons employed, per diem for self and others, and after plots and description lists were filed. Ironically, even then he was to be paid only when and if there were available funds not already appropriated.

[220]*The Emporia News*, December 3, 1869, "Executive Committee Report;" *Annual Report of the Superintendent of Public Instruction*, Kansas, 1863-1870, "Ninth Annual Report, 1869," p. 84. Some evidence that five sections of land were to be sold appeared in the two above reports. An Illinois buyer dealing through a Salina firm was to pay $6.50 per acre. No contracts had been signed, however, nor any money transacted.

An interesting chart showing that three quarters sections had been sold appeared on page nineteen of the Board of Commissioners 1873 report.

Acres	Price	Am't	Am't Pd	Comm	Net	Interest	Total
160	$6.00	$960.00	$96.00	$28.80	$67.20		
166.82	5.00	834.10	83.41	25.02	58.39		
160	6.00	960.00	96.00	28.80	67.20		
					$192.79	$86.40	$279.19

In their report (1874), they stated that no additional lands had been sold. (No mention of land sales is made in the Board of Director Minutes for 1873 or before.)

An 1872 Land Sale bill which, according to the Minutes of January 11, 1872, was drawn up by the Normal Board of Directors, superseded the 1866 Act. Published on March 19, 1872 in the *Kansas Daily Commonwealth*, Section five of the Act declared the 1866 land sale law "hereby repealed." Instead of the $1.25 per acre minimum of the earlier law, a $5.00 minimum was legislated. (In 1877, the legislature passed an act to reorganize the State Normal School at Emporia and to provide for the sale of its land. Lands were to be sold under the 1872 law, but the minimum price per acre was reduced to three dollars. The act also reaffirmed that there were to be no appropriations to the school in the future. [The 1877 Act may be found on p. xxi of the Appendix.]) The amount of the initial payment, however, was decreased from one-third to one-tenth of the purchase price, and interest of ten percent on the remaining balance could be paid at the option of the purchaser. The earlier bill had required that the balance of the purchase price be paid in two equal installments with ten percent interest from purchase date.

The land agent was to be under the control and direction of the Board of Directors who were to pay him no more than three percent of his sales. Gone were the protective requirements spelled out in the 1866 law. Instead, the agent was to "give such security for the faithful performance of his duties as the Board of Directors may approve." Section four, however, stipulated that all money from sales, principal and interest, was to be deposited into the state treasury where it could constitute the Normal School fund. That money received as principal was to be invested according to law; and interest received was to be subject to the order of the president and secretary of the Board of Directors for the sole purpose of supporting and maintaining the Normal School. Presumably, it was this section that negated Sections three and four of the two earlier appropriation acts deeming the cost of the first building a loan to be repaid from land sales. (See pp. xix and xx of Appendix for the 1872 Land Bill in its entirety.)

The Board of Directors had requested in 1868 and again in 1869 that the legislature release the Normal School from its obligation to repay the building appropriations of 1866 and 1867 with no specific legislative response. Of particular interest, therefore, is what the 1873 Board of Commissioners had to say on the subject.

> When these loans were made it was not expected, or not thought probably by many of the legislators that the State would ever be recompensed; . . . .

Later, the state cancelled all claims against the Agricultural College and soon stopped referring to appropriations as loans "until now the appropriations are made from year to year without provisions for refunding." (Board of Commissioners Report, 1873, pp. 19-20.)

[221]*The Emporia News*, January 1, 1869, "Principal's Report for 1868."

[222]*Ibid.*, June 11, 1869.

[223]*The Laws of the State of Kansas Passed at the Ninth Session of the Legislature, 1869*, pp. 21-23, 207, and 208; *The Emporia News*, January 22 and February 5, 1869. Although the deficiency in Norton's 1868 salary amounted to $1200, a special bill, "An Act in relation to the salary of the Associate Principal of the State Normal School," provided but $900 in scrip, an amount which was "just, due, and unpaid." That Act was approved January 21, 1869, and published in the *Daily Kansas State Record*. The remaining $300 was taken care of in the regular appropriation bill of 1869. Principal Kellogg, also, was allowed the $500 deficiency

in his 1868 salary at the same time. The act giving the "one additional section" to the Normal School endowment lands took effect March 1, 1869.

[224]*The Emporia News*, July 2, 1869. Women graduates were Mattie J. Nicholls and Martha P. Spencer, both Lyon Countians who were members of the "original eighteen;" Matilda Upton, Allen County; and Mary L. Williams, Douglas County. The men were Charles T. Cavaness, Thomas Ticer, and J.N.D. Brown of Lyon County; Houston L. Poplin, Anderson County; and Thomas Stewart, Allen County. Teachers in June, 1869, were Kellogg, Norton, Watson, and Gorham of the Normal, and Plumb of the Model School.

[225] *Ibid*. The affirmative, debated by a Miss Medill of Leavenworth and Mr. Ball of the local vicinity, had the emotional support of the audience according to Stotler, but the negative, taken by Miss Thayer of Burlington and Mr. Hurlburt of Emporia, gave the better arguments.

[226]*Ibid*. Stotler quoted from Thacher's own report of the festivities, including comments on the graduate essays and essayists. One of the essayists, Thomas Ticer, lost his thread of thought and had to forego his conclusion. The audience, however, according to the account was sympathetic. The essayists were Martha P. Spencer, Matilda Upton, and J.N.D. Brown.

Thursday morning activities opened with an anthem "The Lord Our God is Full of Might," and a prayer by the Reverend G.C. Morse. (The Reverend Peter McVicar was listed in the advance program.) After a choral number, Charles T. Cavaness presented the negative point of view towards "Compulsory Education." Miss Spencer spoke about the "Educational Labors of Horace Mann," and Mr. Ticer "The Wealth of a Nation." A quartet sang "A Home on the Rolling Sea" followed by three more essays: "The Educational Horoscope" by Miss Upton; "An Appreciation of the Scientific Basis—a Pre Requisite to Successful Work" by Houston L. Poplin; and "Duties of Parents in Regard to Schools," Mary L. Williams. The school chorus sang "Fling Out the Joyful Banner" preceding the final three essays: "Responsibility to Law," Thomas Stewart; "Nobility and Responsibility of the Teachers' Vocation," Mr. Brown; and "The End of the Beginning," Martha J. Nicholls. A choral number, "The Breaking Waves Dashed High," ended the morning program. (*Ibid.*, June 18, 1869.)

[227]July 9, 1869. According to an earlier note in *The Emporia News*, July 2, 1869, the women teachers of the Normal, Gorham, Watson, and Plumb, also attended the Manhattan meeting. They apparently traveled with another group.

[228]*Ibid.*, January 1, 1869, "Report of Board of Visitors;" also *Ibid.*, August 20, 1869, for the editorial.

[229]*Ibid.*, December 3, 1869, p. 1, "Principal's Report."

1868			
4		Graduates	
12		Senior	
16		Middle	
85		Junior	
36		Prep. And Model	
153		Total for Year	
	78	Females	102
	75	Males	96
113		Future Teachers	

Other relevant information concerning the 1869 enrollment was that the average age of the students, who came from nineteen counties and seven states, was 19 years.

[230]*The Emporia News*, February 5, 1869. Preston B. Plumb and E.P. Bancroft accompanied the two visiting legislators on the second day of their inspection tour. According to Stotler, he and other Emporians called on the committee the evening of their first day (Monday) at the National House. At the end of the inspection, Voss addressed the faculty and students. He was highly complementary to them. Rankin, too, spoke in complimentary terms. He said, however, that the state needed an additional Normal School in the northeast section, probably Johnson County, as soon as one could be afforded.

[231]"Report of the Joint Committee on the State Normal School," 1869 newspaper clipping, Normaliana Collection, W.A. White Library.

[232]*Ibid*. The amount requested did not include $900 of Norton's back salary. See Footnote #222.

[233]*The Emporia News*, December 3, 1869. The Board of Visitors for 1869 were S.J. Crawford, E.B. Peyton, and W.R. Brown. They visited the Normal on November 2, 1869. The executive committee was comprised of Eskridge, Morse, and Stotler who had replaced Rogers early in the year.

Second on Kellogg's want list was the need for more boarding facilities, a concern that already has been discussed in the section on the Boarding House Association. Other wants were (3) record books for the preservation of statistics and the history of the institution; (4) chemistry apparatus, especially for visible illustrations; (5) window blinds for assembly and recitation rooms, the curtains having worn out; (6) more fencing, trees, and shrubs for landscaping.

234*Ibid.*, December 24, 1869. The celebration of the arrival of the Union Pacific Southern Branch Railway (later called the "Katy") was on December 21, the same day as the Normal School examinations which continued through December 23.

235*The Emporia News*, February 4, May 13, and July 22, 1870. The first cars of the Santa Fe arrived in Emporia on Thursday, July 21, 1870; but by mid-May, regular train service between Topeka and Osage City had begun. Emporians taking the stage could make connections with trains at Osage City. That fare from Emporia to Topeka was four dollars.

236*Ibid.*, January 21 and 28, 1870. The National House which had been sold by Hunt to Colonel Robinson late in 1869 and since enlarged by twenty-six sleeping rooms, was full. According to the latter issue of the newspaper, "Between noon and midnight on Saturday last, 50 guests registered at the Robinson House, and 100 guests took dinner there on Sunday." Both the Madison and the Buckeye Houses had opened late in the year but were already crowded. The latter was sold in April, 1870, to be enlarged. (*Ibid.*, April 8, 1870.)

237*Ibid.*, February 11, 1870.

238*Ibid.*, February 25, 1870. Emporia already had surpassed the necessary 2,000 mark in population to qualify for a city of the second class.

239*Ibid.*, February 4, 1870. In the piece "Our City Parks," the editor declared Washington Park to be the most unsightly square of the 168 in the original town plot. A ravine passed almost directly through the center of it, necessitating that it be bridged or filled up. He gave a lengthy argument for disposing of the square as a park if possible.

See also *Ibid.*, March 25, 1870; *Proceedings of the City Council*, City of Emporia, Kansas (Office of the City Clerk). According to the April 9, 1870 Proceedings of the first city council, the town company gave the city the privilege of choosing alternate lots in Washington Park, located from Eighth to Ninth Avenues between Merchant and Mechanic Streets. The park included the east side of Merchant and the west side of Mechanic. Not until after the park ceased to be did Commercial Street bisect the area.

In choosing their sixteen lots, the city council committee began with the north lot on what is now the west side of Commercial Street, thence south, selecting alternate lots with a 25 foot frontage; then beginning with the south lot on the east side of Commercial Street and going north, selecting alternate lots as before. (See maps of the original town site and book I A of Lyon County Land Records, Register of Deeds Office.)

[240]June 3, 1870. Stotler rebutted Justice's plea by urging citizens to vote bonds. Stotler maintained that Justice had trumped up the remonstrance and that the boarding house keepers had never seen the plea. Stotler also believed that not one private boarding house would close if the bonds passed. He thought it essential to provide the houses to prevent crippling the usefulness of the Normal. "There is no telling how soon the school may be taken from us and located at some point which will furnish these facilities [cheap self-boarding] if we do not do so."

Other bonds for street improvements, water works, and a fire department were also being considered for a total of $94,000. At the May 28 public meeting, Preston B. Plumb and Judge R.M. Ruggles spoke out against those bonds. Eskridge and Mayor H.C. Cross spoke in favor.

[241]*Ibid.*, June 10 and 24, and July 15, 1870.

[242]*Ibid.*, July 29, 1870; Proceedings of the City Council, August 1 and 22, 1870. There was only a light turnout on July 26, probably because little advance information about the second election appeared in the newspapers. A total of 140 votes were cast (88-52).

The special council committee consisted of E. Borton, R.D. Thomas, and G.W. Frederick.

[243]*The Emporia News*, August 26, September 23, October 28, November 18 and 25, 1870; and the 1889 *History*, p. 122. One boarding house for the women was located on the southwest corner of Ninth and Commercial; the other one, occupied by men, was across the street seventy-five feet or so from the corner.

[244]Although Kellogg included cisterns in his 1870 report, published on December 30 in *The Emporia News*, they were not yet constructed. The city council did not authorize the taking of bids for cisterns until their March 6, 1871 meeting. (Proceedings of the City Council.) Sidewalks were authorized on September 26; privies were authorized on November 14; and steps to the front door of the east boarding house, December 26.

A lengthy story, "Emporia During 1870," which appeared in the January 6, 1871 issue of *The Emporia News* paints a less positive picture of the two frame structures located at what then was the north end of Commercial Street. The writer was blunt in denouncing the architecture as nothing to speak of. In fact, he declared their external appearance to be horrible.

[245]*Ibid.*, December 9, 1870, "Official Reports of the State Normal School, 1. Principal's Report." This report also may be found in *Kansas Public Documents, 1870*, pp. 155-172.

[246]*The Emporia News*, February 4, 1870.

[247]*Ibid.*, May 20 and 27, 1870.

[248]*Ibid.*, June 17 and 24, and July 1, 1870. In the Fish and Kayser Thesis, v. 1, p. 29, the authors state that "the [commencement] exercises were changed from June to December [in 1870] in order to accommodate some of the teachers." Their source (Thesis, v. 2, p. 50) was the June 24, 1870 issue of *The Emporia News*.

While it is true that some of the teachers were convenienced by the change, a more likely reason for postponing commencement, perhaps, was that Kellogg was attempting to extend the length and depth of the academic program in order that the classics and foreign languages could become a part of the curriculum. (Individuals from the Normal faculty and the executive committee were involved in the Crewell Town Company which had been formed to found a town by that name at the confluence of the Arkansas and Walnut Rivers in Southern Cowley County. Shortly, the name of the townsite was changed to Arkansas City.) In this respect, it is significant that not only was the 1870 graduation in December, but the 1871 graduation likewise was scheduled for December (see footnote #269). Unforeseen developments again changed the schedule, however, and the 1871 commencement was cancelled entirely, leaving the 1870 commencement the only one in the history of the school to be held in December until quite recently. In 1970, winter commencements were added to the school calendar which already called for May and August commencements. The latter was discontinued in 1979.

As early as March 21, 1870, a permanent organization was effected, officers of which were H.B. Norton, president; C.V. Eskridge, vice president; W.R. Brown, secretary; and L.B. Kellogg, treasurer. Their executive committee consisted of Eskridge, H.D. Kellogg, brother to L.B.; and Captain G.H. Norton, brother to H.B. (*The Emporia News*, March 25, 1870.) Sometime before October, Stotler replaced Brown as secretary. (*Ibid.*, October 7, 1870.)

By June, plans were being made for a grand Fourth of July celebration on Max Fawcett's claim near Arkansas City. A large party was to leave Emporia in covered wagons and ambulances on June 29, take eatables along, camp out at night, make short journeys and long rests, and to return after the Fourth at their leisure. Whoever wished to sign for the trip could do so. The celebration itself was to include music, a big dinner, an oration by H.B. Norton, toasts and short speeches by Kellogg and others. (*Ibid.*, June 17 and 24, 1870).

Kellogg, moreover, participated in the State Teachers meeting in Wyandotte during the final week of June. Mrs. Gorham and three Normal students also attended. (*Ibid.*, July 1, 1870.)

[249]*The Emporia News*, September 9, 1870.

[250]*Ibid.*, September 23 and October 28, 1870.

[251]*Ibid.*, December 23, 1870.

[252]*Ibid.*, December 30, 1870. See the 1870 Principal's Report for information on Henry West.

[253]*Ibid.*, December 30, 1870 and January 6, 1871. Mr. Spangler was hired as an assistant at the Normal School for $90 per month. Miss Storrs continued studying the classics, at the same time teaching one class in the Normal and one in the Model School. Mr. Bales went to Fort Scott to direct a colored school for $65 per month, and Miss Hawkins became principal of the public schools in Cottonwood Falls for $60 per month. Miss Duren returned to her home in Garnett, preferring to wait until spring to begin teaching even though she had a choice of two or three positions.

[254]Although there is no mention in the minutes of these resignations, Kellogg in his 1870 Principal's Report mentions them. Regarding Norton, he wrote the following:

> At the close of the third quarter [term], H.B. Norton, associate principal, resigned. Ill health, coupled with a desire for an active, out-door life, constituted the motive inducing the resignation. Professor R.B. Dilworth of Leavenworth, accepting the invitation of the Board of Directors, has been performing the duties of the vacant position during the present third term.

[255]*The Emporia News*, January 20, 1871; Minutes, June 22, 1871. Board members who took the oath of office in June were John W. Horner, Chetopa; E.S. Stover, Council Grove; Harvey Bancroft, S.B. Riggs, and E.P. Bancroft, Emporia; and State Superintendent H.D. McCarty. Edwin Tucker of Greenwood County, the sixth newly-appointed member, apparently was absent from the meeting.

[256]January 13, 1871. The only missing phrases were those extolling the Principal and his faculty as was Stotler's practice, not that the omission was of any particular significance except in the light of what was soon to occur. Earlier (*Ibid.*, January 6, 1871), Kellogg had resigned his editorship of *The Educational Journal*, probably because with Norton gone he could not afford the time for the job. He also had advertised for sale some of his speculative land near the Normal (*Ibid.*, November 11, 1870), and had purchased *The Arkansas Traveler* in Arkansas City. In announcing the latter, Stotler had been complimentary about Kellogg's capabilities and the future of that paper under his guidance (*Ibid.*, December 30, 1870).

[257]*Ibid.*, December 30, 1870 and January 20, 1871; also Minutes, January 18, 1871. Present at the meeting were five of the nine members: Governor J.M. Harvey, State Superintendent McCarty, S.S. Prouty, the Reverends C.R. Rice and R.M.

Overstreet. Kellogg, an honorary member, also was present. The executive committee report, signed by Stotler [no longer on the board by January 18] and Eskridge [not present on January 18] had recommended substantial increases for the faculty: Principal, $2500; Preceptress, $1800; Professor of Natural Sciences, $1800; (2) assistant teachers, $2000 [$1000 each]; Principal of the Model School, $1200; Janitor, $500; and back pay of $500 for the preceptress, making a total of $10,300 for salaries. Action of the board, however, cut the total amount to $7,400. Kellogg's salary was to remain at $2000; Preceptress, $1200; Professor of Natural Science, $1600; one assistant teacher, $900; Principal of the Model School, $1000; Janitor, $500; and $200 in back pay for the preceptress.

[258]Minutes, January 25, 1871; *The Emporia News*, February 10, 1871. Seven hundred dollars from the executive committee's recommendations were not reinstated, including $200 each for the professor of natural sciences and the preceptress, and $300 in back pay for the preceptress. At the second board meeting, however, Kellogg's $500 increase was restored; the assistant teachers' salary increased $100; a second teacher at $1000 included; $400 added to the preceptress' salary; and $200 to the Model School principal's salary. Present for the second meeting were Governor Harvey, J.E. Hayes, treasurer; McCarty, Eskridge, Overstreet, Prouty, and Kellogg. Absent were L.D. Bailey, T.S. Huffaker, and Rice. The latter was the only member at the first meeting to be absent from the second meeting.

An error appears in the 1889 *History* concerning the dates of service to the Board of Directors for S.S. Prouty. According to the chart (p. 29), Prouty's term ended in 1870. However, he was very much a part of the board until the middle of 1871, probably May 16. The Minutes for January 25 show that it was Prouty who moved that the legislature be asked to make the appropriations recommended by the board. The motion carried. Minutes of the called meeting, as voted by the board, were published in *The Topeka Commonwealth*.

[259]*Ibid.*, February 10, 1871. In this issue also, a notice appeared that Mrs. A.M. Philbrick, an 1865 graduate of Salem, Massachusetts and a teacher in Albany, New York, had been hired as the extra assistant teacher. The 1889 *History* apparently erred in stating that her length of service to the Kansas State Normal was from 1869 to 1873 (pages 37 and 52). There is no mention of her in the Minutes before June 22, 1871, when her claim for discount on state scrip was disallowed. Nor does her name appear in Kellogg's Reports. The Kansas State Normal Catalog lists her for the first time in 1871-72. (The Thesis has her listed as having taught from 1869 to 1873, the source of which, in all probability, was the 1889 *History*.)

[260]*Ibid.*, February 17, 1871.

[261]*Ibid.* Kellogg in his article admitted to a six year friendship with Stotler who had always been a friend of the Normal. In this instance, however, he thought Stotler's usual good judgment had deserted him.

[262]*Ibid.*, February 24, 1871. Kellogg was notably small of stature, a fact that apparently had never hindered him in operating the Normal; nor had he been demeaned because of it previously.

[263]*Ibid.* According to Stotler, Kellogg and Gorham [the preceptress] were the only faculty members dissatisfied with the salaries set by the first board. Kellogg, he maintained, had informed him of that at the called meeting to which Stotler had been summoned.

[264]*Ibid.* This was an unfair criticism since in the early years students came for brief periods, dropped out to teach, or left because of illness, lack of funds, et cetera. What one time would have given a fair count? It is well, however, that through the years a more sophisticated system has evolved. Today's enrollment figures, in all six of the state universities, become official on the twentieth day of classes.

[265]*Ibid.* Many of the exchanges were first published in the *Daily News*, a short lived paper that Stotler had begun in 1870, primarily to get national news to his subscribers while it still was news. Thus in his weekly issues, there often appeared more than one article on the board controversy. In the February 24 issue, appeared three such articles authored by Stotler, Overstreet, and Kellogg. Not until a month later did Eskridge enter the contest.

One point of interest is that although in "The Small Controversy" Stotler said he opposed an extra teacher, he earlier had wholeheartedly approved Kellogg's proposed expansion of the curriculum, especially in the field of mathematics and languages.

[266]*Ibid.*, March 3, 1871. Stotler's usual writing style was to use "we" meaning himself.

[267]*Kansas Daily Commonwealth*, January 24, 1871, "State Normal School: Appropriations Asked For Salaries Reduced The Reasons Why!", p. 4, c. 4. On January 25, another story "State Normal School," p. 4, c. 3, appeared refuting much of the above story, terming it misleading. The author is unknown, but it sounds like Stotler while he still was rational on the subject. Minutes of the called meeting appeared in the January 26 issue of *The Commonwealth*.

[268]*The Emporia News*, March 24 and 31, 1871; September 1 and 8, October 6, 13, and 20, 1871; Minutes, January 25, 1871. At the second board meeting in January, Overstreet had stood alone against increasing salaries. Before adjournment, he moved that an itemized account of expenses for fencing be filed with the board

secretary. That motion prevailed. In the intervening months before Eskridge was again elected to the legislature, Overstreet insinuated time and again that Eskridge had been dishonest in his handling of the fencing project. The contention was that a portion of the fence dividing the Normal grounds from the Eskridge property should have been paid in part by Eskridge, not the state. In all probability, it was this verbal mudslinging between Overstreet and Eskridge that prompted the authors of the 1889 *History* to ignore the entire newspaper wrangle of 1871, and the authors of the later Thesis to dismiss it with the proclamation that it was valueless as history. (V. 1, p. 30.)

Although in the Minutes of July 24, 1871, the executive committee of the Board of Directors exonerated Eskridge of any wrongdoing in handling the fence project, Overstreet continued his newspaper harangue on the subject. One positive result of the heated verbal exchange was a more businesslike approach to the accounting of incidental fees taken in by the Normal School. By Eskridge's own admission, he and Kellogg had often paid for items out of their own pockets, later reimbursing themselves when there were sufficient funds in the incidental account. Thus, when the matter of the party fence was finally cleared up, Eskridge held a two year old due bill of $22.39 in his favor. Overstreet, who openly rejoiced at having succeeded in his goal to effect a change in the local members of the board and in the faculty, maintained that the incidental fund, during the late administration of affairs here, had been

> . . . little else than a scrap trough where odds and ends are poured in and poured out with little or no regard as to whence they come or whither they go.

He also rejected that "We now have a Board of Directors and a Faculty for the State Normal School under whose auspices everything connected with the institution promises a glorious success." Eskridge, however, accused Overstreet of nearly ruining the school "necessitating all of the new (able) board members to do their utmost to restore it to its former stature."

[269]*Ibid.*, April 21 and May 19, 1871. *The Emporia Tribune* was a short-lived paper which eventually was bought up by Stotler. Very few issues are extant.

[270]*Ibid.*, June 2, 1871. In the *Kansas State Normal School Catalog, 1870-71*, for the academic year ending December 31, 1870, the calendar for 1871 lists the end of the spring term as June 22 with oral examinations and a public meeting of the Literary Society. The third term of 1871 was scheduled from September 11 to December 21 with graduation and the anniversary oration scheduled for the final afternoon. Oral exams were scheduled for that morning and a reception that evening.

[271]Minutes, June 22, 1871; *The Emporia News*, June 30, 1871. Later at the evening session, Harvey Bancroft was elected treasurer of the board even though State

Treasurer Hayes, according to the law, was to serve in that capacity. Appendix, p. iii, sec. 3, and 1889 *History*, pp. 23 and 130.

[272]Minutes, June 22, 1871. Stover made both motions regarding instructions to the executive committee. Riggs moved for a committee to study the retention of faculty, review salaries, et cetera.

[273]*Ibid.*

[274]*Ibid.*

[275]*The Emporia News*, June 30, 1871. J.C. Greenough, Westfield, Massachusetts Normal School had been selected on June 22 to replace Kellogg. He, however, refused the offer.

[276]*Ibid.*, July 7, 1871. According to the Minutes of June 22, 1871, Mrs. Gorham was asked to resign "with a view to secure a harmonious faculty for the ensuing year." Stotler in the above issue said it was a mistake on his part. He lamely explained that he had gained his impression during a conversation with a member of the board.

[277]*The Emporia News*, April 28, July 28, and August 11, 1871. In a letter from Parkersville, Kansas (November 16, 1871) to the *Junction City Union*, "Santagio" described Hoss as "a full grown man." *The Emporia News*, November 24, 1871, "How They Do Things at the Normal," a reprint.
[278]*Ibid.*, August 18, 1871. In all probability, the increase was for one term only. The published notice of the opening of the winter term on January 2, 1872, listed tuition of non-teachers at $6.00 per term. (*Ibid.*, December 15, 1871.)

[279]*Ibid.*, September 15, 1871. The speech by Hoss indicated that his philosophy of education was strikingly similar to that of his predecessor. His list of needs for success of the Normal included nine essentials: suitable buildings; suitable apparatus; library for reference; model or training school; boarding facilities; harmonious faculty; honorable, orderly, and industrious student body; cooperation of state educators; and harmonious board of trustees. The first five had always been of primary concern, whereas the last four had not been problems in the Kellogg years. Only recently had they become a source of grave concern.

[280]*Ibid.*, September 22, 1871.

[281]*Ibid.*, November 3, 10, and 17, 1871. A visiting lecturer of note who addressed the citizens and students alike in Bancroft Hall, October 26, 1871, was Sojourner Truth. She was about 84 years of age at the time. Also, see *Ibid.*, February 23,

1872 for one interesting result of the Health lectures. The school "let" a contract for vaccinating the Normal students and faculty [presumably smallpox]. Physicians were asked to bid. The lowest offer was $3 per dozen [students] with the privilege of "corralling the lot and applying the virus [sic] wholesale." The name of the successful bidder was not revealed.

[282]Minutes, December 14, 1871. Action of the Board of Directors established a permanent chair of languages at the Normal, naming Lamprey to fill that chair at a salary of $1600 per year. Inasmuch as a full time language instructor was one of the urgent needs listed by Hoss in his first annual report, it is apparent that the board wasted no time in complying with his request.

[283]See footnote #276 for "Santagio's" report. His reference to Hoss as president instead of principal of the Normal appears to have been the earliest of record. When the Board of Directors replaced Kellogg, they hired Hoss as principal. Not until January 11, 1872 did they refer to him as president. Minutes of that date record that the annual report of President Hoss was read. *The Emporia News* published that report on December 22, 1871 as the "Report of the President of the Normal." Stotler, however, was still referring to him as professor in December news items, a title he had used consistently since Hoss first arrived in Emporia. Prior to his arrival, Stotler had referred to him as the new principal. In all probability, it was Hoss himself who first assumed the title of president, using a visiting reporter and his first official report as a means of making the change.

[284]Minutes, June 22, 1871.

> On motion by H.D. McCarty, it was ordered that the scholastic year of this Institution shall commence on the first day of September, and end on the thirty-first day of August, with the usual vacations.

[285]*The Emporia News*, December 8 and 15, 1871. In the annual report of the executive committee, published in *Ibid.*, January 19, 1872, and approved at the annual board meeting but never entered in the space provided in the Minutes, there is a salary of $600 provided for a teacher of vocal music and penmanship for 1872. T.G. Jones, who according to the 1889 *History*, p. 48, was a very able musician and composer, took the job. By the end of the year, he was being recommended for a salary of $1,000. Thus, in less than a year after Kellogg was dismissed, the faculty with no model school to operate had increased to six members.

In the published circularly of December 15 which advertised the next term there appeared for the first time specific prerequisites for entering the Normal School proper. The new board had instructed the executive committee to draw up such regulations. (Minutes, June 22, 1871.)

> All applicants are expected to read readily in some standard Fourth reader—define parts of speech and explain and apply rules and principles in arithmetic as far as common fractions. Others will be helped in preparatory classes as far as practicable.

[286]*Ibid.*, December 8, 1871.

[287]Minutes, December 14, 1871.

[288]*The Emporia News*, January 5, 1872. Ninety-seven of the 120 students were pledged to teach.

[289]*Ibid.*, January 5 and 12, 1872. The newspaper had undergone some major changes just prior to the new year. Stotler, who had bought Williams' half of the paper in June, 1871, thereby becoming once again sole owner of the establishment, soon purchased the short-lived *Emporia Tribune* and formed a new partnership of Stotler, Rowland, and Graham. (*Ibid.*, October 20, 1871.) During the holiday season, *The Emporia News* closed shop temporarily in order to move into new quarters in the upper story of the new Williams' building on the Northeast corner of Sixth and Commercial Streets. Their first new issue of 1872, a ten column newspaper, was published on January 5. Their larger coverage was welcomed by the state exchange papers, according to the congratulatory comments reprinted within its pages. The only other Emporia paper at the time was the *Emporia Ledger*, a Democratic paper started by R.M. Ruggles in June, 1871. (*Ibid.*, June 16, 1871.) Stotler had suspended his daily *News* on August 11, 1871.

[290]*Ibid.*, January 12, 1872. Stotler explained that he was copying the article because he believed the recipient [Hoss] deserved the compliments.

[291]*Ibid.*, January 12 and 19; February 2, 1872.

[292]*Ibid.*, January 19, 1872.

[293]*House Journal Proceedings of the Legislative Assembly of the State of Kansas, 1872* (Topeka, KS: S.S. Prouty, State Printer, 1872), pp. 77 and 157; *The Emporia News*, January 19, 1872.

The committee revealed that not only were there not enough seats in the assembly room for all of the students, but that one class had to wait until the other classes had met and recited before it could do likewise, a situation that wasted much time. There was no room for a library nor for scientific apparatus, and the school suffered as a result.

[294]*Ibid.*, February 2, 1872; Council Proceedings, January 27, 1872.

[295]*Ibid., House Journal, 1872*, p. 357 and pp. 384-385.

[296]*Ibid.*, February 9, 1872. The full course of study was published in the advertisement of the spring term. When adopted by the board, it had been presented as a recommendation of the faculty. Space was provided in the Minutes for that recommendation, but was never copied therein.

[297]October 13, 1871 and March 29, 1872. Lumber for the Hoss residence came from Jay and company; woodwork was by J.Q. Reed, architect and contractor; stonework and chimneys by Douglas; plaster by Frances McCain; plain painting by Pythian; ornamental painting and grain work by Sonnedeker. A summer kitchen and woodhouse were yet to be added. When completed, the home was expected to cost in the neighborhood of $6,000. Hoss paid $1,200 to George Southwick of Marion County for the 5-acre plot in September, 1871. (Lyon County Register of Deeds office, Range Book #1, 10-19-11, Numerical Index, p. 497; Deed Record Book S, p. 13.)

[298]*Ibid.*, October 18, 1872. The Hoss residence and acreage eventually was taken into the city limits, but not until after it had changed hands several times. When Hoss and his wife Harriet returned to Indiana late in 1873, they sold their property to J.K. Finley. Four years later, he in turn sold it to T.J. Maltby. In March, 1881, George W. deCamp, a newcomer from Pittsburgh, Pennsylvania, purchased the property. He and his wife Nancy gradually subdivided the tract, but the family kept the homestead at 502 West Twelfth until the late 1950s. The Church of Christ edifice now stands where the original Hoss home stood for eighty-five years. (Deed Record Books V, p. 195; X, p. 60; #12, p. 580; #28, p. 114; #16, p. 343; #259, p. 371; and #262, p. 307.)

[299]Greenwood Abstract Company, Lyon County Register of Deeds Office, Abstract Research: Land Patent, May 7, 1860 Filed December 19, 1865; District Court, Lyon County Archives, Appearance Docket B, pp. 139, 242, 270-271.

[300]Lyon County Register of Deeds, Deed Record Book Q, p. 604; Deed Record Book T, p. 22. The unsatisfactory quit claim was filed on March 4, 1872; the second one on March 28. It was several years before the Indian Float issue was finally settled in behalf of the defendants.

[301]Minutes, March 8, 1872; Council Proceedings, February 20, March 25, and July 22, 1872.

[302]*The Emporia News*, February 16, 1872.

[303]*Ibid.*, Minutes, February 23, 1872. The three architects or builders who appeared at the late February meeting were E.T. Carr, J.G. Haskell, and Charles Wheelock.

[304]Minutes, March 8, 1872. The executive committee was instructed by the board to advertise for proposals under the direction of the architect, E.T. Carr.

[305]*The Emporia News*, April 19 and 26, 1872. According to the May 3 and July 26, 1872 issues of *Ibid.*, John McDonald made a permanent move from Independence to Emporia where he soon opened a wood manufacturing plant at the foot of Commercial Street. Second and third lowest bidders were an unidentified Leavenworth firm and John Hammond of Emporia.

[306]Minutes, April 24 and June 20, 1872. The three bidders were asked to submit separate bids on $42\frac{1}{2}$ inch and 48 inch boilers. See also *The Emporia News*, May 3, 1872. A Mr. Pollard of Emporia was given the contract for making 750,000 bricks for the Normal School building. Excavation and stonework was awarded to the Emporia firm of Champlin and Hughes who were to put about 20 men to work immediately. The stone was to come from a quarry near Cottonwood Falls. The June 24, 1872 issue of the paper stated that Champlin and Hughes had opened a new quarry on the A.T.S.F. Railroad two miles east of Cottonwood Falls. They were shipping 3 cars per day to Emporia for foundations, watertables, etc., of the Normal School building.

[307]*Ibid.*, March 22 and April 5, 1872.

[308]*Ibid.*, June 14, 21, and 28, 1872.

[309]In all probability, the Chetopa article was written by J.W. Horner, editor of the *Advance*, former president of Baker University, and a current member of the Normal School's Board of Directors.

[310]Minutes, June 20 and August 7, 1872; Council Proceedings, February 20 and July 22, 1872.

[311]*The Emporia News*, July 12 and 19, 1872. His lectures were at Neosho Falls, July 22; Humboldt, July 23; New Chicago [Chanute since January 1, 1873], July 24; Parsons, July 25; and Chetopa, July 26.

[312]*Ibid.*, August 9 and 30, 1872. Arrangements to board the students were made with Professor Jones. See Minutes for June 20 and August 7, 1872, and Annual Report of President Hoss for the Academic year ending June 21, 1872. In June, the Board had voted to establish a chair of mathematics and to suspend temporarily the chair of languages, an indication perhaps that languages could be handled

better by other members of the existing faculty than could mathematics. In August, the Board hired Babcock and voted for some unknown reason to allow Lamprey to draw his salary through August 31.

[313]*Ibid.* The Board considered four desk styles, three of which were from Kansas: McDonald of Emporia; Shomon and Purcell, Iola; and an unidentified manufacturer of Leavenworth. All three Kansas desks were declared to be "extremely cozy." See also *Ibid.*, September 13 and 27, and October 25, 1872, for progress of work on the Normal building.

[314]*Ibid.*, November 1, 1872. Except for Champlin and Hughes' stonework, the Normal building, including most of the partitions, was of Emporia brick, laid by Pope and Keeler. Roofing, both tin and slate, was by O.P. Bowman of Emporia. Benson acted as overseer. Frank McCain supervised the plaster job, and Brewer was general manager for the overall contractor, McDonald. Wheelock, supervising architect, personally inspected all materials. Miller and company of Leavenworth had the contract for plumbing and heating. Gas, steam, and waterpipes were all in place by November.

[315]Minutes, September 23, 1874; October 12, 1875; and November 16, 1876.

[316]The annual report, dated November 14, 1872, was published in the November 22 issue of *The Emporia News*. During the school year ending in June, 72 men and 118 women had been enrolled for a total of 190. There had been two seniors; three juniors; 44 in the second year; and 99 in the first year; 19 in the academic course not pledged to teach; and 23 in the preparatory class. Twenty-two Kansas counties were represented, and eight states.

Of the 1872 fall term, Hoss declared there was evidence of increased prosperity. All but 14 of the students in attendance were preparing to teach. Standards had been raised and ten of the 132 applicants had failed the entrance exams. [Presumably, those ten entered the preparatory department.]

[317]*The Emporia News*, December 20 and 27, 1872. In the January 24 issue of the paper, readiness of the new Normal building was promised for mid-February. Apparently, the patience of the public finally was exhausted, for when the middle of February arrived and the building still was not ready, a large crowd determined to see the building anyway. (See *Ibid.*, February 21, 1872.) According to the news account, the new Normal building was a popular place "last Sabbath" [February 16]. A thousand people must have taken a peep at its various rooms and viewed the landscape from the tower from which Americus, Plymouth, the Neosho Rapids windmill, and everything for fifteen miles around could be seen. In vain did McDonald [the contractor] lock doors and fasten windows to keep people out.

[318]Entered into the Minutes of May 6, 1873 is the following statement from M. McCoy, the statehouse engineer:

I have examined today [May 6] the heating apparatus of the Normal School and after having obtained a pressure of 72 pounds of steam, let the steam in the registers and kept up a heavy fire for an hour and a half. At the expiration of that time, there was 15 pounds pressure with all the fire I could possibly make. I think it would be impossible with the boiler now in use to keep the rooms farthest from it warm on a cold day, in its present condition. I think it is very necessary that there should be valves placed in the drip pipes in the engine room for several reasons: first, that the engineer could drain all of the registers by the valve in the engine room, whereas at present, he has to go to every register, and they cannot be regulated, as they now are without, some having too much drain which would necessarily heat the water too hot in the cistern for the pump to handle. I think the upper floor might be drained to the boiler which would be a great saving.

I do not think the boiler is of sufficient capacity to supply the registers. In the upper rooms, the thermometer stood at 78° with the windows closed. [Temperature outside was 70° degrees.]

Respectfully Submitted
M. McCoy

[319]Horner, Tucker, and Hoss were the only holdovers on the board.

[320]At the May board meeting, resignations of Emily F. Brewer, T.G. Jones, and S.S. Babcock were read. Brewer and Jones applied for reelection; Babcock did not. Apparently, neither Dilworth nor Philbrick turned in resignations.

[321]Minutes, August 6, 1873. Miss Smith was offered the principalship after Ella M. Stewart declined the offer. Mary F. Hapgood, Adrian, Michigan, was elected to the position of preceptress, but there is no record that she ever accepted. The executive committee eventually hired Mrs. Morse.

[322]*The Emporia News*, March 28 and June 20, 1873.

[323]Minutes, October 15, 1873. President Pomeroy in his 1875 annual report described the heating system as totally inadequate:

> Much inconvenience and considerable suffering and sickness resulted from the defective working of the present system during the fall and winter terms of the past year.

The Board of Visitors' report for the same year stated that so deficient was the heating system that it had been necessary to close the school on a cold day "this term." See "Emporia Normal School," 15th Annual Report, pp. 195-202, *14th-16th Annual Report Superintendent of Public Instruction*.

The first mention of the problem in *The Emporia News* was in the issue for December 3, 1875 in the following note: "The Normal School furnace makes a very successful refrigerator. It was put in by a Leavenworth firm."

[324]*Ibid*. The tribute read:

> Resolved by the (Board of) Regents of the State Normal School at Emporia, Kansas, that in parting with Geo. W. Hoss, LLD., President of our Institution for the past two years, we recognize in him an able and efficient Executive officer; a gentleman of high Christian character, of rare intellectual culture, and a thorough organizer and disciplinarian. He has merited and received our confident and support, and to him is largely due the prosperity of our Institution. We shall bear with us pleasant remembrances of our intercourse with him as an Educator and true gentleman.

[325]*The Emporia News*, November 21 and December 12, 1873. By November 13 when Hoss submitted his annual report, there were 171 students currently enrolled in the Normal department and 47 in the newly-opened training school for a total of 218 students. Nine applicants were rejected during the fall term.

Eight Normal students were getting daily practice teaching under Principal Rose Smith of the Model School. In order to get the Model School in full operation despite a dearth of funds, the Normal had accepted the entire seventh grade from the city schools. Other applicants over 15 years of age were also eligible to attend provided they could pass entrance examinations in spelling, reading, geography, arithmetic, and English grammar. (*Ibid*., August 29 and September 5, 1873; Minutes, August 6, 1873.)

[326]*Ibid*., October 31, 1873.

[327]December 19, 1873.

[328]*Ibid*. The silver, consisting of a cake basket, fruit stand, pickle stand, card receiver, and a pair of goblets, was purchased from T.M. Fry, local jeweler. Stotler described the pieces as being heavy, beautiful, and costing nearly $100 [an amazing sum considering faculty salaries at the time and the general scarcity of cash].

[329]*Ibid*., December 26, 1873. A brief note in the January 9, 1874, issue read: "The Normal School students think that 'J.L.D.' stands for 'Jackass of Low Degree' . . . , *Ledger*. It does. He took his degree in Normal Lyceum. J.L.D." Three weeks later over the same initials, an article appeared in *The Emporia Ledger* telling of a free lunch given on a Friday evening by the Lyceum at which rowdyism held sway. On Monday morning, the Normal president [Dr. C.R. Pomeroy] locked the hall and

put the key in his pocket, stating that the hall looked worse than any saloon he had ever seen. According to the writer, it was doubtful whether the Lyceum would be able to meet again. It did continue meeting, however, with apparently no further reports of high jinks. A month later, Cr. C.E. Lewis addressed the society on the sublimity and importance of education. The title of the speech was "If the flowers of summer bloom not, there will be no fruit in autumn." (*The Emporia News*, February 27, 1873.)

[330]*Ibid.*, December 12 and 19, 1873. As there is no record that Pomeroy ever purchased the Hoss property, he must have rented it during the years he and his family lived there. Hoss offered his property for sale late in 1873, and according to records in the Lyon County Register of Deeds office, J.K. Finley purchased the property on December 16, 1873, receiving the warranty deed on March 2, 1874.

[331]1889 *History*, pp. 39-40.

[332]March 6, 1874. Pomeroy's sermon concerned the importance of engaging in God's service while one is young. The reviewer (probably Stotler) was obviously impressed with what he had heard. "Now," the title of the review, was also the key word of the sermon, he claimed; and he proceeded to apply Pomeroy's words to some of Emporia's projects that needed doing now, utilizing nearly a full column for the piece.

[333]*The Emporia News*, March 13, 20, and 27, 1874. The first night's entertainment consisted of musical and literary numbers. On the second night, a drama "Among the Breakers" was given. Although the 1889 *History*, pp. 63-64, indicates that the Lyceum was successor to the Normal Literary Union and that the Philadelphi was a new organization, it seems logical that the latter—whose membership included members of the former Union, and whose public performances seemed more akin to the Union's than did those of the Lyceum—was really the progeny of the Union. At any rate, the Philadelphi won possession of the organ which had been purchased by the Union's efforts. (It is unfortunate that all records of the early societies were destroyed in the fire of 1878.)

[334]*Ibid.*, April 3, 1874.

[335]*Ibid.*, April 10, May 1, 8, and 15, 1874.

[336]*Ibid.*, May 22 and June 5, 1874; Minutes, June 17, 1874, and June 13, 1876. Upon recommendation of the faculty, a fifteenth member of the class of 1874, G.L. Kennedy, was graduated from the Elementary course in 1875, according to the Minutes for June 1, 1875. While the Elementary course was a two-year program, a preparatory year was necessary for most of the students.

Awarding of degrees during the early period of the Normal School seems to have begun and ended with Pomeroy's administration. (1889 *History*, p. 25.) An incorrect reading of the aforementioned history in all probability accounts for the false statement that appears in the Thesis v. 1, p. 41: ". . . there is no record to indicate that these degrees were ever given."

[337]June 26, 1874. Pomeroy's text for his sermon was from the New Testament (I John 2:14); "I have written unto you, young men, because ye are strong."

[338]*Ibid.* Other graduates of 1874 and titles of their speeches were Eva L. Howard, Americus, "The Nobility of the Teachers' Vocation;" Dora Wilson, Windham, Ohio, "There's Room Up Higher;" Mary L. Dickerson, Marion Center, "Our Influence;" Anna M. Stinson, Waushara, "Elementary Science;" Nettie Thurston, Manhattan, "Wrecks;" Nellie Spaulding, Wathena, "Man and Nature;" Ansel Gridley, Jr., Oxford, "The Demands of the Age Upon Young Men;" Hattie Ward, Emporia, "Girls;" Sadie Rogers, Princeton, "Stepping Stones;" Jennie R. Campbell, Plymouth, "Knowing More; Or When Will the End Be?"; Annie Melville, Sturgis, Michigan, "Shams;" and Lillian A. Norton, Arkansas City, "High Places."

Gridley was loudly cheered and bouquets thrown at the Misses Cole, Norton, Rogers, and Dickerson.

[339]*The Emporia News*, July 17 and 24, August 28, 1874. At a Presbyterian meeting, Pomeroy spoke on the relationship of the Sunday School to the church. A basket meeting [which today would be referred to as a basket dinner] held near the confluence of the Neosho and Cottonwood Rivers six miles S.E. of Emporia, at which Pomeroy preached, was held on August 23.

Of the eight educators listed on the program of the institute, held September 1-3 at the Normal School, four were from the Normal faculty (Pomeroy, Norton, Carmichael, and Sprague). L.B. Kellogg, also, was listed on the program. Attendance, however, was considered meager. (*Ibid.*, September 4, 1874.)

[340]*Ibid.*, August 21, September 4, 11, and 18, 1874; Minutes, June 17, 1874. Miss L.E. Sprague, who had taught during the spring term, was hired as principal of the training or practice school. Her assistant was Miss Irene Gilbert of Winona, Minnesota. Mrs. J.D. Lee, graduate of Mt. Holyoke and teacher at Carlton College, Minnesota, was hired to teach music. [These three women who remained at the Normal but a year or so continued careers in teaching after leaving Emporia.] Norton returned from his leave of absence for the fall term.

[341]*Fourteenth-Sixteenth Annual Report of the Superintendent of Public Instruction*, pp. 154-161.

[342]*Ibid.*

[343]*The Emporia News*, September 18 and 25, October 23 and 30, 1874. The ranting politician was a Mr. Wilcox, candidate for District Clerk. Stotler took the occasion to point out the extra services to the state rendered by the Normal faculty, such as assisting with institutes throughout the state; yet they were paid less than those at the university. To suppress the school now, would be the "height of folly."

Probably, one reason for the attack upon the Normal at this particular time was that a study of appropriations to the various state institutions from 1866-1873 had just been made public. According to that report, Kansas State Normal had received a total of $142,297.17. That figure, however, does not include the assistance given by the citizens of Emporia and Lyon County. (*The Emporia Ledger*, February 5, 1874.)

[344]*Ibid.*, November 27, December 4, 11, and 18, 1874. Officers were H.B. Norton, president; Miss Cornelia Slack, vice president; George A. Whitney, secretary; Miss Lama Gordon, treasurer; Frank Kizer, curator. Plans were to hold public meetings monthly, a schedule adhered to at least through the first year. Second and third public meetings were held in February and March, 1875. (*Ibid.*, February 5 and March 12, 1875.) According to the 1889 *History*, p. 64, however, public meetings were held but once each term.

[345]*Ibid.*, December 11, 18, and 25, 1874. The initial charge of $3.00 per term, set by the Board of Directors, apparently deterred many parents from enrolling their young children in the practice school, thereby resulting in the charge being cut by half. [Originally, the use of textbooks was free.]

[346]*Ibid.*, January 1 and 8, 1875; *14th-16th Annual Report Superintendent of Public Instruction* (15th Report), "Emporia Normal School," pp. 195-202. In addition to Mr. and Mrs. Pomeroy, faculty members were S.C. Delap [Norton's replacement], P.J. Carmichael, Mrs. Morse, Misses Mary A. Dickason, music; Rebecca Buchanan, drawing and penmanship [both replacements for Mrs. J.D. Lee]; Irene Gilbert [Miss Sprague's replacement]; and Effie Partch. The two assistants who taught preparatory students were Mrs. S.C. (Marion) Delap and Ansel Gridley.

[347]*Ibid.*, February 5, 1875; *Kansas Public Documents, 1874* (Topeka, Kansas State Printing Works, George W. Martin, Public Printer, 1875), pp. 3-38.

[348]*The Emporia News*, March 5, 1875. Serving in the House in 1875 were two men from Labette County: J.J. Woods, a farmer, and R.W. Wright, physician. It seems probable that Woods was the one to whom Stotler referred. Both men, however, voted for the appropriation bill as amended. The vote was 54 − 15. (*House Journal*, 1875.)

[349]Minutes, September 23, 1874 and March 9, 1875. Music and drawing continued to be taught by one teacher for the rest of the school year; but in June the Board voted to pay the sum of $750 for both a music teacher and a drawing-penmanship teacher. By the fall term, the Misses Mary Dickason had been hired for music and Rebecca Buchanan for drawing. Although Miss Dickason did not remain longer than a year, Miss Buchanan seems to have remained until 1880. (1889 *History*, p. 43.)

At the end of the spring term, a sum of $50 which remained in the salary fund was divided between Mrs. Morse and Miss Gilbert, the two women teachers whose salaries had been reduced by 18½%. By Board decision, each was to receive her $25 for the fall term. (*Ibid.*, June 1, 1875.)

[350]*The Emporia News*, March 26, 1875. It is this writer's opinion that Stotler, whether or not by design, misrepresented the facts regarding the employment of Mrs. Pomeroy. She had taught a full term at the Normal by the time Stotler wrote his editorial. He had already announced her appointment early in January (footnote #345). Moreover, her appointment had taken place before the legislature cut appropriations. According to the Minutes, the position in languages was decided upon as early as September 23, 1874, at a salary of $1600. In December, the executive committee was instructed to fill the position.

[351]*Ibid.*, April 16, 1875. Another to leave for a more lucrative position was Mrs. J.D. Lee, teacher of music, drawing, and penmanship for the past year. She left in June for a position in the Mankato, Minnesota State Normal School at a salary of $1000. (*Ibid.*, May 21, 1875.)

[352]*Ibid.*, June 11, 1875. The watch, an Elgin, was purchased from T.M. Fry, local jeweler. O.A. Shattuck of the post office jewelry store did the engraving.

[353]*Ibid.*

[354]*Ibid.*, May 14 and June 4, 1875. Among the 24 candidates were ten from Emporia. All areas of the district, except Topeka, were represented.

[355] *Ibid.*
[356] *Ibid.*, June 18, 1875. The Latin motto can be translated thus: "If we protect the steps, the end will crown the work."

[357]*Ibid.*, July 30 and August 27, 1875.

[358]*Ibid.*, October 15 and 29, 1875. According to Stotler, the performance was scheduled to be repeated in Council Grove.

[359]*Ibid.*, November 19, 1875.

[360]*Ibid.*, December 17, 1875. See the December 10 issue for the closing of the term schedule.

[361]*Ibid*, December 17, 1875. Officers of the Sumner were Ansel Gridley, president; Miss Emma Davis, secretary; and Joseph Hill, treasurer.

[362]*The Emporia News*, January 14, 21, and 28, 1876. Stotler first reported enrollment to be 250, but was corrected the following week. In the Emporia *Ledger*, January 20, 1876, appeared the following:

> Last week we stated that the students in the Normal had attained the unprecedented number of 340. *The Commonwealth* [Topeka] published the item, but made the number 840. This shows how stories will sometimes grow, and nobody to blame.

[363]Minutes, October 12, 1875.

[364]*The Emporia News*, January 28, 1876. The committee included Senators Thomas Bartlett, Allen County; Thomas L. Johnson, Leavenworth; W.L. Parkinson, Franklin; Representative P.P. Elder of Franklin, chairman of the House committee; J.E. Duncan, Harvey; J.C. Stone, Leavenworth; E.S. Pierce, Lincoln; H. Berry, Chautauqua; T.B. Tomlinson, Atchison; and George N. Nichols of Cloud.

[365]*Ibid.*, February 18, 1876.

[366]March 3, 1876.

[367]*Ibid.* See also the *Emporia Ledger*, March 2, 1876.

[368]*Laws of Kansas, 1876*, p. 37. It is interesting that the same legislature dictated that Kansas University organize a Normal department. See pp. 41-43 for "An Act making appropriations for the state university for the fiscal year ending November 30, 1876, and providing for Normal department." On p. 42 at the end of Sec. 1 of the Act is the following provision:

> . . . for finishing necessary recitation rooms in new university building, five thousand dollars; Provided, that the regents of the university shall immediately organize a normal department in said university, and open the same for the reception of Normal students, and detail one or more instructors to conduct the same.

Although the university, according to its 1864 charter, was to have a normal department as one of its six components, nothing had been done about the matter until after the 1876 legislature acted. Thereupon, the university regents agreed to open a normal department by April 1. After operating for eight years, the department was abolished by the 1885 legislature, but the program survived unchanged except for a change in name. (*The University of Kansas: A History* by Clifford Stephen Griffin, pp. 130-132.)

[369]March 3, 1876.

[370]P. 894. Bill #450 was introduced to locate a Normal School in the southwestern part of the state.

[371]*Ibid.*, p. 913.

[372]*Ibid.*, pp. 248-249. According to p. 1323, Eskridge's substitute appropriation bill failed by a single vote (44-45) to be considered further by the legislature.

[373]*The Emporia Ledger*, March 9, 1876. During the visit of the Methodist ministers and lay leaders to the Normal School on March 2, they were formally welcomed by a senior student, Ansel Gridley, and treated to an exercise in calisthenics by the class of Miss M. Davis, and a choral recitation of "The Song of Hiawatha" by Irene Gilbert's pupils from the Model School. Bishop Peck, who addressed faculty and students, revealed that both Mr. and Mrs. Pomeroy had been students of his many years before, when they were children. See also *The Emporia News*, March 10, 1876.
[374]Minutes, March 15, 1876. Present at the meeting were J.H. Crichton, M.M. Murdock, A. Sellers, H.C. Cross, and C.R. Pomeroy. The executive committee consisted of C.B. Butler, Cross, and Pomeroy.

[375]*The Emporia News*, March 17 and 24, 1876. Closing of the term exercises included the usual written examinations, March 16, 17, and on Monday, March 20. President Pomeroy delivered the term sermon in the Methodist Church on Sunday morning, and the oral exams were Tuesday and Wednesday, March 21 and 22. A letter written to Stotler gave a positive review of the exercises. The spectator spoke highly of Mrs. Pomeroy's English grammar orals and those of Miss Buchanan in Drawing. Miss Dickason's music groups were also complimented.

Of particular interest in the March 24 issue was a reprint of an article from the Jefferson City, Missouri *Daily Journal* to the Topeka *Commonwealth* inviting Kansans to attend Missouri's Normal Schools.
[376]*The Emporia Ledger*, April 27, 1876.

[377]*E-News*, April 7, 1876. Debaters were I.T. Way and S.C. Delap, affirmative; P.J. Carmichael and Ansel Gridley, negative.

[378]*Ibid.*, May 5, 1876.

[379]*Ibid.*, advice that apparently was not heeded. See the issue of June 9, 1876: "Trees were doing well, but students seemed to forget Kellogg's advice. The Board should tend them over the summer."

[380]*The Emporia Ledger*, May 4, 18, 25, June 1, 8, and 15; *The Emporia News*, May 5, 26, June 2, 9, and 16.

[381]*E-News*, June 16, 1876.

[382]*The Emporia Ledger*, June 22, 1876.

[383]*Ibid.*, June 29, 1876.

[384]*Ibid.*, June 22, 1876.

[385]See 1889 *History*, Part II, p. 64. In the 1872 Catalog, Mrs. Caveness is mistakenly listed as an 1870 graduate.

[386]*E-News*, June 16, 1876; Board Minutes, June 13, 1876. Graduates of the Normal Course were Ansel Gridley, Jr., Oxford; Joseph H. Hill, Osage City; Ella Murdock, Laura Gordon, and Hattie Ward (Scientific) of Emporia. Elementary course graduates were Addison W. Stubbs, Joseph Clayton, Hiram T. Pickett, Lizzie Janney, and Flora A. Bennett of Emporia; Buel T. Davis, Maggie M. Davis, and Roxanna Davis of Hesper; Allie A. Gordon and Emma C. Gordon, Eureka; Sarah Romigh, Cottonwood Falls; O.B. Wharton, Reading; and William Sherwood of Burlington.

[387](1) The Faculty shall be discharged at the close of the present term, with the exception of the President, who is retained, without salary, to represent the Board of Regents, and to conduct the Normal School.

(2) The President is hereby authorized to continue the Normal School for the fall and winter terms of the ensuing year, employing such teachers as he may deem necessary, and to charge a tuition fee of $5 per term for the preparatory year, and $7 for more advanced studies, and also an incidental fee of $2 per term, provided that the Board of Regents shall not be responsible for any expenses incurred in conducting the school and that the buildings and premises be maintained in good shape.

(3) The textbooks in the Normal may be used by students, subject to the provisions previously made for rental, the money thus accruing to be applied in liquidating the debt incurred in their purchase.

(4) The Board of Regents engage to ratify the educational work of the Normal during these terms upon satisfactory evidence of its thoroughness.

(5) The Executive Committee are empowered to make such additional arrangements as they deem necessary for prosecuting successful the work of the

Normal, provided they do not involve the Board of Regents or the State in financial obligations.

[388]*E-News*, June 30, and July 7, 1876.

[389]*Ibid.*, July 14, 21, and August 4, 1876.

[390]*Ibid.*, August 11, 1876; *The Emporia Ledger*, August 3, 1876.

[391]August 18, 1876.

[392]*E-News*, September 8, 1876; *The Emporia Ledger*, September 7, 1876. Rates for the Model School were $5 for advanced pupils and $3 for lower grades. Books could be purchased at cost or rented as to the Normal students.

[393]*E-News*, September 29, 1876. Signed "A Student." The *Fourteenth to Sixteenth Annual Report Superintendent of Public Instruction*: "Emporia Normal School," Report of the Board of Regents, pp. 158-172.

[394]*E-News*, December 8 and 15, 1876. President Pomeroy gave the Term Sermon at the Methodist Church on Sunday, December 10, as part of the closing of the term festivities. A reprint in the latter issue from the *Eldorado Times* lauded the flourishing condition of the Normal considering the circumstances. "Now that the school is over all of its trouble, if the legislature does its duty this winter, it will rank among the very highest educational institutions in the West." There also was a reprint from the *Winfield Courier*, stating that in spite of last winter's "bad treatment" at the hands of the legislature, the Normal is reported to be in good condition considering. The editor hoped that the next legislature would appropriate sufficient amount to enable them to take their place with similar institutions in the West.

[395]*Ibid.*, November 24, 1876.

[396]*Ibid.*, December 15 and 29, 1876.

[397]Miscellaneous expenses approved by the legislature on March 7, 1877 and published on March 8: "To the Board of Regents of the state Normal School at Emporia for the following purposes; for repairing building (work already done), two hundred dollars; for repairing and resetting boiler, three hundred dollars; for blackboards and material, two hundred eighty dollars; for painting roof of building, one hundred dollars.

[398]Board Minutes, March 2, 1877.

Appendix

An Act to Establish, Locate and Endow a State Normal School.

Be it enacted by the Legislature of the State of Kansas:

Location. SECTION 1. That there be and is hereby established and permanently located at the town of Emporia, in Lyon Co., a State Normal School, the exclusive purposes of which shall be the instruction of persons, both male and female, in the art of teaching, and in all the various branches that pertain to a good common school education, and in the mechanic arts, and in the arts of husbandry and agricultural chemistry, and in the fundamental laws of the United States, and in what regards the rights and duties of citizens; *Provided,* That a tract of land, not less that twenty acres, adjacent to said town of Emporia, be donated and secured to the State, in fee simple, as a site for said Normal School, within twelve months from the taking effect of this act.

Com'rs appointed. SEC. 2. That the Governor of the State is hereby empowered to appoint three commissioners, which commissioners, or a majority of them, shall meet at Emporia, aforesaid, on or before the first day of September, 1863, and, having taken an oath to faithfully discharge their duties, shall proceed to select the aforesaid site, and see that a good and sufficient deed be made to the State for the same, which deed shall be duly recorded in the records of the Recorder of Deeds for Lyon county, aforesaid, and deposited with the Auditor of State; and on the site thus selected by the commissioners aforesaid, the State Normal School shall be forever located; and said commissioners shall make a full report of their proceedings to the Governor on or before the first day of January, 1864.

Lands donated. SEC. 3. That all lands granted to the State of Kansas, and selected by said State, adjoining, or as contiguous as may be to each of the salt springs belonging to said State, and granted by the fourth sub-division of the third section of an act of Congress entitled, "An act for the admission of Kansas into the Union," approved, January 29th, 1861, save and except the salt springs, and the section of land upon which each of the said salt springs are located, and one additional section, are hereby set apart and reserved as a perpetual endowment for the support and maintenance of the Normal School established and located by this act.

Money to be invested. SEC. 4. That all moneys derived from the sale, rent or lease of the lands aforesaid, shall be invested in stocks of the United States, the State of Kansas, or some other safe and reliable stocks, as the Legislature may determine, yielding not less than six per centum per annum upon the par value of said stocks, and that the money so invested shall constitute a perpetual fund, the principal of which shall remain forever undiminished, and the interest of which shall be inviolably appropriated by the Legislature of the

State of Kansas, to the support and maintenance of the Normal School established and located by the provisions of this act, and to the further purpose of constructing and keeping in repair a suitable building or buildings for the said Normal School; but to no other purpose or purposes whatever.

SEC. 5. The Legislature may, at any time, alter, amend, or repeal this act, but such alteration, amendment or repeal shall not cause a removal of said Normal School, nor operate as a diversion or diminution of the endowment fund herein provided for.

SEC. 6. This act to take effect and be in force from and after its publication; and immediately after the approval thereof by the Governor, it is hereby made the duty of the Secretary of State to cause this act to be published once in the *Emporia News*, a newspaper published in Lyon county, Kansas, which shall constitute such publication.

Approved, March 3d, 1863.

THOMAS CARNEY,
Governor.

I hereby certify the foregoing to be a true copy of the enrolled Law now on file in my office, and that the same was published in the *Emporia News*, (Emporia, Kansas,) for March 7, 1863.

W. W. H. LAWRENCE,
Secretary of State.

AN ACT to organize the State Normal School.

Be it enacted by the Legislature of the State of Kansas:

SECTION 1. That the State Normal School, established and located at Emporia, in Lyon county, Kansas, upon the site selected by the commissioners in pursuance of an act of the Legislature of the State of Kansas, entitled "An act to establish, locate and endow a State Normal School," approved March 3d, 1863, shall be under the direction of a board of directors, and shall be governed and supported as hereafter provided.

B'rd of directors —how constit'd.

SEC. 2. The board of directors shall consist of nine members, six of whom shall be appointed by the Governor; and the Governor [Secretary] of State, State Treasurer and State Superintendent of Public Instruction shall, by virtue of their office, be members of said board.

State treasurer treas'r of board.

SEC. 3. The State Treasurer shall, by virtue of his office, be treasurer of said board, and the members thereof shall annually select one of their number president, and one of their number secretary.

Directors not to be interested in contracts.

SEC. 4. No member of said board of directors shall, during his continuance in office as a member of said board, act as the agent of any publisher or publishers of school books or school library books, or become interested in the publication or sale of any such books, as agent or otherwise; and the Governor of this State is hereby authorized and required, upon satisfactory evidence being produced to him that any member of said board is employed as such agent, or is interested in the manner aforesaid, by and with the advice of the State Superintendent and State Treasurer, to remove such member of said board from office, and appoint another member in his place, to fill such vacancy.

Principal and assistant teachers.

SEC. 5. Said board of directors shall have power to appoint a principal and assistant, to take charge of said school, without expense to the State, and such other teachers and officers as may be required in said school, and fix the salary of each, and prescribe their several duties. They shall also have power to remove either principal, assistant or teacher, and to appoint others in their stead. They shall prescribe the various books to be used in such school, and shall make all the by-laws necessary for the good government of the same.

Experimental school.

SEC. 6. Said board shall also establish an experimental school in connection with said Normal School, in which the pupils shall have opportunity to practice the modes of instruction and discipline inculcated in the State Normal School; and said board shall make all the regulations necessary to govern and support the same, and may, in their discretion, admit pupils free of charge for tuition, and without expense to the State.

Regulations.

Sec'y of board to notify Sup't Pub. Instruction.

SEC. 7. As soon as said Normal School is prepared to receive pupils, the secretary of the board of directors shall notify the Superintendent of Public Instruction, who shall immediately give notice of the fact to each County Clerk in the State.

SEC. 8. The board of directors shall ordain such rules and regulations for the admission of pupils to said Normal School as they shall deem necessary and proper. Every applicant for admission shall undergo an examination in such manner as may be prescribed by the board, and if it shall appear that the applicant is not a person of good moral character, such applicant shall be rejected. The board of directors may, in their discretion, require any applicant for admission to said school other than such as shall be by law entitled to admission free, and who shall, prior to such admission, sign and file with said board a declaration of intention to follow the business of teaching common schools in this State, to pay or secure to be paid such fees for tuition as the said board shall deem reasonable.

SEC. 9. That each representative district in this State shall be entitled to send one pupil each term of twenty-two weeks of said school, said pupil to be recommended by the representative of the district to the board of directors; the person thus recommended shall be admitted free of tuition : *Provided*, the applicant shall be of good moral character, and shall sustain a satisfactory examination, and sign a declaration of intention to follow the business of teaching common schools in this State : *And provided further*, that pupils may be admitted without signing such declaration of intention on such terms as the board of directors may prescribe; and said board of directors are hereby authorized to make such order as they may deem proper for the separate education of white and colored pupils in said institution, securing to them equal educational advantages.

SEC. 10. After said Normal School shall have commenced its first term, and at least once in each year thereafter, it shall be visited by three suitable persons, not members of said board, to be appointed by the Superintendent of Public Instruction, who shall examine thoroughly into the affairs of the school, and report to the Superintendent their views with regard to its condition, success and usefulness, and any other matters they may judge expedient. Such visitors shall be appointed annually.

SEC. 11. It shall be the duty of the Superintendent of Public Instruction, once at least in one year, to visit said Normal School, and he shall annually make to the Legislature a full and detailed report of the doings of the board of directors, and of all their expenditures and the moneys received for tuition, and the prospects, progress and usefulness of said school, including so much of the reports of said visitors as he may deem advisable.

SEC. 12. Lectures on chemistry and comparative anatomy, physiology, astronomy, and on any other science, or any branch of literature that the board of directors may direct, may be delivered to those attending the said Normal School, in such manner and on such terms and conditions as the said board may prescribe.

SEC. 13. As soon as any person has attended said institution twenty-two weeks, said person may be examined in the studies required by the board in such manner as may be prescribed, and if it shall appear that said person possesses the learning and other qualifications necessary to teach a good common school, said person shall receive a certificate to that effect from the principal, to be approved by the Superintendent of Public Instruction; and as soon as any person shall have completed the full course of instruction in the State Normal School, he *Diploma granted.* or she shall receive a diploma, which, when signed by the President of the institution, State Superintendent of Public Instruction, and the board of directors of said school, shall be evidence that the person to whom such diploma is granted is a graduate of the State Normal School, and entitled to all the honors and privileges belonging to such graduates, and such diploma shall serve as a legal certificate of qualification to teach in the common schools of this State.

SEC. 14. The board of directors are hereby authorized to make such by-laws and regulations as they may deem proper *By-laws.* for the well ordering and government of said school and board of directors in the transaction of their business: *Provided,* the same be not repugnant to the constitution or laws of this State or of the United States: *And provided further,* that the same may at any time be altered or abrogated by the Legislature. Said board of directors shall have power to transact all necessary business at any meeting, a quorum being present, and meetings may be called in such manner as their by-laws shall prescribe, and a quorum shall consist of a majority of the board. The first meeting may be held at such time and place as may be directed by the State Superintendent of Public Instruction, and no publication of notice thereof shall be necessary, and the attendance of a quorum shall render valid the proceedings of such meeting, and all process against such board shall be served on the president or secretary.

SEC. 15. The members of the board of directors, appointed *Directors to hold office three yrs.* in pursuance of section second of this act, shall hold their office for three years and until their successors are appointed, and any vacancy which may occur in said board by death, removal, resignation or otherwise, shall be filled by appointment by the Governor.

SEC. 16. That the board of directors provided for in this act, be and they are hereby authorized and empowered, in the name of the State, to receive by gift, grant or donation, any *Grants and donations.* property that may be given, granted or donated to said institution, for the purposes of said institution; but said board of directors shall have no power to make any contract or incur any indebtedness in the organization or control of said institution, either in the name of the State, or for which the State may be made liable.

SEC. 17. This act to take effect and be in force from and after its publication in the statute book.

Approved February 16, 1864.

THOMAS CARNEY,
Governor

¹

Kansas State Normal School.

The Board of Directors of the State Normal School respectfully announce to the friends of Common Schools throughout the State, that the first term of this Teachers' School will commence on Wednesday, the 15th of February, 1865, at Emporia, Lyon County, and continue for 19 weeks, under the care of L. B. Kellogg, late of the State Normal University of Illinois.

DESIGN OF THE SCHOOL

The object of the Normal School, is to prepare teachers for the Common Schools of the State.

COURSE OF STUDY.

The studies pursued will be those taught in the Common Schools, to which will be added the different branches of a complete English education, together with so much of Latin and Greek as are necessary to a full understanding of our own language. In every department constant reference will be had to the best methods of teaching the subjects under consideration.

ADMISSION.

By the provisions of the Act establishing the School, each Representative District is entitled to gratuitous instruction for one pupil, who is to be recommended by the Representative of that district, and is to file with the Principal of the school a declaration of his intention to become a teacher in the State.

For the first term other students than those entitled by law to gratuitous instruction may be admitted free of tuition, provided they file a declaration of their intention to become teachers.

Applicants for admission must be, if males, not less than sixteen years of age; if females, not less than fifteen.

EXPENSES.

TUITION: Free for those designing to become teachers; for others, 50 cents per week.

Good board may be secured in private families at from $3.50 to $4.50 per week.

Application for admission may be made to the Secretary of the Board of Directors, or the Principal, of whom further information respecting the school may be obtained.

G. C. MORSE, Sec'y. B'd.
L. B. KELLOGG, Principal.

Emporia, February 1st, 1865.

N. B. It is desirable that every student be present on the first day of the term.

Published in The Emporia News prior to the opening of school: on February 4 and February 11, 1865.

STATE NORMAL SCHOOL,

EMPORIA, KANSAS.

ORDER OF EXERCISES

At the Close of the Present Term, June 27th and 28th, 1865.

TUESDAY.

Examination of classes will occupy the forenoon and afternoon.

In the evening, addresses by His Excellency Gov. Crawford, Prof. I. T. Goodnow, Superintendent of Public Instrutcion, L. B. Kellogg, Principal, together with recitations and songs by the students.

WEDNESDAY.

Examination of classes will be continued during the forenoon.

In the afternoon, Judge D. G. Brewer, of Leavenworth, will deliver an address before the student teachers and friends of Education.

The exercises will be closed in the evening by

THE STUDENTS RECE'PTION

AT THE NORMAL SCHOOL ROOM.

The examinations of each day and the exercises generally, will be open to the public.

Teachers and friends of education throughout the State are invited to be present.

The next term of this school will begin on Wednesday, September 13th, 1865.

The announcement concerned the first of many annual anniversary exercises scheduled in the early years of the Kansas State Normal School. From The Emporia News, June 17 and 24, 1865.

vii

This Ad announcing the
opening of the fall term of the
Kansas State Normal School
appeared in The Emporia News,
September 9 and 16, 1865.
Although this was the second
term in the history of the school,
it was the first of three terms
in a new school year.

THE STATE NORMAL SCHOOL,

EMPORIA, KANSAS.

BOARD OF DIRECTORS:

Hon. C. V. Eskridge, Rev. O. C. Morse, Sec.
Hon. T. S. Huffaker, Hon. James Rogers,
Prof. J. M. Rankin, Judge J. W. Robbutt.

EX OFFICIO MEMBERS:

His Excellency, Gov. S. J. Crawford, President.
Hon. William Spriggs, Treasurer.
Hon. I. T. Goodnow, State Sup't Pub. Instruction.

L. B. KELLOGG, Principal.
H. B. NORTON, Assistant Principal.

OBJECT.

The design of the Normal School is to assist
in providing good Teachers for the Public
Schools of the State.

HISTORY.

The School was organized by act of the Legislature, approved February 16th, 1864, and was
opened for the reception of students February
16th, 1865. Eighteen were present. The number increased until, at the end of the term, forty-
two names had been placed in the class books,
and forty-two students had received instruction.
The studies were, in theory, a review of the elementary branches taught in our schools, but included much more than is usual with such studies,
amounting, in some cases, to nearly an original
investigation. The term closed on the 27th and
28th days of June.

CALENDAR.

The School Year of forty weeks is divided as
follows: First term, commencing on Wednesday, September 13th, 1865, continues fourteen
weeks. Vacation, one week. Second term,
twelve weeks. Vacation, one. Third term,
twelve weeks. Students are admitted at the
beginning of each term; those from a distance
should make arrangements to reach Emporia the
day preceding the opening of each term.

ADMISSION.

By the provisions of the Act of Organization
each Representative District in the State is entitled to gratuitous instruction for one pupil, to be
chosen by its Representative. The Principal is
authorized to receive, free of tuition, other students who intend to become teachers, and a limited number who do not, on payment of a reasonable tuition fee in advance. Pledges will be
required of those who are to teach.
Students are required to be, if males, seventeen, and if females, sixteen years of age. This
rule may be suspended in favor of pupils who
intend to complete the course of study before
teaching, and manifest sufficient maturity of
mind.
Applications for admission may be made to
the Principal, or O. C. Morse, Secretary of the
Board, at Emporia, and should be forwarded as
soon as possible.

EXPENSES.

A contingent fee of five dollars a year will be
required of each student, to meet incidental
expenses.

BOARDING.

Board can be obtained in families at reasonable rates. Arrangements will be made for boarding in clubs, for such as may desire it, thereby
securing a great reduction of cost. A large
Boarding House is about to be erected for the
use of Normal students, which will be completed as soon as practicable.
Assistance in procuring boarding places will
be given to students if desired. Call upon Rev.
O. C. Morse or the Principal.

MISCELLANEOUS.

The course of study includes all branches
necessary to a thorough English Education.
Latin and Greek are optional.
Most of the text books are furnished by the
State. Students are advised to bring with them
such books as they have, but not to purchase
others until they arrive.
Good order and thorough discipline are neces-
sary, and will, therefore, be insisted upon.
Physical Exercises will be had daily.
Students who wish will have opportunity to
take music lessons.

EMPORIA, Kansas, September 9th, 1865.

SENATE BILL No. 45.

AN ACT FOR THE PAYMENT OF THE TEACHERS AND PROFESSORS OF THE STATE NORMAL SCHOOL, THE STATE AGRICULTURAL COLLEGE.

Be it enacted by the Legislature of the State of Kansas:

SECTION 1. That two thousand dollars is hereby appropriated to the State Normal School, to be used by the directors exclusively for the salaries of teachers for the year eighteen hundred and sixty-five; also, three thousand and two hundred dollars to the State Agricultural College to be used by the regents exclusively for the payment of teachers and professors for the year eighteen hundred and sixty-five; Provided, That a part of such appropriation shall be expended in the publication of two hundred catalogues of all the scholars taught in such school, which catalogue, shall give the age of each scholar, and the grade of studies, and their place of residence. Such catalogue shall be laid upon the tables of the members of the Legislature at the opening of the session.

SEC. 2. That the professors of the Agricultural College of the State of Kansas, shall annually, during the months of January and February deliver a course of lectures on agriculture and agricultural chemistry, and said lectures shall be free to all who may desire to attend, and there shall be at least five lectures in each week of said months.

SEC. 3. The Auditor of State is hereby authorized to issue warrants on the State Treasurer in favor of the Board of Directors of the State Normal School, also in favor of the Treasurer of the Board of Regents of the State Agricultural College, in accordance with the provisions of this act, said orders to be drawn quarterly on presentation of the certified accounts of the several teachers and professors, for services rendered, and shall be marked severally with the names of the several institutions in whose favor they are drawn.

SEC. 4. This act to take effect and be in force from and after its publication once in the KANSAS EDUCATIONAL JOURNAL.

Approved February 14th, 1865.

S. J. CRAWFORD, Governor.

I, R. A. Barker, Secretary of State, do hereby certify that the above is a true and correct copy of the original on file in my office.

In testimony whereof, I have set my hand and fixed the official seal of my office, this 23d day of February, 1865.

R. A. BARKER, Secretary of State.

DEDICATION HYMN
by
H. B. Norton

The ancient night is almost gone;
    Deep echoes to awakening deep,
As ever westward, ever on,
    The banners of the morning sweep,
And new-born states their arms outspread
    O'er mountain heights and plains afar,
As westward still the nations tread,
    And westward rolls the iron car!

The opening era points the way,
    And makes the mission-work sublime,
Which molds the infants of today
    To giants of the coming time.
And joyfully we gather here,
    To consecrate, with solemn praise,
A fane which earnest souls may rear
    To gladden all the future days.

By all the progress and the might
    Which other ages shall unfold—
By all the brilliant beams that light
    The Future's skies of morning gold—
By all that sheds a cheering ray
    Upon the path the Past has trod—
We dedicate its walls, this day,
    To Truth, to Freedom, and to God!

The above poem was first published in The Emporia News,
December 22, 1866.

xiii

CLASS SONG

Now our feet stand on the threshold
    'Tis the hour expected long;
And our hearts are sad, yet hopeful,
    As we sing our parting song;

Sad to leave these Halls of learning,
    Sad to leave our friends so dear,
Sad to think no more we gather
    As we oft have gathered here.

But the world lies broad before us,
    And our goal far yonder stands;
Bright-winged Hope is smiling o'er us,
    Earnest work awaits our hands.

From the School-house by the roadside,
    Or the crowded city street,
Youthful voices loud are calling:
    Forth we go with willing feet.

Aid us, O our Heavenly Teacher;
    Lead us on our devious way,
Till Thy Hand shall grant diplomas
    On Life's Graduation Day.

Be it enacted by the Legislature of the State of Kansas:

SECTION 1. That the sum of fourteen thousand dollars be and the same is hereby appropriated to the state normal school, to be expended under the direction of the board of directors thereof, as follows: Five thousand six hundred and fifty dollars, or so much thereof as may be necessary, for the completion of the building now in occupation by the school; fifteen hundred dollars, or so much thereof as may be necessary, for furniture and apparatus for the school; four thousand dollars, or so much thereof as may be necessary, for teachers' salaries for the ensuing year; for the use and operation of a model school, one thousand dollars; for fencing and ornamenting grounds, one thousand dollars; for well or cistern and outbuildings, eight hundred and fifty dollars.

SEC. 2. The auditor of state is hereby authorized to issue warrants upon the state treasury in favor of the parties to whom any of the funds appropriated in section first of this act may be due, upon filing with him a detailed statement of materials furnished, labor or service performed, duly sworn to by the party claiming the same, and approved by the board of directors.

SEC. 3. That all of the aforesaid sum of fourteen thousand dollars not used for the payment of teachers, shall be taken and deemed a loan by the state of Kansas to the state normal school, to be reimbursed to the state from funds derived from the sale of the lands granted and set apart for the support of said school, by act of the legislature, approved February 26th, 1866.

SEC. 4. That none of the funds derived from the sale of said lands shall be used for any other purpose, until the loan of the state is paid.

SEC. 5. This act shall take effect and be in force from and after its publication once in the Leavenworth *Evening Bulletin.*

Approved, February 19, 1867.

Published in the Leavenworth *Evening Bulletin*, February 26, 1867.

An act to provide for the sale of lands set apart for the support and maintenance of the state normal school.

Be it enacted by the Legislature of the State of Kansas:

SECTION 1. The board of directors of the state normal school are hereby authorized to sell, as hereinafter provided, the lands set apart for the support and maintenance of said school, in pursuance of an act entitled "An act to establish, locate and endow a state normal school," approved March 3d, 1863, at a price not less than one dollar and twenty-five cents per acre, the one-third in hand, and the remainder in two equal installments from the time of sale; and, in the sale of timber lands, the one-half of the purchase money shall be paid at the time of sales, and the balance in two equal annual installments, with interest from the date of said sale at the rate of ten per cent. per annum, the interest to be paid annually in all cases; and in the event of a failure on the part of the purchaser or purchasers of any of the land aforesaid, to pay the interest, or installments, as they become due and payable, he or they shall forfeit the amount of purchase money, and interest, paid on the sale of the said lands aforesaid, and the title to said lands, forfeited as aforesaid, shall revert to the state, for the uses and purposes of said school, as fully and effectually as if the same had never been sold; and, on the payment, by the purchaser or purchasers, of the whole amount of the purchase money and interest, of any of the lands sold as aforesaid, the governor of the state of Kansas shall be required to issue a patent, signed by him and attested by the seal of the state, vesting in the purchaser or purchasers the title, in fee simple, to the lands so sold as aforesaid.

SEC. 2. The said board of directors are hereby authorized and empowered to appoint an agent to sell said lands, in pursuance of the provisions of the first section of this act, who shall have power to make and execute contracts for the sale of the lands aforesaid, to receive and receipt for all moneys arising from the sale of such lands, and to do and perform everything necessary to comply with the provisions of this act, but who shall at all times be subject to the control and direction of the board of directors, and shall receive such compensation for his services as shall be allowed by said board.

Sec. 3. The said agent, before he enters upon the duties of his office, shall take an oath to faithfully discharge his duties as such agent, and shall execute a bond to the state of Kansas, with two or more sureties, to be approved by said board of directors, in the penal sum of ten thousand dollars, conditioned that he will faithfully discharge his duties as such agent, and pay over, on receipt of the same, all moneys received by him, to the treasurer of said board of directors, which bond shall be filed in the office of the secretary of the state.

Sec. 4. So soon as the amount appropriated by the state for the purpose of erecting a building for said normal school shall be realized from the sale of the lands aforesaid, it shall be the duty of the treasurer of said board to reimburse the state in the amount advanced by the state for the purpose aforesaid, and the balance realized from the sale of said lands shall be applied, under direction of the board of directors, for the support and maintenance of said school; and all orders upon the treasurer shall be signed by the president and secretary of the board; and, in case there should be any balance remaining in the treasury at the end of each year, after reimbursing the state, as aforesaid, and defraying the current expenses of said school, the same shall be invested by the treasurer, under the direction of the board of directors, in state or United States stocks, or in such other manner as will best subserve the interest of said school.

Sec. 5. Whenever any purchaser or purchasers shall have paid the whole of the purchase money on any lands sold in pursuance of this act, the secretary and treasurer of said board of directors shall certify the same to the governor, which shall be sufficient evidence to authorize him to issue a patent to said purchaser or purchasers.

Sec. 6. This act shall be in force from and after its publication once in the Leavenworth *Conservative*.

Approved, February 26, 1866.

Published in the Leavenworth *Conservative*, March 10, 1866.

CHAPTER CLXXXIX.

STATE NORMAL SCHOOL—LANDS—SALE OF.

AN ACT to provide for the sale of lands set apart for the support and maintenance of the State Normal School.

Be it enacted by the Legislature of the State of Kansas:

Board of directors SECTION 1. The board of directors of the State Normal School are hereby authorized to sell, as hereinafter provided, the lands set apart for the support and maintenance of said school, in pursuance of an act entitled "an act to establish, locate and endow a State Normal School," approved March 3, 1863, at a price not less Terms of sale. than five dollars per acre. One-tenth of the purchase money shall be paid in cash at the time of sale, and the remainder may remain on interest at ten per cent. per annum, at the option of the purchaser, under such regulations regarding the payment thereof as the board of directors may prescribe. Any interest which may become due, under the provisions of this act, shall be subject to such penalty as the board of directors may prescribe, not exceeding twenty-five per cent. of the amount, and in the event of a failure on the part of the purchaser or purchasers to pay such interest within three months after the same shall become due, he or they shall forfeit the amount of purchase money and interest paid on the purchase of said lands, and the title to said lands shall revert to the state, for the purposes and uses of said school, as fully and as affectually as if the same had never been sold, and any contract or agreement in writing entered into with such purchaser, by the board of directors or their authorized agent, for the sale of such land, shall be null and void.

Duty of Governor SEC. 2. It shall be the duty of the Governor of the state to issue a patent, signed by him, and attested by the seal of the state, vesting in the purchaser or purchasers the title, in fee simple, to the lands so sold as aforesaid, upon the certificate of the secretary and treasurer of the said board of directors, that the whole of the purchase money and interest has been paid, upon any sale of lands made in accordance with the provisions of this act.

SEC. 3. The said board of directors shall have power to appoint an agent to sell said lands, under the provisions *May appoint agent.* of this act, who shall have power to make and execute contracts for the sale of such lands, to receive and receipt for all moneys arising from the sale of such lands, but who shall be at all times subject to the control and direction of said board of directors, and who shall give such security for the faithful performance of his duties as the board of directors may approve, and who shall receive for his services such compensation, not exceeding three *Compensation.* per cent. on the amount of the sales made by him, as may be allowed by the board of directors.

SEC. 4. All moneys derived from the sales of land, under the provisions of this act, both principal and inter- *Money paid into state treasury.* est, less the amount of commissions allowed by the board of directors for the sale thereof, shall be paid into the state treasury, where it shall constitute the "State Normal School fund," for said institution. The amount thus *Principal; how invested.* received as principal of the fund, shall be invested by the treasurer of state, as provided by law, in the bonds of the State of Kansas, or of the United States, and the amount received as interest, both from purchasers of the *Interest.* lands as aforesaid and from the interest on the bonds as aforesaid, he shall hold subject to the order of the president and secretary of the board of directors, for the sole uses and purposes of the support and maintenance of the State Normal School: *Provided,* That the said agent *Proviso.* shall not purchase himself, or associate himself with others, or be in any way interested, directly or indirectly, in the purchase of or sale of any of the said lands.

SEC. 5. An act entitled "an act to provide for the sale of lands set apart for the support and maintenance of the State Normal School," approved February 26, 1866, is hereby repealed.

SEC. 6. This act shall take effect and be in force from and [after] its publication once in the *Kansas Daily Commonwealth.*

Approved March 1, 1872.

I hereby certify that the foregoing is a true and correct copy of the original enrolled bill now on file in my office, and that the same was published in the *Kansas Daily Commonwealth* March 19, 1872.

W. H. SMALLWOOD,
Secretary of State.

CHAPTER CLXXIX.

STATE NORMAL SCHOOL, EMPORIA.

An Act to reorganize the state normal school at Emporia, and to provide for the sale of its land.

Be it enacted by the Legislature of the State of Kansas:

Number of regents, and by whom appointed. SECTION 1. That the state normal school at Emporia shall be governed by a board of regents, hereby created, consisting of six persons, who shall be appointed by the governor and confirmed by the senate. Three of the regents first appointed shall hold office for two years, and three for four years, and until their successors are appointed and qualified. All subsequent appointments shall be for four years.

SEC. 2. That all suits effecting [affecting] said normal school, its property or its endowment, shall be in the name of the state.

SEC. 3. That the instruction in the normal school shall be confined to the various branches of an English education, and the method and art of teaching.

Duty of regents. SEC. 4. It shall be the duty of the board of regents to sell, or cause to be sold, under the provisions of chapter one hundred and eighty-nine of the session laws of eighteen hundred and seventy-two, the lands belonging to said institution, at not less than three dollars per acre; and no appropriation shall be made for this school in the future.

SEC. 5. This act shall take effect and be in force from and after its publication in the *Commonwealth.*

Approved March 7, 1877.

I hereby certify that the foregoing is a true and correct copy of the original enrolled bill now on file in my office, and that the same was published in the *Commonwealth* March 13, 1877.

THOS. H. CAVANAUGH, *Secretary of State.*

CHAPTER XLI.

STATE NORMAL SCHOOL—EMPORIA.

AN ACT making an appropriation to the State Normal School at Emporia.

Be it enacted by the Legislature of the State of Kansas:

School building. SECTION 1. That the sum of fifty thousand dollars, ($50,000,) or so much thereof as may be necessary, be and the same is hereby appropriated, to be used under the direction of the board of directors of the State Normal School at Emporia, for the purpose of building a new normal school building, in addition to and connected with the building now occupied by said institution.

Title to be examined. SEC. 2. That no part of said appropriation shall be drawn until the board of directors, with the attorney general, shall have examined into the title of the land upon which it is proposed to erect said building, and shall have filed a statement with the auditor of state. that in their opinion the State of Kansas is possessed of a good and valid fee simple title to said land.

SEC. 3. That no part of the money appropriated by this act shall be drawn until the city of Emporia shall Condition have by its mayor and council authorized the issuing of the bonds of said city in a total sum of not less than ten thousand dollars, ($10,000,) payable at such time as said city council may determine, not exceeding ten years from the date of such bonds. The proceeds of such bonds to be expended under the direction of the board of directors to aid in furnishing and finishing said building; and said mayor and city council are hereby authorized to issue such bonds and provide for the payment thereof and the interest thereon.

SEC. 4. The auditor of state is hereby required to draw his warrants on the state treasurer, on the presentation of bills approved by the executive committee of the board of directors of said school for the purposes aforesaid.

SEC. 5. This act shall take effect and be in force from and after its publication in the *Kansas Daily Commonwealth.*

Approved February 12, 1872.

I hereby certify that the foregoing is a true and correct copy of the original enrolled bill now on file in this office, and that the same was published in the *Kansas Daily Commonwealth* February 18, 1872.

W. H. SMALLWOOD,
Secretary of State.